The Symbolic Function
Psychoanalysis and the
Philosophy of Language

Gemma Corradi Fiumara

BLACKWELL
Oxford UK & Cambridge USA

Copyright © Gemma Corradi Fiumara 1992

Gemma Corradi Fiumara is hereby identified as author of this work in accordance with Section 77 of the Copyright, Designs and Patents Act 1988.

First published in Italian as *Funzione simbolica e filosofia del linguaggio*, Editore Boringhieri 1980. English translation by Brian Keys.

First published in this translation 1992

Blackwell Publishers
108 Cowley Road, Oxford, OX4 1JF, UK

Three Cambridge Center
Cambridge, Massachusetts 02142, USA

Library of Congress Cataloging in Publication Data

Corradi Fiumara, Gemma.
    [Funzione simbolica e filosofia del linguaggio. English]
    The symbolic function: psychoanalysis and the philosophy of language / Gemma Corradi Fiumara.
        p.   cm.
    Translation of: Funzione simbolica e filosofia del linguaggio.
    Includes bibliographical references and index.
    ISBN 0-631-17317-X – 0-631-18372-8 (pbk.)
    1. Language and languages – Philosophy.   2. Semiotics.   3. Thought and thinking.   4. Cognition.   I. Title.
    P106.C59713   1992
    401'.41 – dc20   91-22289
                                                                                        CIP

British Library Cataloguing in Publication Data

A CIP catalogue record for this book is available from the British Library

Typeset in 10½ on 12 pt Baskerville by Graphicraft Typesetters Ltd.
Printed in Great Britain by Biddles Ltd, Guildford, Surrey

This book is printed on acid-free paper.

Contents

Contents   vii

To Romano, Linda and Michele

1

Language and Symbolization

Purposes and Scope of the Book

With an intent to focus on the issue of the symbolic media involved in cognition and interaction, two common points of philosophical departure ought to be dispensed with: in the first place, attention is directed away from 'objects' as such (almost as if, paradoxically, we were not even considering reality) and, secondly, any inquiry regarding the 'intellect' is avoided (almost as if, in a pre-philosophic fashion, we were not concerned with the nature of thought). This choice of approach originates from a shared suspicion that classical ways of access cannot ultimately be reconnected with a study of the linguistic tools which sustain our cognitive life. A concern for the symbolic media of cognitive and interactive processes is in fact not primarily directed to 'objects' or 'subjects' but specifically to the complex network of relations which exist between language(s) and reality in the making. And questions of interaction – of which cognition is a superb variant – refer to a set of links which constantly point both to the *development* of knowing subjects and to the *construction* of possible realities.

Viewed in this way, the inquiry addresses an area which stays at an equal distance from both 'intellect' (mind, reason, spirit) and 'reality', and which thus provides a fertile field of research in which the risk of gravitating towards the extremes of either 'pure thinking' or 'empirical realism' is perhaps avoided. It is a question of exploring our growing propensity towards *making* truth, and our decreasing obligation to *find* it, either in the 'creative flow' of the spirit or in the 'solidity' of the world.

Attention is thus increasingly drawn to the basic ways in which symbolization allows propositions to be formulated, rather than being focused on specific utterances as such.

It is our symbolic potential for generating language which allows for the formulation of new purposes which could not have been construed prior to some kind of appropriate symbolization; such purposes may include the *task* of representing something which is thought to be out there as well as the *aspiration* to create something new which only springs to life by means of our novel symbolic instruments.

It would also be appropriate to draw attention to the merits of methodological approaches which try to forgo any pretensions to settling questions of a theoretical nature regarding matters of priority between thinking and reality. 'One may give whatever answer one wishes to such general questions,' remarks Filiasi Carcano, 'and one will always be able to find philosophers who "decide" in the same or in a contrary way.'[1] Philosophical inquiry which revolves around language posits instead working hypotheses which diverge from investigations tacitly addressing the structure of reality or the nature of the mind. In the general area of linguistic philosophy there can in fact develop a concern for those basic symbolic functions which provide tools for intersubjective relations as well as for shaping possible experiences of the world. These functions, however, do not unfold in an area of public linguistic lucidity, since they in fact range from the obscure depths of our affective life to the formal 'creative' abstractions of metalinguistic levels.

I believe that the tendency to separate desires and abstractions is a variant of a common inclination to assume that the mind, and even nature, have their own essential structure to which philosophy has, or 'ought to' have, a privileged access. Such a tendency may derive from a custom of reinforcing the choice of one of the prestigious epistemic vocabularies with which we encode our world view; that choice may ultimately serve the purpose of strengthening individual cultural identities, as if ethological problems of human territoriality were fully transposed on to the level of abstract interactions.

This book tries to show how language can be investigated if we take up the demand for a mode of reflection which tries to avoid defensive splittings and which connects affects and thoughts. Davidson remarks that 'Beliefs, desires and intentions are a condition of language, but language is also a condition for them. On the one hand, being able to attribute beliefs and desires to a creature is certainly a condition of sharing a convention with that creature.'[2]

This work is not an attempt to discuss language with respect to specific thinkers, theories or schools which can somehow be kept distinct by means of appropriate shifts in vocabulary; it is an effort to discuss our linguisticity by focusing on interactive humans, living from infancy to senescence 'within' one brain with differing hemispheric roles, and 'within' one mind (intellect, self, spirit, consciousness, ego) where affects and reasons are inextricably interwoven. And the comparative cultural plasticity of humans appears to be closely associated with the inchoate modes of symbolizing one's attitudes. Frequently pointing to affects in his philosophy of psychology, Wittgenstein remarks: 'The thing is, language has a multiple root; it has not a single root, but roots.'[3]

The symbolic schemes which follow one another in the process of hominization[4] (and which may even coexist within the same culture or person) actually *speak* and *teach* in the sense that they impart specific directions regarding the world and our relation to it. Such symbolic frames may differ on fundamental issues which will act in concert so as to shape subsequent cognitive patterns. For it is our basic symbolic formations which 'tell' us with intensity and immediacy whether danger comes from inside or outside, whether the individual exists or only the group does. Our inchoate symbolizations even 'tell' us whether words themselves are tools or weapons, precious or worthless. In this fashion not only are the boundaries of what is knowable established on the basis of what our symbols intimate, but also potential areas of cognition are placed out of reach inasmuch as limits of significance are defined, beyond which it is not even possible to think. Of course language is influenced by inventions and innovations, but 'little and slowly', according to Whorf, 'whereas *to* inventors and innovators it legislates with the decree immediate.'[5] Even before we decide to inhabit a specific epistemology and become one with its language, we may have gone through several epistemological migrations: such experiences should indeed provide us with respect for our symbolic versatility rather than with a determination to argue cogently from the premises we have settled in.

Drawing upon Cassirer, we might tentatively define symbolic language as a general function of mediation whereby every possible area of perception and discourse is articulated.[6] And yet, long before the notion of symbolic forms can provide an 'answer', it first poses a question as to the combination of mediating tools within a unified symbolic function. Ricoeur, too, suggests that it is symbolization which sets the 'common denominator'[7] of possible modes of forming objects and of giving sense to reality; and the symbolic domain expresses moreover the non-immediacy of the manner in which we apprehend our world. Ricoeur even insists that the very fact that symbolization is used in such diverse fields as mathematics and religion, physics and music, seems to confirm that the notion of symbol 'has the species of universality'.[8]

At least in its intentions, philosophical inquiry of the linguistic type does not give in to the attraction of those philosophies which are in some way ultimately linked to idealism in general, nor does it drift in among philosophies rooted in physicalism at large; in other words it tries to do without points of departure such as 'thought' and 'reality', 'knowledge' and 'truth'. Debates on truth in general are thus gradually replaced by discussion of truth-conditions. But if we abandon some of the reassuring vocabulary suggesting the idea of a world with fixed laws and of a reason – or even a language – with its 'eternal' structure, we might ultimately come to confront the disquieting options of constructive *or* destructive modes of symbolization. There is now perhaps a tacit philosophical expansion which includes not only questions of truth or falsity but also a growing concern for matters of enhancing life or degrading it.

A Concern for the Symbolic Function

On the path of epistemic awareness we may start out thinking of objects as things that can be seen or handled. The Latin term *obiectum* is related to the idea of something that we can throw or that can be thrown in front of us. The magnitude and quantity of objects progressively extends from things that we can grasp, catch, throw and better control by means of 'knowledge', on to ever greater and abstract dimensions. The object-symbolization may thus extend to the planet we inhabit. An indifferent, unaffective approach to our phatic function may result in divisive objectifications of everything we deal with. In the language of Quine:

> We persist in breaking reality down somehow into a multiplicity of identifiable and discriminable objects.... We talk so inveterately of objects that to say we do so seems almost to say nothing at all; for how else is there to talk? It is hard to say how else there is to talk, not because our objectifying pattern is an invariable trait of human nature, but because we are bound to adapt any alien pattern to our own in the very process of understanding or translating the alien sentences.[9]

By way of illustration, one may invoke quotations from the front covers of two prestigious journals, *National Geographic* and *Dialogue*.

'The Geographic asks: "Can we save this fragile earth?"';[10] on the holographic cover, a crystal earth shatters after being hit by a bullet, indicating that we might face an equally shattering environmental apocalypse unless we change our ways. Similarly, 'Can we save the earth?' is used on the front cover of *Dialogue*[11] as a general title for a section on the earth and its energy. It is indeed a logocratic missymbolization that makes us speak of the earth as of an object that *we* can or cannot save. In our pseudosymbolic immaturity we exhibit a propensity to ignore that our 'need' is to save ourselves rather than the earth. The assertive, non-listening quality of our linguisticity compels us 'to talk so inveterately of objects'[12] that we think that *we* can 'spare' the planet-object while it is possibly the dominating quality of our symbolizations that is conducive to damaging it. As long as we adhere to the symbolic paradigms which are interwoven with our linguistic games (or *jeux de massacre*) and forms of life (or ways of extinction), it will be difficult to 'save the earth' inasmuch as the symbolic expression of the project leads us into the opposite direction. Our obstinate philosophical language may infiltrate and sabotage even the most enlightened and illuminating of cultural enterprises. The excellent quality of the above-mentioned journals is thus subtly conditioned by symbolic premises which create the very problem that they try to eradicate. If we speak of the earth as of an object that we could shatter like a crystal sphere, then we are bound to ignore that in fact even if we rendered the planet uninhabitable it is the human species which might disappear, not the earth. In spite of our symbolic decrees, we are not the masters of the object-earth (that we can save or waste) but rather we are dependent upon it so significantly that if we damage the earth we primarily endanger the human species while the planet's life would probably continue undisturbed.

In order to 'save the earth' we should perhaps first acknowledge the binding power of those 'object-symbolizations' which may be conducive to the deterioration of our habitat and possibly even to the extinction of one more species, that of the 'philosophical' humans who passively adhere to a domineering linguisticity intent upon 'breaking reality down ... into a multiplicity of objects'.[13] As we are the authors of that language, we erroneously use it as a source of authority in the unwarranted equation between authorial and authoritative prerogatives, which begin to emerge more clearly in an extended perspective. By means of a methodological effort to avoid the alternatives underlying certain types of philosophic tradition, one escapes a 'dilemmatic power' which illusively makes such exclusive choices seem worthwhile through the spontaneous onset of cognitively reassuring attitudes. Such attitudes might include the tacit 'awareness' of belonging to a more enlightened school of philosophy, or the equally reassuring certainty of being in a position to single out cultural practices to be regarded as 'antagonistic' or as the locus of blindness or futility.

The priority assigned to language assumes relevance for methodological reasons in the sense that what comes to be highlighted is the approach to any of the problems which might arise in the course of philosophical reflection. Inquiry regarding the symbolic function might in fact constitute the starting-point of the philosophy of language inasmuch as its outlook is open to the integration of all forms of linguisticity.

Through a laborious process aimed at regaining awareness and responsibility for our linguistic tools, it may be possible to understand that some, perhaps many, of the key positions which 'enliven' philosophic disputes, namely those seminal metaphors or assertions which philosophers attack and defend, are not necessarily to be seen as bearers of competing projects within the same general outlook, but rather as proposals for different and possibly complementary pursuits.

Our concern for the symbolic function enables us to regard alternative vocabularies as more like instruments for making an open-ended spectrum than like component elements of a superepistemology to be brought to completion.

The speakers in a phatic community are often in contrast not because their positions are conflicting (that is, at the limit, logically incompatible), but because they often think that they are so, partly because of a non-critical use of language. When one looks for the motives of such a misleading dilemmatic attitude, it may be seen that linguistic activity occurs over a range of performance, from speaking as an individual within a community, to being 'spoken' by it in the sense of allowing oneself to be spoken through by the background-epistemology with which one establishes a symbiosis which is as polymorphous as it is elusive. Ryle suggests that utterances often appear to be contradictory answers to the same question, when in fact one is speaking without fully realizing that one is referring to different things. Ryle points out: 'The two sides are, at certain points, hinging their arguments upon concepts of different categories, though they suppose themselves to be hinging them upon different concepts of the same category, or vice versa.'[14] This is so inasmuch as the latent 'matrix' of certain symbolic paradigms which are used symbiotically, and without being sufficiently differentiated, stands in the way of a clearer perception of our symbolic tools as the *means* whereby our knowledge is organized. Possibly to a similar effect, Wittgenstein remarks that, whenever 'Idealists, Solipsists and Realists' engage in philosophical dispute, 'the one party attacks the normal form of expression as if they were attacking a statement; the others defend it, as if they were stating facts recognized by every reasonable human being.'[15]

It is 'imagined' that the interlocutor has an alternative theory of knowledge, mind or language, whereas it may simply be the case of an attempt to dispense with certain standard disciplines. Departing from a 'school' or one of its paradigms cannot be equated with arguing against it – although this is often the general appreciation of the dynamics; even in philosophy, 'away' from something is regarded as 'against' something. It may instead be an attempt to foresee the possibility of a form of philosophical endeavour in which the vocabulary inherited from a particular tradition would ultimately appear pointless.[16]

The Multiplicity of Languages

As we know, the phenomenon of perception does not amount to mirroring 'real' things (whatever their ontological status may be); nor may knowledge be explained in terms of a linear approximation to a given aspect of reality. Once we concede that even physical sciences 'indicate' that there are no ultimate entities, such as particles or waves, having an autonomous existence independent of the observer who constructs such phenomena, we may opt for a propensity to explore perspectives, namely outlooks originating in those selfsame symbolic modes which characterize our primal relations with the environment.[17] As an alternative to any reductive outlook or epistemological monopoly (underpinned by reassuring symbolic paradigms according to which reality, or reason, is 'nothing but ...'), we may conceive of knowledge, including the most exact scientific sort, not as being *the* perspective of philosophy but as one of the perspectives envisaged by humans: that is to say, one of the possible symbolic modes of building oneself a universe with which to be conversant. Thus Cassirer, elaborating on Leibniz's thought, affirms: 'In his view, the logic of things ... cannot be separated from the logic of signs. For the sign is no mere accidental cloak of the idea, but its necessary and essential organ. It serves not merely to communicate a complete and given thought-content, but it is an instrument, by means of which this content develops and fully defines itself.'[18]

The idea that 'objects' are the result of an elaboration and not given facts emerges ever more clearly from disparate sources in culture: philosophic accounts generally prevail according to which reality is seen as the outcome of symbolic work. As is argued in Lugarini's analysis of Cassirer's contribution, our different languages 'turn out to be so many "worlds" generated by the functions to which they correspond and within which take shape just as many peculiarly specified and distinct "pictures of reality"; the emphasis shifts from knowing to doing, from awareness to performance. The numerous ways of human ingenuity function as sources of different worlds, each of them as relevant as is the scientific-cognitive domain.'[19]

These same lines of argument seem corroborated by an incisive remark expressed by Moore: 'I do not think that the world or the sciences would ever have suggested to me any philosophical problems. What has suggested philosophical problems to me is things which other philosophers have said about the world or the sciences.'[20]

It is possible to glimpse within the complexities stemming from the many questions thronging the cultural horizon (the 'things which other philosophers have said about the world or the sciences') an ancient concern linked to the deep levels of symbolization through which the very act of relating is generated, and which originally confers a meaning to reality. And this concern with our inchoate possibility, or impossibility, of establishing some means of interactive relation assumes an increasingly salient role as it ultimately proves to be one of the essential motivations for a philosophy of language. We thus propose to examine which of the features of language constitute suitable, or unsuitable, tools for shaping some liveable reality. And when we speak of reality, or of our fellow speaker, we are not referring to the world in itself or to the other's ontological status, as if these were assumptions to be posited without reference to the symbolic travail of our awareness, but rather to the sort of reality which the individual laboriously carves out day by day in the form of a construct negotiated within the limits of what may be said, thought and done within his symbolic horizon.

It was of course an important juncture in the itinerary of Western thought when the apparatus of metaphysics – and hence of its normative role in logic and ethics – was challenged and posed as a problem, for this meant that it could no longer do duty as a source of criteria for evaluation and judgement. The central concerns of philosophic inquiry seem then to gravitate towards the problem of how 'objects' of experience are built up, namely towards problems regarding our creative and constructive pursuits as distinct from research into the criteria ruling accurate description. What accounts for the need to bring to light the latent normative role of certain epistemologies is our incipient awareness of how potentially destructive they can be for the complexity of nature and, above all, of human life; this complexity, in fact, may be detrimentally coerced within the dictates of definitional provisions. As Cassirer points out:

> The unity of knowledge can no longer be made certain and secure by referring knowledge in all its forms to a single common object which is related to all these forms as the transcendent prototype to the empirical copies. But instead a new task arises: to gather the various branches of science with their diverse methodologies – with all their recognized specificity and independence – into one system, whose separate parts precisely through their necessary diversity will complement and further one another. This postulate of a purely functional unity replaces the postulate of a unity of substance and origin.[21]

Inquiry into the multiplicity of languages is closely associated with the experience of a growing variety of vocabularies; for it is such plurality that allows for a richer encoding of reality and also constitutes a measure of our detachment from language, whereby the way is opened to 'imagining' more than one linguistic model for any of our problems and thus an opportunity for patterning the relationship with reality along different lines. If, through inertia, as it were, one goes about unwittingly applying the vocabulary originally imposed by one's culture, there is a risk of fixing a certain cognitive paradigm, the very rigidity of which makes it impossible to construct a more complex experience; or such terms may be automatically introduced in the discussion of a problem, ultimately making its solution impossible.

Attention to the role of language in the construction of reality entails that the linguistic function is not to be envisaged as a smooth, automatic process. We advance in a realm of possibilities; and not only is the situation open to diverse lines of development, but it also admits of drastic regressions, distortions and self-defeating goals.[22] Thus the role performed by language in determining the type and the hierarchization of relations may come across to us more cogently. Of course, if there were no world to experience, there would be no language with which to speak about such a pole of reality, be it a person or a thing. Philosophically speaking, though, the salient point is the impossibility of a world of 'facts' and 'persons' in the absence of a symbolic potential to form significant *relationships*. Cassirer thus describes the approach: 'If the object of knowledge can be defined only through the medium of a particular logical and conceptual structure, we are forced to conclude that a variety of media will correspond to various structures of the objects, to various meanings for "objective" relations.'[23]

The increasing awareness of virtually being able to choose among different languages leads to some major epistemological shifts, in the sense that the very prospect of being in a position to make a selection among various vocabularies could imply the construction of more than one 'world': a different language might even give rise to a different 'science'. Such reflections allow us at least to force the problem to its limits and to direct attention not so much to the comparative efficacy of vocabularies as to the 'genetic' role of language, namely to our symbolic function at the basic level of the inchoate paradigms which engender different formulas for the construction of a liveable reality.

Constructive versus Descriptive Language

Although inferior to most living beings with regard to the survival value of their innate instinctual abilities, humans owe their successes and their evolution to an intelligence which may be conceived of, at least in part, as the capacity to create and use a meaningful symbolic system.

In Cassirer's philosophy, the concept of symbol stands for the most universal constituent of reality, that is the totality of elements which, in whatever form, *indicate* or *represent* meaning. Such an attempt at definition will undoubtedly appear extremely generalized. And, of course, not everyone subscribes to a philosophic position whereby all knowledge and relations are of a mediated nature. None the less, to the extent that knowledge is held to be a mediated (as opposed to immediate) 'grasp' of reality, it should also be allowed that it is symbolic in that it relies on symbols, these being the means (discursive, mathematical or other) whereby knowledge is achieved.[24] There seems to be no doubt that our specific way of gaining experience of the 'objective' world does not emanate from any unspecified 'outwardness'. Classically, it is thought to spring from a process involving diverse and correlated procedures whereby we form a 'synthesis' of multiple inputs. One of the contributions of psycho-analysis to philosophic inquiry could perhaps be traced in its capacity to reveal how mental development occurs by organizing diversified 'universes', world views or types of reality. Hence the need for a closer scrutiny of the symbolic activity underlying processes whereby disparate universes of perception and discourse are constructed.

Infant development, for instance, offers us a few significant hints: the young human often asks, 'What is this?', and not, 'What do you call this?' We may hypothesize that in the beginning, at the dawn of thought, that which the thing *is* and what it is *called* converged within a single process from which it transpired that an objective world was conquered thanks to the support of verbal signs. We may thus argue that the symbolic action carried out in naming performs the task of stabilizing, as it were 'fixing', perceptual conglomerations, long before those same verbal signs come to be attributed to them by way of 'names' available for purposes of description. Perceptual selec-tivity, therefore, which is fixed and made permanent by language, may be conceptualized neither as a duplicating function (that is to say, as a way of mirroring a previously established organization of reality) nor as a procedure for making conscious semantic attributions.[25]

An over-circumscribed way of theorizing the process by which reality is symbolized, described by Wittgenstein as the 'ostensive teaching of words',[26] leads to a view of the symbolic function which is rather static, as a result of its being informed by a fragmentary, linear system of causation too far removed from life's dynamics. Such an approach to the problem of language is not of much use in 'explaining' the complexity of our countless and inchoate inter-actions. The ostensive linguistic pattern (name–named) is therefore to be seen as *one* of the approaches to the problem of the symbolic function. Though it does represent something of a 'step' towards a philosophy of language, such an approach does not allow us to go many steps further. Without a doubt, the ostensive conception of language is among the primal means by which a model of reality is worked out, but it is obviously insufficient by itself. And since it remains within the confines of the name–named pattern, it tacitly confirms the uninspiring assumption of a previously established reality which language is accurately to mirror and label.

Virtually every contribution in the field of hermeneutics testifies to the extent to which subtlety and perspicacity are required in each interpretative effort if one is to avoid devaluing the specific qualities of any forms of symbolization by smoothing them to fit patterns of meaning alien to both the accretive evolution of thought and to the complexity of the individual. Every interpretation which unduly curtails expression initiates a chain of negative equivalents of language, or missymbolizations, involving disrupting and restrictive consequences. We may hypothesize, therefore, that any expressive process is truly symbolic to the extent that it is metabolic and contributes to the formation of an open system of relations which does not bar the way to the construction of reality: whenever construction is impeded its function could be described as 'dia-bolic'.[27] In summarizing his comparative studies on language, Whorf adopts positions which converge with certain aspects of psychoanalytic theory and linguistic philosophy: 'Every language is a vast pattern-system, different from others, in which are culturally ordained the forms and categories by which the personality not only communicates, but also analyzes nature, notices or neglects types of relationship and phenomena, channels his reasoning, and builds the house of his consciousness.'[28]

Generating versus Using Language

As he redirected philosophic inquiry to encompass the everyday use of language, Wittgenstein embarked upon a critique of the logical atomism underlying the pursuits of the *Tractatus*.[29] As his new approach supplants inquiry dealing prevalently with an ideal language – conceived as an instrument capable of avoiding the inaccuracies and the ambiguities of ordinary language – it concomitantly 'upgrades' ordinary language, thus providing additional scope for philosophical inquiry. Everyday language, as a consequence, is no longer seen as an inferior access to philosophic research. Within such a widened framework, the 'logic' of one's ratiocination ceases to look like a smooth, transparent calculus of sentences. It comes across, instead, as a conglomeration of a number of 'rules' regarding which there has come to be a certain degree of negotiation by virtue both of the ways in which we go about surviving as well as of the characteristics of our humanity. As Filiasi Carcano suggests, in Wittgenstein's later view, speakers are not isolated subjects but performers of linguistic acts who agree to participate in a variety of linguistic games within certain forms of life.[30]

Once ordinary language has been redeemed as an acceptable starting-point, it also allows for a philosophic space within which it is possible to advocate the study of the very dawn of language, of our primal symbolic functioning and of the ways in which language presides over the basic paradigms of intersubjective relations.

Shaping reality and forming personal interactions can thus be regarded as deriving from a unified symbolic function. And yet, whenever language subjects us either to virtual chaos or to excessive restrictions, it becomes necessary to bring about a crisis in the form of a suspension of certain strategies which have become inner obstacles or sources of unbearable confusion. Even a crisis may then be knowingly accepted as a pause, as a hiatus in our unliveable linguisticity. And if we focus on the linguistic dimension of relational issues, and direct attention to the affective and cognitive scope of the symbolic function, we may expect to regain a fruition of language in the sense of exploring and laboriously experiencing those primal vicissitudes whereby we developed the sort of language we use to interact at differing levels of maturity.

When inquiry follows such a propensity one is working in a more complex and hazardous setting. One is not abiding by the traditional conception of living beings who simply use a *given* symbolic apparatus in order to refer to a *given* reality. In this work, in fact, I shall be prevalently concerned with humans as the creators of symbols, and not merely with humans as users of symbols.[31] I shall thus approach the study of language, not merely as the mirror of a pre-existing order of meaning, but as a generator of significance. Language will be regarded neither as a cohesive block nor as a static entity. It is in fact likely that at least some of our difficulties may derive from an unduly static and cohesive notion of man's linguistic life. When we try to overcome our naïvely realistic conception of language and to break through to a richer awareness of the symbolic processes under-lying the construction of our reality, we are involved in a laborious operation for the recovery of our developmental history, that is intent upon an 'unnatural' retrieval of our own perilous cognitive origins: at such early stages, in fact, insight may have been more threatening than obtuseness. It almost seems that, when we gaze beyond factual and logical boundaries, we confront the profound obscurity not only of our cognitive origins but also of our affective roots. Perhaps this is one of the reasons why human beings, the symbolic animals *par excellence*, sometimes cling to naïve forms of verbal realism and thus can hardly comprehend the role performed by symbolization in their cognitive and affective life.

2

The Concept of
Linguistic Community

Symbolic Paradigms and the Roots of Knowledge

Within the purview of contemporary culture we are induced to witness disquieting human phenomena and transformations which potentially make us feel 'alien' even in our own shared languages. It would thus be appropriate to enquire not only into the modes by which 'revolutionary' outlooks are somehow expressed but also into our basic propensities for those inchoate paradigms[1] which sustain the network of our different linguistic communities. Of course the idea of a linguistic community is rather vague, since it may extend from the 'private language' of twin infants to our 'Greek logos', regarded as a philosophical mother-tongue generating the scientific languages of the West.[2] Moreover, a linguistic community may represent a phase in the life-cycle of a philosophical school, or indicate scholarly research inspired by influential thinkers: indeed, it may characterize a world view, however extended or minimally shared.[3] Starting from such premises, our efforts are directed towards studying the symbolic function as the complex of means for establishing communal basic modes of relating with persons and things. As Dummett points out: 'The role of language as the vehicle of thought is *secondary* to its role as an instrument of communication: it could not serve the former purpose unless it served the latter; and, as serving the latter purpose, it is as much of its essence to be imbedded in a social practice, to be the shared possession of a community.'[4] And, as Wittgenstein seems to suggest, even questions of truth hinge more on agreement in 'form of life' than in 'agreement of opinions'.[5] It is moreover suggested that any piece of discourse is the truth only inasmuch as it is an '*unmoving* foundation of ... language-games'.[6] Looked at in this light, a number of questions may be seen as having to do largely with symbolization, in the sense that they derive from ways of expressing early interactive 'decisions'. The crux of certain problems may thus be seen as depending upon the symbolic paradigms on the basis of which our *way* of articulating interrogatives is organized. And even in discourses at the highest levels of abstraction (as distinct from the purely expressive and descriptive domain), when our language reaches 'argumentation', there still is a tendency to 'forget' that certain assumptions have no fully conscious, or no mutually agreed-upon, meaning; they are in fact rooted in the serious complexity of what we call 'social practice'.[7] The question at issue may 'simply' be that of a set of semantic choices emanating from our inchoate paradigms of symbolization to which we are vitally linked, they being the foundation of our social development and, as such, unlikely to be readily forsaken.

An interdisciplinary approach to the study of the symbolic function may help us identify those basic paradigms, those minimal prerequisites of relatedness and structure, which support the development of our diverse ways of conceiving 'theories'. And once a symbolic paradigm has been fully articulated within an accepted frame of reference, considerations which question its heuristic validity generally come to be deemed unfounded. Cultural outlooks may well differ as to their fundamental paradigms, and yet in each micro- or macro-culture there often is a tendency to propose them as transculturally valid criteria for the assessment of general cognitive processes.

The choices made among differing symbolic schemes turn out to coincide ultimately with decisions regarding diverse forms of relation. When a cognitive choice really stands for a particular type of object-relation, and that relation is rooted in primal affective interactions, it will not be easily transformed by means of arguments emanating from a different cognitive framework, deriving in turn from its own profound roots. And when the basic assumptions underlying diverse cognitive approaches are compared, it is easy to find oneself involved in circular arguments, inasmuch as the cognitive derivatives of a given symbolic framework are often used to support the basic structure of the framework itself.

The continuing allegiance to a basic symbolic paradigm may be borne out by cursorily retracing the variegated history of hominization. It is in fact admissible to posit that even the prevalence of certain forms of perception (for instance, visual versus auditory) rests upon some sort of symbolic scheme without which reality could not be suitably established, and the individual would have to cope with a world as menacing as it is unpredictable. Any symbolic framework whatsoever, be it ever so elementary or primitive, proves handy for coming to terms with a potentially chaotic universe.

Cassirer remarks that 'The process of language formation shows for example how the chaos of immediate impressions takes on order and clarity for us only when we "name" it and so permeate it with the function of linguistic thought and expression. In this new world of linguistic signs the world of impressions itself acquires an entirely new "permanence", because it acquires a new intellectual articulation.'[8] And further on in the same work: 'In the symbolic function ... of consciousness ... certain unchanging fundamental forms ... disengage themselves from the stream of consciousness; the flux of contents is replaced by a self-contained and enduring unity of form. Here, however, we are not dealing with an isolated act, but with a progressive process of determination.'[9]

In the extreme version of this perspective, even an attack on symbolic links – namely an attempt to induce confusion and disruption (as is reported in the more serious forms of mental pathology) – may turn out to be, paradoxically, an active effort for organization, preferable to being passively absorbed by incomprehensible situations. For in this case it is a subjective nucleus of the self which is producing disorder, as opposed to being overwhelmed by what is perceived as a chaotic milieu. The cognitive value of any basic symbolic scheme in fact interacts with primal patterns of our relations. And such fundamental symbolizations, besides having a cognitive scope, are also latently normative, in the sense that they establish the premises on the basis of which it is decided which entities the world does or does not contain. Such symbolic paradigms function as the bases from which specific modes of knowledge can be derived. If 'reality' is too complex and enigmatic to be known or constructed 'by chance', recourse to primal symbolic frameworks is as indispensable as are observation and verification. In fact, the historians of our 'scientific thinking' show us that when a scientist assimilates a paradigm he 'acquires theory, methods and standards *together*, usually in an *inextricable* mixture. Therefore, when paradigms change, there are usually significant shifts in the criteria determining the legitimacy both of problems and of proposed solutions'.[10]

The structuring power of a symbolic paradigm (which probably also implies some measure of unexplained coercion) is thus discussed by Kuhn:

> The coherence displayed by the research tradition ... may not imply even the existence of an underlying body of rules and assumptions

that additional ... philosophical investigation might uncover. That scientists do not usually ask ... what makes a particular problem or solution legitimate tempts us to suppose that, *at least intuitively*, they know the answer. But it may only indicate that neither the question nor the answer is felt to be relevant to their research. *Paradigms may be prior to, more binding, and more complete than any set of rules for research that could be unequivocally abstracted from them.*[11]

The history of 'scientific' pursuits seems to indicate also that paradigms do not lend themselves to be easily altered by the ups and downs of research, for the most that positive science can manage is to acknowledge anomalies, crises or static situations. Given a symbolic paradigm, the *interpretation* of experimental data ultimately proves to be engaged in the constitution of phenomena originating from the paradigm. The act of interpreting data can do no more than extend the structure of the paradigm: by no means can it amend its structure. It is therefore a legitimate concern to try to investigate the vicissitudes of our symbolic potential inasmuch as they shape the format (the design) of those interactive pursuits of which cognition is a relevant variant.

Fixity and Mobility of Symbolic Paradigms

Even ordinary language may exhibit a tendency to be pervaded by a complex of dominant meanings. The standardization of prevailing clusters of significance observable in a community's linguistic customs constitutes a tendency which may culminate in a conglomerate terminology hinging on a single term: a hypostasis. Words may come to be isolated in such a way as to transform them into 'absolute' concepts. And concepts become 'absolute' – unbound – in the sense that they can no longer be influenced by whatever may occur in human doings. There is a concomitant (and ultimately anti-symbolic) tendency to ignore various usages of terms and to overlook certain nuances (or 'anomalies') which might otherwise prove quite pertinent; such potential sources of mutation, however, can be even marginalized on account of their scarce linguistic lucidity. And this (scarcely philosophic) propensity tends to become dominant and self-defining. Inasmuch as a symbolic paradigm brings order, one may become accustomed to the 'name' standing for the paradigm, and, the next thing one knows, the paradigm has become 'visible' – hence amenable to being decreed 'transcendental' or even further dignified. True, a categorizing function is brought into play which allows us to avoid dissipating reality into an 'excessive' multiplicity of features or a mere cultural contingency; but, when such a progression becomes automatic and unwitting, other opportunities for linguistic development are passed up and the hypostasis of meaning ultimately serves the purpose of ignoring the world's complexity and our own.

It may be worth our while to focus critical attention upon basic symbolic paradigms, because of the crucial role they play in establishing the assumptions which guide research in general. Out of a solid framework of assumptions laid down beyond any 'reasonable' doubt – assumptions of a conceptual, theoretical and methodological nature – a set of criteria is derived whereby one can 'establish' what the world is and what kind of science belongs therein. And the researcher addressing a specialized branch of any sufficiently mature science may with reasonable confidence direct his search towards problems arising *both* by virtue of the criteria derived from fundamental assumptions *and* by virtue of rules acquired within a certain discipline.[12] The greater cogency of certain basic paradigms guiding semantic attributions, as compared to the rules according to which a particular science or discipline proceeds, may be highlighted through reference to the history of scientific thought. According to Kuhn, even though it has no need to be entirely regulated by a set of operating rules, positive science, none the less, is a highly controlled activity: 'That is why ... I introduced shared paradigms rather than shared rules, assumptions and points of view as the source of coherence for normal research traditions. Rules, I suggest, derive from paradigms, but paradigms can guide research even in the absence of rules.'[13]

Even though research is carried out invariably under the banner of a particular paradigm, it is nevertheless the ability to discard the paradigm itself which makes it possible to surpass the boundaries of knowledge allowed by it. On the contrary, if we enclose ourselves within a paradigm we prevent the adoption of different assumptions capable of fostering innovative research. When a tentative statement of a paradigm becomes available – and there is a commitment to defend it – some clear instances may be offered indicating the nature of the cognitive practices of those subscribing to the paradigm, that is to a specific mode of seeing reality. Although such examples and 'proofs' may exhibit a high degree of efficacy, I believe that the philosophical point at issue is a recognition that even such arguments may not exceed the qualitative level of persuasion. A given symbolic paradigm can never become cogently convincing – either logically or statistically – for the thinker who is unable to 'join the club'.

Among philosophers and other thinkers it is common to point out the basic futility of pursuing what would appear as a fertile concern, namely the discussion of fundamental principles. When a number of 'principles' have been established at the expense of others, it is almost impossible to discard them.

Whorf, for instance, suggests that 'common sense' as its name shows and 'practicality' as its name does not show

> are largely matters of talking so that one is readily understood. It is sometimes stated that Newtonian space, time and matter are sensed by everyone intuitively, whereupon relativity is cited as showing how mathematical analysis can prove intuition wrong.... Laying the blame upon intuition for our slowness in discovering mysteries of the Cosmos, such as relativity, is the wrong one. The right answer is: Newtonian space, time and matter are no intuitions. They are recepts from culture and language. That is where Newton got them.[14]

Although in many relevant respects scientific research broadens knowledge, in other ways, however, it may be a source of powerful frames of reference within which it is extremely difficult to concede epistemological status to certain enigmatic, disturbing or 'irrelevant' phenomena which cannot be fitted into the explicative scheme. In this sense, research exerts a subtly inhibitory function upon such cognitive developments as may not yet be related to reference paradigms of a sufficiently 'visible', consensual and productive nature. It is the very ability to gain access to or invent symbolic levels of a metalinguistic and interepistemologic order which makes it possible to question the general equilibrium of a conceptual field, revising and renaming those time-honoured assumptions which seemed placed out of reach.

Anomalies such as an unexpected, disturbing phenomenon are all the more clearly visible (and cannot be 'hidden' by blind spots) to the extent that they are allowed to cast doubt upon the overall framework and go against cognitive expectations. 'What is important about depicting anomalies?' asks Wittgenstein. 'If one cannot do it, that shows that you do not know your way around concepts.'[15] The stubbornness and seriousness of an anomaly are precisely what bring about the occasion to revise fundamental symbolic patterns. And after our repeated attempts to make the 'disturbing' phenomenon fit within the available cognitive edifice have failed, the thing to do is to come to grips with the manifest anomalies, raising doubts about the framework itself, for the reason that there is no way to reconcile such anomalies with the underlying symbolic pattern.[16] At the occurrence or reappearance of an anomaly, a number of questions which could formerly be considered wholly irrelevant, or side-issues, may prove the harbinger of new modes of inquiry and open up new symbolic domains.

I am thus trying to advocate a greater measure of tolerance for marginalized 'theoretical' or interepistemic discourses: they may not be scrupulously clear inasmuch as they are peripheral with respect to standard vocabularies, epistemologies or forms of life; yet they may be sufficiently inspiring to provoke the emergence of problems which would have been otherwise vulnerable to obscurity. Such questions may come to the fore not only as a result of 'normal' research, but possibly as the direct outcome of creative symbolizations which cannot adequately be vouched for.

On the strength of this transformed symbolic framework, a seeker may not only adopt new cognitive tools and look in other directions; he may actually provide himself with an awareness of things new, even when he applies traditional methods of inquiry in fields already examined. Observations which once only yielded factual matters pointing to a *quaestio facti* may then be conducive to the challenge of a *quaestio iuris*. In contexts which had been thoroughly familiar, different structural forms may dawn upon the mind instantly, with the result that the customary world of relations may seem, in certain respects, to bear no similarity to the one in which one *lived* previously. When a new symbolic paradigm is accepted and we come face to face with previously quite familiar situations, we now learn to capture, as it were, a fresh Gestalt in them. Under such conditions it will seem to be impossible, in certain respects, to obtain a mutual transposition or translation of the cognitive process itself, with the epistemological approach of a previous phase.

Paradigms, furthermore, are not passive containers of experience; rather, they are the active principles by means of which the process of formation and unification of reality in the making is carried out. In fact, whenever a new angle from which to observe things can be discerned, there is an effort to think out and plan suitable investigations for the purpose of confirming, correcting the new perspective.

The research carried on within a given 'scientific' tradition works in precisely this fashion; the various contributions are a result of the *choice* of the problems which may be solved within the range of the available conceptual tools, and such tools are themselves closely associated with a given perspective. A research tradition allows one to single out those problems that may be defined within the purview of existing knowledge and tools, with the result that one knows beforehand at least the *type* of result that one intends to achieve and consequently chooses the instruments and the logical structuring most suited thereto. Research carried on within a tradition, therefore, may not altogether ignore the assumptions which constitute the tradition's reference grid. However, what Bunge names as the 'maturation of science',[17] like any other maturational process, holds in store some not inconsiderable transitions and upheavals which bear upon the human being not only cognitively but also affectually. Throughout the history of scientific thought, one comes across periods of relatively gradual development, as well as periods of deep and drastic transformation; such fateful passages cannot be accounted for sufficiently in terms of the refinement and proliferation of scientific data. There probably exists no empirical basis which is enough in itself to decide the fortunes of a scientific theory. In my opinion, the decisive evolutionary factor, as regards both the history of knowledge as well as the growth path of the individual, may be traceable to a willingness to accept and work through the loss of previously acquired conceptions. And concepts are not simply philosophical elements amenable to various systematizations: they are constitutive factors of our identity which can only be discarded at a high cost. In Whitehead's language, they are 'fundamental assumptions which adherents of all variant systems within the epoch *unconsciously* presuppose'.[18] From this point of view, then, the capacity to evolve seems more rooted in an affective disposition to endure losses than dependent on any set of cognitive contingencies.

The Question of Anomalies: A Connection between Wittgenstein and Freud

In an effort to investigate the cognitive and affective roots of our symbolic potential it is perhaps appropriate to invoke a connection between Wittgenstein and Freud. From the notes taken by Rhees of his conversations with Wittgenstein, we learn that the latter had read Freud in his early life and that he continued to consider himself as one of his disciples or followers.[19] This has been regarded as somewhat surprising but perhaps it may appear more plausible and thought-provoking upon closer scrutiny. I shall thus attempt to propose a few remarks on possible connections between Freud's approach to the life of the mind and Wittgenstein's investigation of human linguisticity.

Once again, Wittgenstein's remarks may be invoked: 'What is important about depicting anomalies precisely? If you cannot do it, that shows you do not know your way around concepts.'[20] If we do not know our way around concepts when failing to depict anomalies accurately, perhaps we have not sufficiently mastered the vocabulary of the epistemology that we inhabit, or else we may be trying to deal with concepts which are alien to the anomalies that we are trying to face and consequently we can only 'depict' them roughly and not at all 'precisely'. And yet, if we disregard our aspiration to precision and specificity, we may go on describing anomalies in a gross fashion and thus continue illusively to 'find our way around' concepts. In my view the question at issue is one of opting for a greater or lesser interest in anomalies and as a consequence for a greater or lesser measure of accuracy in trying to understand them and in our way of *inhabiting* a conceptual network.

Whatever else can be said about Freud and psychoanalysis we can easily grant that, at least in theory, there is a demand for the utmost attention, precision and interest in all kinds of anomalies. And what are called psychic anomalies can be 'seen' not by experimental means but rather through experiential ways primarily linked to the linguistic behaviour of individuals.

Of course it is not easy to suggest which aspects of Freud's work might have especially elicited the interest of Wittgenstein. We do not know whether it was the interpretation of dreams, early affective development, the language of illness, the vicissitudes of instincts or the so-called 'talking cure' that primarily inspired Wittgenstein to the point of telling Rhees that he thought of himself as a follower of Freud. I am inclined to believe that it is not one specific contribution which is responsible for inspiring Wittgenstein, but rather Freud's approach to the life of the mind through his fascination with anomalies, and his determination to place question marks as deep down as he possibly could. The demand for this approach is nowhere better reflected than in his remark: 'One keeps forgetting to go right down to the foundations. One doesn't put the question marks deep enough down.'[21]

The concern for anomalies is not related to a humane attitude or an inclination to tolerate exceptions, errors, heresies. I believe that

Wittgenstein, instead, is basically urging us to cultivate a taste for precision. He is not interested in anomalies *per se*, but in the *effort* to depict them with ever greater attention. Everything functions correctly within any powerful epistemology, or standard vocabulary, and there is nothing wrong with its success except that it leaves out a great deal of the specificity of human expressiveness. From within a standard vocabulary certain features of a cognitive field can, in fact, be seen with extreme clarity at the cost of ignoring other potential aspects of human linguisticity. Such aspects may all too easily be regarded as sheer anomalies. The tendency to address problems which can be illustrated in terms of linguistic examples such as 'buying newspapers', 'ordering meals' or 'directing taxi drivers' may be 'suggestive' of an extremely thin sector of language. We might easily be sceptical about such highly selective examples inasmuch as a significant proportion of humans (or at least in certain stages of the life-cycle) have no connections with buying, ordering or directing, in spite of their legitimate claim to language and communication. In this sense, we should advocate the inclusion of communicative instances unfolding outside of such limited standard activities. This is possibly achieved not so much by reaching for the 'abstractions' of metaphysics, spirituality, hermeneutics or soft-minded philosophy, but rather by disregarding those barriers towards forms of language that may appear at the beginning or at the end of the life-cycle, in marginal(ized) conditions or in any variant of post-Kraepelinian psychic 'pathology'. If we wish to continue moving about elegantly within our standard vocabulary, and if we intend to produce convincing combinations of concepts, we should stay at a distance from anomalies and especially anomalies of mind and language.

Inasmuch as we think of Wittgenstein as the thinker who epitomizes philosophy of language, we can point to a further link which connects Wittgenstein and Freud. Although Freudian psychoanalysis is an emanation of medical disciplines, it has no direct concern with the body of the person and the primary instrument of work in the linguisticity of the individual, and the therapeutic practice entirely relies upon symbolic interaction. And of course the 'secret' of analysis is attentive, persistent listening[22] to whatever the other is trying to say and in whichever way.

'Anyone who listens to a child's crying', remarks Wittgenstein, 'and understands what he hears will know that it harbours dormant psychic forces, terrible forces, *different from anything commonly assumed*. (Profound rage, pain and lust for destruction.)'[23] Further: 'A whole world of pain is contained in these words. How *can* it be contained in them – It is bound up with them. The words are like an acorn from which an oak tree can grow.'[24]

It is telling that the term 'infant' etymologically means someone who cannot speak. Newborn humans are referred to as infants, the non-speakers. When they 'learn' to speak they may perhaps face one of two extreme confrontations, almost as if parental figures were saying to them, 'This is language, baby, and you had better learn it quickly if you want to survive', or, on the other hand, 'Let us see how we can best interact and then perhaps you, the infant, could even teach me some new ways in language.'[25]

To the extent that a newborn human does not embody a dominant epistemology, there is a fertile field for observing so-called anomalies and for attempting precision in describing them. 'If in life we are surrounded by death, so too in the health of our intellect we are surrounded by madness,' remarks Wittgenstein.[26]

If psychoanalysis is to be regarded as a hermeneutic practice rather than as a science, it confronts primarily connections between propositions and other propositions, motives and further motives. As a hermeneutical enterprise it does not focus on connections between signs and causes. If we posit something called the unconscious, which is the 'primal cause' of both normal and pathological behaviour, then we would be faced with a variant of what Heidegger calls traditional metaphysics, where the unconscious may function as a substitute for time, being, prime matter, the logic of history or the transcendental cognitive apparatus. And of course Wittgenstein could not be a disciple of Freud in this quasi-metaphysical sense.

If we approach Freud in a different, non-metaphysical, non-causalistic perspective, and become interested in his propensity to be fascinated with anomalies of all kinds, to be intrigued not so much by the mechanisms of memory but by the act of forgetting, not so much by the process of perception but by our capacity to create blind spots and even our ability not to listen, it is more than plausible for Wittgenstein to proclaim himself a disciple of Freud; he in fact teaches us to appreciate the language of illness, silence, confusion – a language that we can hardly approach and cope with, a language that may ultimately induce a feeling of silliness. 'Never stay up on the barren heights of cleverness, but come down into the green valley of silliness,' urges Wittgenstein.[27] The practice, endurance and appreciation of our own silliness is perhaps advocated by Wittgenstein as a philosophical condition enabling us to confront something for which we are theoretically and linguistically unprepared, and whereby we run the risk of not knowing what to say – of making fools of ourselves. 'For a philosopher there is more grass growing down in the valleys of silliness than up on the barren heights of cleverness,' insists Wittgenstein.[28]

In view of the enormous complexity and depth of the human mind and of our linguisticity, I believe that we should be more readily willing to recant favoured assumptions, to discard vocabularies and desert powerful epistemologies in favour of the anomalies with which we may wish to interact. I thus believe that the term 'mentation' is possibly more appropriate than the word 'mind', as the latter can be suggestive of some sort of Cartesian staticity and lucidity. The term 'mentation' allows more easily for the notion of growth and lack of development and for an image of our inner world which is vulnerable to obscurity and subject to illness. Moreover, as Wittgenstein basically teaches us that language is not an object that we can control, the term 'linguisticity' may be preferable to 'language'. The word 'language' is so profusely employed in contemporary philosophy that we almost regard it as one of the familiar objects in our profession, perhaps as the sum total of all our utterances, actual and potential. The diction 'human linguisticity' possibly evokes a greater measure of humility and thus improves chances for the cultivation of precision.

Cultural Transformations: A Kuhnian Approach

As transformations of a symbolic paradigm are usually connected with shifts in perception, one cannot reasonably expect that an awareness of such transformations will emerge from within a sector of normal research, in which the mode of inquiry is more geared to knowing an aspect of the 'world' than to dealing with the epistemological structure of experience itself. For standard investigation addresses the complexity of the 'real' and not the complex interaction created between symbol and 'reality'. The following observations by Kuhn as regards changes in the conception of the world are thus pertinent to the philosophic question of envisaging extracultural and, in this circumscribed sense, metalinguistic levels of discourse. Kuhn remarks:

> Looking at the moon, the convert to Copernicanism does not say, 'I used to see a planet, but now I see a satellite.' That locution would imply a sense in which the Ptolemaic system had once been correct.

Instead, a convert to the new astronomy says, 'I once took the moon to be (or saw the moon as) a planet, but I was mistaken.' That sort of statement does not recur in the aftermath of scientific revolutions. If it ordinarily disguises a shift of scientific vision or some other mental transformation with the same effect, we may not expect direct testimony about that shift.[29]

Hence, the search for the basic modes of cognition is conducted within the context of an inquiry which does not address an aspect of the world but the forms of the relationships established between symbolic paradigms and object-constructs. If, for example, Gallileo could look at certain phenomena in a way radically different from that in which they had been 'seen' previously, one cannot but ask how such a radical transformation in the way of seeing things came about. Obviously we ought to acknowledge Gallileo's individual talent,

> But ... genius does not here manifest itself in more accurate or objective observation of the swinging body. Descriptively, the Aristotelian perception was just as accurate.... Rather, what seems to have been involved was the exploitation by genius of perceptual possibilities made available by a medieval paradigm shift. Gallileo was not raised completely as an Aristotelian. On the contrary, he was trained to analyze motions in terms of the impetus theory, a late medieval paradigm which held that the continuing motion of a heavy body is due to an internal power implanted in it by the projector that initiated its motion.... It was a view made possible by the transition from the original Aristotelian to the scholastic impetus paradigm for motion. Until that scholastic paradigm was invented, there were no pendulums, but only swinging stones. Pendulums were brought into existence by something very like a paradigm-induced gestalt switch.[30]

To the extent that the 'late medieval paradigm' was not properly 'Aristotelian', it was able to function as an *external*, metalinguistic sort of discourse, potentially conducive to the cultural transformations brought about by the 'genius' of humans.

The Growth of Expressive Modes

The celebrated saying of the early Wittgenstein, 'Whereof one cannot speak, thereof one must be silent',[31] might well sound like a rather 'constraining' philosophic principle within the scope of an inquiry directed towards an understanding of humans' constant effort to give expression to the 'inexpressible'. It may in fact take years of dialogic work to bring about a sufficiently 'authentic' two-way relationship to enable precisely those inner histories that least lend themselves to 'utterance' to find some way of coming to be expressed (and thus processed), so that they do not continue to be embodied in impoverishing forms of regression. For it is often very difficult – and at times wellnigh impossible – to speak about, for example, one's own uselessness or unworthiness to be in the world, about the incomprehensible 'voices' that persecute the mind, or of the fear of disintegrating. It is a question of expressing the unutterable suffering that one lives through and laboriously survives, by trying to convey and render intelligible to others our primal inner experiences. We are faced with our most trying vicissitudes and wallow in exasperation at precisely those times when we cannot manage to 'utter' in some way our inner conflicts – when 'we must pass over in silence what we cannot speak about'.[32] Aggressiveness and rage are by their very nature nearly unutterable in that their 'explosiveness' tends to elude containment by symbolic means, these being the function which creates connections and relationships, whereas aggressive affects tend to split, lacerate and fragment. The support of a far-sighted awareness of profound vicissitudes may enable us, therefore, better to appraise the philosophic difficulties attached to widening the domain of what is utterable, since that would ultimately involve the cognitive retrieval of obscure experiences hardly amenable to being framed and metabolized in symbolic discourse.

Names, for instance, bring a measure of order to experience, by giving 'objects' a feeling of familiarity; this is underscored by the sense of discomfort which we experience when confronted with something we are *not* able to name: in the extreme, something of an indescribable, unpredictable nature, such as defies rationality and customary classification. Ethnologists point out that, in certain cultural outlooks, to know a thing's name is to possess that entity, to be able to work magic, so that the thing's real name has to be kept secret and revealed only under certain conditions. When someone persists in trying to 'know' what it is that 'makes' that person 'feel bad', or what this 'illness' is called, we may be witnessing an exasperated reliance upon magical remedies. Grasping a name may thus be regarded as a first step towards a measure of control.

In the course of especially difficult stages of 'therapy', or at any rate somewhere along the path to maturity, the individual will be struggling to get across how much he is hounded by destructiveness inside himself – unutterable, inexpressible, not silent but mute – and will somehow ask for help in facing a 'terror' which he can neither utter nor explain. And resorting to some name borrowed from the jargon of psychopathology comes down to nothing more than a lame, defensive ploy involving magic expectations. It is an attempt to contain the disturbing complexity of mental events and bridle them with a name picked up in a purely imitative fashion. Whereas the enormous maturational momentum sparked off by the experience of being able to express oneself, and of having oneself understood, is of such relevance that it cannot be sufficiently appreciated in an integral cognitive perspective. A hypothetical suffering subject might make the following (unphilosophical) comment about Wittgenstein's celebrated statement: 'But if it is precisely what I cannot manage to utter that incapacitates and poisons my cognitive and interactive life, why then is it precisely about such things that one ought not to speak?' A first, historically oriented, reply might be to point out that the statement's 'restrictiveness' is probably related to a positivistic attitude, still too intimately associated with the polemic against metaphysics and with its radical, pioneering spirit.

We can agree, furthermore, with the arguments put forward by Hamburg[33] in a study wherein he proposes a more critical interpretation of Wittgenstein's statement. Such an 'imperative maxim' hinges basically on the meanings attached to 'One cannot' and 'One must'. But let us ask which criteria determine what 'can' or 'cannot' be said, not so much in this or that language as in any language whatsoever. If such criteria are of a syntactic nature, and thus have to do with the rules of logic, then 'cannot speak' refers to the logical impossibility not so much of expressing expectations as of communicating them in ways which do not violate the principles of logically consistent discourse. But, if such is the case, the phrase 'one must be silent' (apparently hortatory) is no longer an exhortation at all, for it represents simply a meaning of a logical nature (unsuited to being put forward in the form of a hortatory guiding principle with a 'therapeutic' potential). The meaning of the celebrated statement, therefore, would be: 'That which cannot be asserted without contradiction cannot be asserted as a communication.' On this premise, the statement in question would be meaningful only at the cost of being useless, or irrelevant, as a hortatory recommendation.[34] If 'Whereof one cannot speak' refers to the actual impossibility of finding or using words in such a way as to indicate a certain cognitive or affective condition, then what is implied by 'one must be silent' is either tautologous or else false.[35] It will be tautologous to the extent that the lack of direct or indirect expressions is synonymous with being silent; it will be false to the extent that the lack of expressions capable of clearly describing a situation has never prevented human beings from employing language for purposes other than description in a strict sense.

That vast area of our language and thought which does not conform to customary norms and standards of expression, those assertions which cannot strictly be either affirmed or denied, but which are none the less always present in mankind, are defined by Carnap as 'analogous to laughter'.[36] However, as Langer suggests, 'There is no eternal decree over means and methods of intelligence. So I will go with the logisticians and linguists as far as they like, but do not promise to go no further. For there is an unexplored possibility of genuine semantic beyond the limits of discursive language.'[37] She suggests, moreover, that 'In this physical, space-time world of our experience there are things which do not fit the grammatical scheme of expression. But they are not necessarily blind, inconceivable, mystical affairs; they are simply matters which require to be conceived through some symbolistic scheme other than discursive language.'[38]

We may point out by way of example how the innovative work of Freud and Jung made it necessary to come to terms with the evidence of inner vicissitudes hitherto considered inconceivable or unthinkable – beyond all possibility of expression. The distinguishing mark of the work of innovators is that it regards as by no means inconceivable certain persistent, embryonic thoughts – however enigmatic and disquieting they may be. On the contrary, innovators tend to centre their method of research ever more upon the systematic effort to listen properly and not to draw back from what might appear unutterable and unthinkable. They attempt to deal symbolically with even the most 'crushing' of problems, through sharing critical discourse on such questions as well as experiential confrontations. One of Freud's major achievements is the formulation of working hypotheses regarding human emotions – hypotheses which previously might well have been unthinkable: no epistemological spaces existed, so to speak, such as would admit the thought that any human being might even harbour destructive desires regarding the persons emotionally nearest to him.

Certain symbolizations may often be regarded as 'indisputable' inasmuch as they are adequate to a system of interpersonal communication – a linguistic community. And, as Whorf suggests, whenever they are adequate linguistically to our social needs, they 'will remain so until an additional group of needs is felt and is worked out in language'.[39] But the question then arises how a 'group of needs' can be felt if it is not to some extent worked out in language. And how can it be sufficiently worked out if it is not 'felt'? The two issues appear to be closely interwoven and a growing attention to the symbolic function may help cultivate a concern for enhancing 'additional' human needs and for working them out adequately to the point where they attain linguistic legitimacy.[40] Such vicissitudes may be re-enacted in individual ontogenies, and a range of attitudes unfolds, spanning from an effort to confine oneself imitatively within current language all the way to allowing oneself to 'feel' new needs and seek suitable symbolizations to share and propound them. Through this latter attitude we could perceive a fuller meaning of the notion of *Bildung*, or self-creation, as a process of (self-)education in the sense of *ex ducere*, of leading out some inner potential in the direction of cultural, symbolic interaction.

The development of language may thus be seen as creating a sort of hiatus diversifying two forms of possibly simultaneous experience extending from the virtual extremes of a lived-through, personal, unutterable experience to the sort of experience which can be properly verbalized – shared. There may be 'facts' occurring in one's inner depth whose reverberations and developments may only in part be channelled into the domain of linguistic, symbolic rule. To the extent that a logocratic culture confers the 'seal' of reality primarily upon those events which are amenable to linguistic systematization, experiences taking place in other areas of the self tend to be further alienated or altogether denied. And yet, however vulnerable to obscurity, they may become vital, autonomous life trends.[41] Efforts to express the unutterable or to think the unthinkable offer the greatest promise of leading to creative propensities. Such efforts, in fact, bring back into focus a virtual line of demarcation which distinguishes between our being 'spoken' or 'thought' by the linguistic community to which we belong,[42] as opposed to our being the cognizant users *and* generators of a language. It is by means of the opportunities for expression offered by a 'transformed' scenario that an individual may embark upon the free and laborious development of his own cognitive world.

3

On Language and Reality

The Gap between World and Language:
A Philosophical Space

One may doubtless consider language as something natural which shares in all the events of the biological world, something within the cognitive reach of various scientific methodologies, such as phonology, glottology and linguistics in general. Yet we ought to concede that language *also* exists 'outside' the natural world, *at least* in the sense that – from a cognitive point of view – it is the heterogeneity and the separateness of the world with respect to language which can confer upon language a variety of semantic values which may be regarded as ranging from 'true' to 'false'. Between language (on the one hand) and nature (on the other), there is, as it were, a gap or intervening space which may be construed as non-physical, non-organic and non-natural. This space, which is both epistemological and hermeneutical, constitutes the specific habitat of philosophic inquiries.[1] In other words, it is a space between the world and that aspect of language (a non-natural aspect of it which is epistemic and interpretative) whereby humans construct cognitive relations with reality.

Cassirer highlights the aspects characterizing the complexity of human linguisticity:

> Even though sensuous and spiritual elements seem to have been inextricably intertwined in the origin of language, this *correlation*, precisely because it is a correlation, does not argue a relation of *one-sided* dependancy between the two.... The characteristic meaning of language is not contained in the opposition between the two extremes of the sensuous and the intellectual, because in all its achievements and in every particular phase of its progress, language shows itself to be *at once* a sensuous and an intellectual form of expression.[2]

As a matter of fact, as soon as the more complex functions of language begin to be addressed, namely as the notion of truth is approached, the symbolic function acts in some respects as an 'alienating' dimension. While even in the most naturalistic construals of language it is necessary to think out some system of relations and aims with respect to which an assertion may be 'valid' to a greater or lesser extent, as one laboriously closes in on a regulative idea of truth (phylogenetically and ontogenetically speaking) there is no chance left that 'true' and 'false' may prove natural properties which can be grasped by a participating awareness. Without some measure of detachment from the natural world, the philosophic categories of 'true' and 'false' could never gain access into culture. The dramatic yet inevitable travail involved in progressing from the use of language to the awareness of it, which derives from just such detachment, is repeatedly referred to by Filiasi Carcano: today's marked insistence on the complex problem of language, symbolism, communication and information is not to be considered an isolated, random phenomenon; rather, it reflects the issue of a biopsychological evolution which has been progressively uprooting mankind from its direct contact with nature and plunging humans into a growing sense of isolation.[3]

All that has been argued hitherto may be led back to an enlightening synthesis offered by Austin, in which he states: 'There must also be something other than the words, which the words are to be used to communicate about: this may be called the "world". There is no reason why the world should not include the words, in every sense except the sense of the actual statement itself which on any particular occasion is being made about the world.'[4] What comes through clearly in contemporary thought is the growing realization that there is no getting away from a symbolic mediation which influences all of our experiences: it separates and (at the same time) connects thought and world, nature and culture. Not only can we no longer rely on a *participation mystique*, but any idea of coming to grips with reality without adhering (with what hopes of success?) to some form of linguistic mediation is also out of the question, with the result that, ultimately, it turns out to be language itself which determines the confines of that which is knowable and of that of which we can gain some awareness.

'Higher' Functions of Language

As we know, language fulfils a number of functions, among which – at the most 'primitive' level – are those of self-expression and of signalling. To the extent, however, that language is not confined to being an instrument of expression or even of communication and description, certain 'higher' functions – those of argumentation – come to light which cannot fit within the boundaries of language when primarily regarded as a natural phenomenon.

As Popper remarks: 'The most important of human creations, with the most important feed-back effects upon ourselves and especially upon our brains, are the higher functions of human language; more especially, the *descriptive function* and the *argumentative function*.' Further:

> The self-expressive function or symptomatic function of language is obvious; all animal language is symptomatic of the state of some organism. The signalling or release function is likewise obvious: we do not call any symptom linguistic unless we assume that it can release a response in another organism. All animal languages and all linguistic phenomena share these two lower functions. But human language has many other functions. Strangely enough, the most important of the higher functions have been overlooked by almost all philosophers. The explanation of this strange fact is that the two lower functions are always present when the higher ones are present, so that it is always possible to 'explain' every linguistic phenomenon in terms of lower functions, as an *'expression'* or a *'communication'*. With the descriptive function of human language, the regulative idea of truth emerges.[5]

At least as far as its epistemological functions are concerned, that complex set of symbolic vehicles which makes up language is essentially both distinct, and qualitatively different, from the natural world. It is the indelible qualitative difference of those functions of language which allows the most diverse forms of philosophical scepticism to raise their heads and which also creates the space which makes it possible and necessary for knowledge constantly to re-elaborate its achievements. In an effort to stave off the perils of scepticism, a number of philosophic trends go to great lengths to mend that 'fracture', that irremediable qualitative difference between reality and language. For that purpose, philosophic inquiry is confined to one or the other side of the troubled linguistic domain. One may opt for a philosophic method wherein language is completely naturalized and treated as an object, in an attempt, possibly, at fusing together nature and culture; or, alternatively, one may attempt to confine philosophic investigation exclusively to the 'symbolic'-formal side. In the latter approach (which is intended to overcome once and for all the laborious passage between the development of language and the construction of reality), clear, distinct paradigms are posited which lie beyond the reach of the troubles afflicting that crucial and tormented relationship between language and reality, culture and nature. Cassirer sums up that problematic relationship as follows: 'Seeing in this context, the way in which we apply the conceptual opposition of "subjective" and "objective" in giving form to the world of experience, in constructing nature, appears to be not so much the *solution* to the problem of cognition, as its perfect *expression*.'[6]

The qualitative difference (or distinctness) of linguistic constructs in the domain of cognitive or interpretative assertions stands at a distance from the language of self-expression and simple description: the former has to do not so much with objects but with the *relationships* which come to subsist between the language of a 'knowing subject' and objects. Popper suggests that 'the autonomy is only partial: the new problems lead to new creations or constructions.... And every such step will create *new unintended facts*; *new unexpected problems*; and often also *new refutations*. There is also a most important feed-back effect from our own creations upon ourselves.... For the new emergent problems stimulate us to new creations.'[7]

Within the potential of human linguisticity, reflection may take the form of a fluctuating process which moves from the world in the making towards the symbol, or from the symbolic level towards reality, in a cognitive ferment of reciprocal give and take. There is a continuous oscillation between symbol and symbolized, between language and world. Filiasi Carcano suggests that there is an underlying twofold process which is essential to an understanding of symbolization. Through language we try to appropriate the world and draw it into ourselves; then, from language, we start back towards the world in the form of an unending rhythmic breathing.[8] It is not so much a question of a 'transition', an inexplicable leap from the objective to the subjective (as in the dualistic view of Kantian epistemology), but rather something we do (or reproduce) within a symbolic medium, something which occurs at a different (biological) level of our experience. In Filiasi Carcano's view, we live on two levels, namely the symbolic (which moves to the fore when the symbolized is not present) and the level of things symbolized which we perceive and use directly and to which the symbol refers.

Metalinguistic Functions

In order to bring into focus the issue of linguistic levels, we may adopt the line of reasoning developed by Danto,[9] whereby it is argued that a linguistic expression such as a sentence may constitute an attempt to describe reality and is therefore to be considered a descriptive sentence. Now, if that sentence – which we may call 's' – is descriptive and refers to reality, it will easily be conceded that another sentence, for instance, ' "s" is true', unlike the above sentence 's', refers not to reality but to the previous sentence called 's'. But it would not be correct to hold that the affirmation ' "s" is true' refers exclusively to the sentence 's', as it would be correct to say that ' "s" is a sentence'. In fact, as Danto goes on to argue, the assertion ' "s" is true' refers not to a sentence but to a *relationship* (or correspondence). In other words, it refers both to the sentence and to reality and it tells us something which the sentence 's' by itself did not tell us, inasmuch as that assertion referred to the world alone, whereas the linguistic expression ' "s" is true' refers to some connection between language and the world.[10]

In my opinion, those aspects of language which gravitate towards 'natural' relations within a physical, organic or social reality could be associated with an expressive or descriptive function of language. On the other hand, those aspects of language which refer to the potential or actual relationship between language and reality may be regarded as the epistemological, philosophical and hermeneutical functions of language. Were the 'philosophic' functions of language to be reduced to the status of purely natural elements, we should be spared, it is true, the labours of scepticism and of philosophic debates, but we might be giving up an evolutionary outlook on our linguisticity. Danto remarks:

> In collapsing the relation between the language and the world into some sort of intra-worldly relation, and hence in collapsing the ultimate differences between philosophical and scientific questions, Naturalists arrived at a picture of what men are which was all right so far as it went, but which lacked a crucial dimension. For men, in so far as they are distinctively men, do not exist only within the world. Never ceasing for a moment to be (complex) bits of the world, they also exist without the world, entering it, so to speak, from across an extra-worldly space.[11]

I believe that this cognitive space is generated by the symbolic function. Indeed, it is conceivable that, were our language made up of semantic elements radically different from those familiar to us (nouns, phrases, classifications, etc.), reality, in turn, would also be arranged differently. And yet the crucial issue of the world–language *relation* would none the less remain unaltered. Although perhaps with different intents, Popper argues to a similar effect:

> With the development of a descriptive language (and further, of a written language), a linguistic third world can emerge; and it is only in this way, and only in this third world, that the problems and standards of rational criticism can develop. It is to this development of the higher functions of language that we owe our humanity, our reason.... This second point shows the futility of all theories of human language that focus on *expression and communication*.... The human organism which, it is often said, is intended to express itself, depends in its structure very largely upon the emergence of the two higher functions of language. With the evolution of the argumentative function of language, criticism becomes the main instrument of further growth.[12]

And there is a specific relation with the world, wherein lies that crucial link which some philosophers have tried, in various ways, to express by proclaiming their effort to find ways of describing reality in a *true* fashion. Despite the myriad roles of language – or, in other words, the great diversity of linguistic games played – these are perhaps of lesser import than the basic issue of constructing objects, that is a sufficiently broad world view; and this we may regard as a common, laborious task for all humans. In the course of the developmental history of individuals, the task of shaping a sufficiently 'large' world leads from the narcissistic use of a parental environment (punctiform, like a source of nourishment) to the conscious recognition of reciprocal relationships such as open up interactive and cognitive prospects.

The Question of Limits

One may discern a submerged travail winding beneath the early Wittgenstein's thinking: it has to do with the identification of the limits of language, of what may be *effectively* expressed, by relegating to the status of 'non-sense' everything which, though expressed, does not come up to the prescribed canons of meaningfulness. We could tentatively say that in the *Tractatus* the limits of language are traced on the basis of the existence of logical models, whereas in the *Investigations* boundaries are decreed by linguistic usage itself and, in the last analysis, by recourse to the notion of 'forms of life'. Yet the shift in the canons of meaningfulness, namely a transition from linguistic patterns to linguistic customs, does not imply a lesser concern regarding the search for limits.

It is also possible, none the less, to interpret Wittgenstein's sustained interest in discovering the *limits* of language not so much as something restrictive, as I previously indicated,[13] but, on the contrary, as a perspective pointing to a tormented awareness of the potential philosophic spaces opening out beyond (or beneath) those very limits. One might well wonder at the theoretical price paid by linguistic clarifications achieved by giving pride of place to the ordinary-language model in its most varied applications, when it may turn out that the 'philosophical' validity of language seems to have been established thanks to the exclusion of vast and deep expanses of human symbolization – *other* forms of life.

A concern with the search for limits may be understood as the negative utterance (or establishment) of those vast expanses for which neither the language of science nor everyday language can find an expression possessed of sense. The very fact that there is, in Wittgenstein's thought, no explicit denial of the meaningfulness of forms of expression not provided for either in consensually accepted usage or by the governing of logic seems in itself a tacit recognition of an irrepressible human creativity. In other words, it is the unveiling of something else which will not be denied, which will not be nullified by any restrictive boundary: on the contrary, it is actually highlighted precisely because it is *other* than that which is contained within the limit itself.

The philosophic proposal of 'silence' concerning any form of thought which cannot be incorporated into a scientific structure (or into a customary practice) is perhaps calling us to a muteness which may none the less be interpreted or, better, *listened to*. While silence may indicate nothing – it may be a void – it may also indicate or evoke all that language, be it ordinary or scientific, cannot manage to say, demonstrate or express.

It is almost as if that 'philosophic silence' which had been so painstakingly achieved within the confines of a philosophy of language resulting in linguistic analysis had proved a 'limitation' which then stirred up an even more energetic 'search' for those forms of thought which venture beyond, so to speak, the bounds of linguistic legitimacy. We do not really know whether there is an intention to reject all the dimensions of thought opening out beyond the anointed languages of science and custom, or whether there is an attempt to distinguish matters that can fit into language from 'topics' which have nothing to do with language inasmuch as they could not live, much less survive, within a domain of *insufficient* symbolization.

4

The Symbolic Function, Error and Awareness

Critical Distances and the Development of Awareness

Since the dawn of reflective thought any 'critique' of knowledge has been construed as an assessment of our cognitive claims and of the reliability of experience, with a view to achieving standards for a more accurate representation and construction of reality. This concern, as we know, is based upon a variety of attempts to theorize the process of elaboration and mediation necessary for (ordinary) experience. And a contribution of psychoanalytic culture to this area of investigation is linked with our renewed appreciation of the affective problems involved, and of the latent emotional factors coming into play.[1] In this perspective, then, the joint issue of knowledge-claims and cognitive theories comes to be regarded as one aspect of the more basic problem of human interactions. The time-honoured problem of knowledge may thus be considered as auxiliary to the broader issue of our interactive life.

The laboriously opened cleavage between the infant's world of fantasy and the domain of reality may be employed for purposes of cognitive development to the extent that another gap comes to be formed within the primal mind. In other words, a second hiatus must form within the developing individual so that some first 'symbolic' element comes to stand out from the background, thus allowing the subject–object relation to be somehow *visualized* with the result that there comes to be, on the one hand, the 'symbol' and, on the other, the subject–object relation to which the symbol in fact refers. It is this additional ability to use symbolic elements which permits the inchoate person gradually to acquire a perspectival view of himself and of *his* relationship with the world. He can engage in interactions and assume responsibility *vis-à-vis* his reality through no means other than such a cleavage or gap or distance, which only at this point begins to perform a proper cognitive role.[2]

Any relation which remains confined within a bipartite apposition – and thus incapable of achieving some grasp of such primal duality – runs the risk of being unable to break free of those fantasmic levels wherein there is no distinction between a signifying element and an object, and even of regressing to the level of 'concrete thought'. Relations patterned along such lines, which are typical of inchoate experience, may perpetuate the infant's confusional subjection to the maternal environment. Through a greater appreciation of the role of human interactions in cognitive growth it may be seen that the aforesaid confusional subjection is to be overcome primarily with the aid of figures which complement the maternal role, all of which may be summed up in the concept of the father-figure.[3] Some form of representation of one's relationship with the maternal environment, as mirrored by the presence of a father-figure, may be introjected by the developing individual and thus made use of for the purpose of attempting a crucial transition whereby the earliest processes of awareness are perspectivally constructed. We are thus confronted with the need for a third relational element corresponding to that further symbolic cleavage within the subject. For the mental 'element' originating from the second cleavage is the factor which allows for the elaboration of a more knowing reference to the two terms of a primal, dual relation, as well as the kindling of the inner perception of one's relation with others. It is in the course of this crucial transition, during which the incipient processes of awareness are organized, that the aforesaid perspectival view of one's relationship with the maternal environment may be taken in and worked into one's inner cognitive processes, thanks to the opportunity of being somehow reflected by an available father-figure.

Similarly, in a dialogic setting, one of the partners may voice comments on the 'mental' state of the other – a condition which he may experience not as a mental state but as (if it were) something quite real. When an attentive listener agrees to deal with a fantasy originating in his interlocutor, the former's response is, at the same time, both empathic and impersonal – distant – in the sense that an effort is made to understand the profound meanings involved in the dialogue and not just its superficial import (which seemingly refers to reality).[4] Responses of the listening interlocutor may thus be employed for the structural foundation of a new, further order of awareness. When someone gives expression to his tormented inner world, in a truly dialogic setting, he is by the same token led, in the first place, to the realization that he experiences (as if they were reality) the images of his own desires; and these 'images' take the form both of idealized 'states' and of catastrophic 'reality' inasmuch as fantasy ideas, which do not provide satisfaction, are inevitably transformed into something disruptive or persecutory. Secondly, the suffering individual has an opportunity to acknowledge the presence of the other person, precisely because the latter's words are the indispensable *optical* instrument for introducing a measure of healthy doubt which constitutes the starting-point for separating the real from the fantastic. The specific relevance of the study of symbols is revealed when the problem of symbol-formation is treated in conjunction with the general problem of suffering and of 'cognitive' error, viewed as a defensive withdrawal from the interactive world. When the human infant is confronted with a condition which calls for sacrifices too great to bear, he may withdraw mentally from the relational world and take refuge in his own inner domain (however empty and hardly liveable). Similarly, when a subject in the making is overwhelmed by the 'goodness' of the mother-figure, his choice is between the utmost passivity, on the one hand, and the rejection of such 'goodness' (and consequent withdrawal into himself) on the other. And it is perhaps in this way that a first step is taken towards assuming a pseudo-cognitive or indifferent attitude.

If, then, we may utilize the notion of a father-figure as the principle of separation which wards off symbiotic reabsorption through allowing the latter process to be visualized and mastered (that is somehow symbolized), we shall also allow that the same father-figure can act as a bulwark capable of shielding the infant against his own recurrent temptations, or fears, of reabsorption into earlier phases of development. A father-figure, or any worthy surrogate, is seen as being indispensable for neutralizing the fear of regressing into the undifferentiated state which alternates and intertwines with bouts of the fear of separation-individuation. Paternal figures are all too often portrayed in rather reductive terms, mainly as somewhat menacing and inhibiting, almost an Oedipal re-edition of the 'bad mother'. This same thesis has been clearly expressed by Loewald when he argues that, in the phase of regressive, fusional pulls, a sufficiently strong father-figure does not at all constitute a further difficulty but rather an essential form of support.

Advancing to a subsequent phase of maturation involves, therefore, the ability to attain a vantage-point from which one may view one's own cognitive self within its relational dynamics. Such a step forward amounts to the acquisition of some early form of meta-language, or second-order language, which, although still 'pre-verbal', is yet the means whereby the individual in the making is able to construct and 'think' the relation between his earliest symbolic forms and that which they stand for.

Clearly, symbolic elements are needed not only in order to communicate with the outside world (synchronically) but also, and above all, in order to communicate with one's own mental depths (diachronically).[5] One might well ask what is meant when we speak of a good relationship with one's own inner affects and cognition. It is probably not a matter of being able knowingly to entertain primal fantasies (such as those which can surface in the course of psychoanalysis), but simply that there is a certain degree of awareness of our own deep-down affects.

As we know, one of the major problems for individuals considered to be 'psychotic' or 'narcissistic' is not just their difficulty in communicating with others, but above all their difficulty in relating with themselves, in the sense that often a share of their (cognitive) structure comes to be cut off from another part, so that the two have no way of communicating.[6] Freud recognized the enormous difficulties involved in the processes of inner communication as well as in the critical perception of our own internal relational vicissitudes and on several occasions eloquently referred to the problem. He argues as follows:

> Our hypothesis is that there are two essentially different classes of instincts: the sexual instincts, understood in the widest sense – Eros, if you prefer that name – and the aggressive instincts, whose aim is destruction. When it is put to you like this, you will scarcely regard it as a novelty.... But it is a remarkable thing that this hypothesis is nevertheless felt by many people as an innovation and, indeed, as a most undesirable one which should be got rid of as quickly as possible. I presume that a strong affective factor is coming into effect in this rejection. Why have we ourselves needed such a long time before we decided to recognize an aggressive instinct? Why did we hesitate to make use, on behalf of our theory, of facts which were obvious and familiar to everyone? We should probably have met with little resistance if we had wanted to ascribe an instinct with such an aim to animals.[7]

Such crucial questioning may well bear witness to the degree of commitment required if one is to take meaningful steps in the odyssey of cognition, namely those steps which constitute the qualitative surge which carries the individual across to the horizon of self-awareness.[8]

The Development of the Idea of Truth

The question how an inner cleavage is achieved whereby one may become aware of one's own cognitive events also represents a relevant issue for those lines of thought which aim at a philosophic concern with knowledge. In his contributions to this area of inquiry, Danto explores the philosophic implications of the emergence of knowledge: he lays stress on the development of two gaps within an original, primitive, undifferentiated state.

> The insertion of a distance between our primary involvement with the world, which created logical space in language for *words* as 'knowledge' and for such a concept as 'knowing that we know', revealed, at the same time, a distance between ourselves and the world with which we were primarily involved. Consciousness is in general an alienating mechanism, in that to be conscious of something is at once to be conscious of a separation of consciousness from that thing *and* to be conscious of the separation; so that when knowledge became self-conscious, as it were, two gaps simultaneously appeared: a gap first between knowledge and its object, and then the gap between this relationship and our knowledge of it, which would be knowledge of *knowledge*.[9]

We might argue that such a process of articulation has to do with both 'suffering' and 'error', in so far as the gap between the subject and his involvement as well as the gap within that same involvement present themselves to awareness only when 'things go wrong', in other words when one realizes that one has got something wrong or made an error. Yet the most meaningful and paradoxical feature is that this maturational process, in and of itself, has no 'practical' (or natural) value, inasmuch as the 'value' of crossing a threshold of awareness can be appreciated only if we adopt a philosophical, or developmental, outlook. For crossing the threshold of the symbolic domain and thus achieving awareness are quite 'useless' to the rest of reality in general, and yet indispensable for purposes of self-creation. Danto asserts as much in the concluding paragraph of his contribution:

> To bring things to consciousness is painful and peculiarly useless, but without it we would not know what we are. Philosophy is the consciousness of consciousness. The philosophy of knowledge is knowledge about knowledge. Such knowledge, too, is painfully attained and

useless. But without it we would not know what we know, nor, fundamentally, who we are. For the space between language and the world is a space within ourselves, since we are within and without the world, and the gap which lies at the core of our being is what defines our essence.[10]

Nietzsche, whose influence on psychoanalytic culture is generally acknowledged, remarks that in an evolutionary perspective 'All instincts which do not discharge outwardly turn inward. This is what I call man's internalization; with it begins to grow in man what later is called his "soul".'[11] There seems to be the suggestion of a remarkable change in viewpoint: the philosophical standpoint has shifted from the 'sympathy' for the unhappy fate of an animal whose instincts become unhinged, to our recognition of the fascinating challenge of the genesis of our 'soul', of man as human. In this light, symbolic structures may be conceived as deciding in favour of internalization and self-creation processes – the growth in man of 'what later is called his "soul" ' – as against mechanisms of splitting and repression. Symbols in fact allow for attempts at successful internalization. Moreover, as Spitz remarks: 'The capacity to use mental operations and communicate them through verbal symbols instead of having to act, instead of having recourse to fight or flight, confers a new measure of autonomy to the child.'[12]

Those symbolic elements by means of which we may perceive our own relationship with the 'other' can begin to take shape when defences by splitting and negation begin to be lowered, in other words when the future individual hazards facing those vexing ambivalences inherent in the experiences of love and hate which inexorably characterize our ontogenetic history. In the project of self-creation one may escape the resulting uneasiness, which involves depression, by regressing to earlier patterns or, in other words, by pinning one's hopes on using mechanisms of denial right to the bitter end as well as a thoroughgoing drastic repudiation of one's own incipient affectual and cognitive awareness. By such means the subject may avoid becoming aware of one of those as yet unmanageable images of himself as destructive or ungrateful that secretly insinuate themselves precisely during transitional phases of maturation. To the extent that such an 'internal policy' works 'successfully', the individual in the making will shut out preliminary 'philosophic' spaces, thereby rendering himself incapable of grasping and perceiving his own emotional-cognitive reality: in other words, he makes himself a prisoner of his own blindness.

The so-called insufficient clarity of certain verbal communications is not a limit but perhaps their very strength. A speaker needs forms of symbolization that he can somehow recant and disavow, in order not to be overwhelmed by responsibility. A developing mind might hesitate to experiment with expressions of creativity, hostility or affection if such symbolizations could not be disclaimed, placed at a distance, with a certain measure of freedom. Should the qualities of intonation and gestures be so accurately identifiable as to make persons responsible for their global expressive modes, the transition from biological life to dialogic existence would perhaps be loaded with an excess of anxiety.

Some individuals find it difficult to deal with reality when the reality involved is their own inner world, which is to say that they find themselves at a loss when it is a question of attempting to articulate their own feelings of suffering. Bion remarks that 'People exist who are so intolerant of pain or frustration (or in whom pain or frustration is so intolerable) that they feel the pain but will not suffer it and so cannot be said to discover it.'[13] Only a *negative* definition may be attempted regarding the condition of a person who is in pain and who is not even capable of asserting that a state of suffering exists in so far as he is unable to be aware of himself suffering (or of his own suffering self). It is precisely when one cannot even manage to experience pain (that is, when one can feel it only in a blunted, benumbed fashion) that one cannot even arrive at the discovery of joy. And to feel pain without either suffering or realizing that it is there may be regarded as corresponding to either clashing head-on with the objects of reality or avoiding any such collisions, without ever developing the capacity to acquire a conscious vocabulary of one's own relations with those objects in the outer world with which one does clash or avoid clashing. To the extent that the impoverishment that ensues from seeking refuge by deafening our inner awareness is avoided (through the interpretative dialogue originally provided by parental environment), the world view being built will turn out to be not only dualistic (i.e. no longer a solipsistic mirroring) but potentially relational, inasmuch as defensive ploys are no longer capable of standing in the way of 'learning' from the sort of experience of which we may have a grasp. When consciousness develops along these lines, what we have is a *reasonable* relational attitude inasmuch as our disposition to avoid suffering does not depend upon mechanisms for ignoring or distorting reality, but upon an effort to come to terms with it through ever-renewed forms of contractual dialogue.

In a synoptic view, we may suggest that, whereas the earliest symbolic formations have to do with external elements, with the appearance of a second inner gap the symbolic elements become capable of also referring to the inner (as related to the outer) world which is being organized. One will thus be able to use a generated (and not acquired) vocabulary in order to create perspectival links with any two aspects of our inner world.

By means of a second inner gap the subject may attain the ability to be conscious of his own relational attitudes. In other words, it is by reaching this further symbolic level that he attains a first measure of awareness and thereby *lets himself know* what he knows. Even in cases of undeveloped or deteriorated mentation, one 'knows' – for example – who one's mother is and 'recognizes' her even though one cannot manage to develop some knowledge of one's own *relationship* with that person. The maturational value of such inner vicissitudes lies, however, in the possibility that the connection between two elements of consciousness is rendered 'abstract' by encoding such inner experiences in some inchoate linguistic form. In other words, a detachment from the stream of affects is thus rendered possible and this provides the subject with a first degree of independence from the sequence of his 'emotional states'. One passes from a world of affective states lived in deafness to a world of situations which are to some extent audible and recognizable.[14] A further developmental benefit consists in the incipient opportunities to perform some type of abstract reflection as a preliminary to carrying out an advantageous interaction with the world. Inasmuch as its function is both retrospective and anticipatory, reflection implies that inner occurrences, such as may be perceived as unfolding chronologically or historically, are relationally placed at a distance and thus become quite different from the absolute, timeless present of primal conditions.

It is only when a first level of awareness comes to separate out that the process of knowledge may take hold as a sequence which can virtually propagate, in open-ended fashion, in the form of an organization of consciousness capable of constructing more complex, truth-oriented perceptions.

The main feature of the notion of 'truth' as a regulative ideal of relations or inquiries is to be recognized more precisely in a growing relation between 'facts' and 'sentences' than in the practical utility or in the reassuring consistency of any discourse or hypothesis. In this sense, both our 'utility' (which may gravitate towards sterile narcissism) and 'consistency' (which may be gratuitously solipsistic or imaginary) could appear less consequential than the efforts of interactive development. We can borrow an example from Popper, who suggests:

> A meta-language is a language in which we talk about some other language. For example, a grammar of the German language, written in English, uses English as a meta-language in order to talk about German. The language about which we talk in the *meta-language* (in this case English) is usually called the *'object language'* (in this case German). The characteristic thing about a meta-language is that it contains (meta-linguistic) *names* of words and of statements of the object language, and also (meta-linguistic) *predicates*, such as 'noun (of the object language)' or 'verb (of the object language)' or 'statement (of the object language)'.[15]

By means of some form of metalanguage, it is possible for us to use an assertion to express a relation between an utterance (in the object language) and a 'fact'. Viewed thus, we may obviously replace the object language with any other language, even with our own language – despite the fact that it is functioning as a metalanguage in the discussion of any 'foreign' language.

It is only when some form of metalanguage is attained that it is possible to embark upon the search for object-related forms of truth in their disparate manifestations. Without metalinguistic tools of some kind we could not even begin to establish a preference favouring a search for object-related truths and would consequently remain dependent upon the sole distinction between conditions of pleasure and displeasure.

It is by virtue of inchoate metalinguistic tools of consciousness that we may develop an ability to make some critical assessment of our relation with the world and thus to enrich our stream of interactions (of which knowledge is a superb variant). Failing the onset of metasymbolic functions, by means of which the very metabolism of our inner life comes to be perceived, there could be no soundly organized mentation.

The Utilization of Errors

As contemporary thought renews itself, we come to be both the onlookers and the participants in a change of perspective. Alongside, and in antithesis to, the tacit assumption that knowledge is a quasi-

'causal' process which determines truth, there is also a tendency to work towards a recognition of knowledge as possibility, effort or project. 'Knowledge' thus could be *one* of the forms of human interaction, no matter how time-honoured and productive it is thought to be. In Rorty's view, for instance, even 'analytic' philosophy could be regarded as one more variant of Kantian cognitive philosophy, a variant characterized by conceiving of representation as linguistic rather than mental, and of assuming that philosophy of language rather than transcendental critique is the discipline which provides the 'foundations' of knowledge.[16]

A postulate common to the majority of traditional theories of knowledge seems to be the assumption that knowledge is basically something 'automatic', so to speak, rather than a laborious, enigmatic, relational process to be developed in time. Although all forms of knowledge are incomplete and all sciences in the process of development, 'classically' based epistemologic views are conducive to an outlook whereby anything accorded the status of 'cognitive' approach or established 'knowledge' automatically rises to so high a level of (alleged) validity that one might feel authorized to take such aspects of knowledge in isolation and consider them as immutable cognitive units in and of themselves.

To the extent that parts of our 'cognitive' structure are still supported by the most archaic forms of relation and thus linked with a world of 'states' or 'conditions', we cannot simply move on to an outlook organized around the interactive processing of our efforts; for the questions formulated tend to be of a static, essentialist cast which seems to flaw and constrain any possible reply. When such an outlook holds sway, just as one might ask, for example, what one's inner illness 'is', it is likewise possible to ask what truth-conditions 'are' and, consequently, what knowledge is. In this fashion, although that basic question, 'What is knowledge?', breaks down into a multitude of linguistic problems, it none the less retains its philosophical 'nobility', so that it stands out as one of the permanent central concerns. Despite the undeniably tentative nature of its countless contributions, even 'scientific' epistemologies often produce the 'optical illusion' of setting up a body of 'definite', although incomplete, truths, with the result that philosophical questions such as *'What is knowledge (or truth)?'* may come to be regarded as legitimate.

Alongside such tendencies, however, there may be a more 'dialogic' outlook wherein various demands and cultural factors converge in such a way that the problem of knowledge, rather than continuing to be considered a noble and essential question, a 'matter of fact', could be viewed as one of the processes of creative elaboration, with the result that the issue cannot be absorbed into the timeless abstraction of a question about the 'nature' of knowledge.

A necessary and laborious transformation of the concept of knowledge from 'process' to 'effort' inevitably implies a new manner of addressing the problem of cognition. It also implies a need to identify the linguistic means suited to capturing the widely diversified dimension of knowledge while abandoning an idea of permanence and entering a more 'historical' scenario of philosophy. The more our outlook is underpinned by an interactive approach, the more the development of a diachronic dimension proves relevant for engendering a potentially far-reaching and complex cognitive dynamics. In the absence of a vivid sense of time or, better, of a 'planning' propensity, the logical space into which we may meaningfully fit the concepts of evolution and criticism of 'knowledge' undergoes a damaging shrinkage.

Phylogenetically speaking, the inestimable relevance of the symbolic function as regards the process of hominization becomes evident not only at the level of expression or communication, but above all – that is in a peculiarly human sense – in language at the level of description and argumentation. Popper believes:

> The linguistic formulation of theories allows us to criticise and to eliminate them without eliminating the race which carries them. This is the first achievement. The second achievement is the development of a conscious and systematic attitude of criticism towards our theories.... The difference between the amoeba and Einstein is that, although both make use of the method of trial and error elimination, the amoeba dislikes to err while Einstein is intrigued by it: he consciously searches for his errors in the hope of learning by their discovery and elimination. The method of science is the critical method.[17]

When we are guided by the 'fascination' exerted upon us by errors – which are neither denied nor rejected but are knowingly accepted and linguisticized as indispensable tools for the general advancement of our own awareness – lo and behold, our impact with the world, or the toughness of life, takes on aspects of genuine creativity. In his own approach, for instance, Fromm suggests that the purpose of knowledge is not so much the achievement of any forms of certainty or control but rather a process of self-creation through our thinking potential.[18] In this perspective, therefore, ignorance becomes as valuable as knowledge inasmuch as both belong to the process of the growth of thinking.

The greater one's reservations regarding 'truth', as some absolute quality which could function as the pivot of cognitive claims, the more the need is felt to compare notes with others in the attempt to explore the genesis and shape of our concerns. It is time to turn even to the 'strangest' of our interlocutors rather than to the 'nature' of our intellect or to the 'ultimate structure' of our favoured epistemology. On the other hand, though, if we view the awareness of 'error' (the experience of things going wrong) as something meaningless and unwelcome, which threatens our habitual view of the world, we may be led to equate the 'notion' of error to the 'notion' of illness. We may form the illusion that both are derivatives of some underlying negativity, absurdity or defectiveness marring the otherwise apparently coherent wholeness of our knowing and living. If we may not properly speak of truth, we may fruitfully speak of error, inasmuch as it is rehabilitated as a relevant factor of the human propensity to 'seek' truth. Similarly, if we assume that the objective of the applied biological and psychological sciences is the attainment of 'human health', it will be seen that research into the dynamics of pathology may contribute more of an insight than mere discourse on the ideal of human sanity.

In my view, neither error nor illness may be adequately understood unless some interactive approach is adopted. Only in relatively recent times has there begun to be an acceptance of the hypothesis that (mental) illness is in some way linked with the life history, relational styles and inner organization of those suffering. In this connection, it is worth noting that in certain cultures illness, not unlike error, is attributed to the power of 'malignant influences'. Even in technologically oriented cultures, traces of such attitudes persist in those instances where error is treated as a contamination of the natural transparency of truth, and illness is pictured by focusing almost exclusively, and thus deceptively, upon the influence of pathogenic agents. It is no coincidence that both such views involve a note of 'menace'. Certain branches of medical science are in fact searching for some metabolite or chemical substance, to be held culpable for psychic disturbances. And physical illness is still largely understood as the result of an invasion from *outside* – no longer, granted, by 'malignant influences', but by known, or merely supposed, pathogens. When the 'pathogen' is thought of as wholly independent of and external to the subject, the majority of illnesses will thus be conceived of as capable of *striking* the subject in an arbitrary fashion, and by no means as expressions of a dynamic situation 'produced' by the individual on the basis of his past history as well as of his personal expectations. Such concepts are perhaps reflected in ordinary language when one speaks, nowadays, of 'being stricken by' or of accidentally 'catching' an ailment; however, one never speaks of either *producing* or *attaining* pathological conditions.

In a not dissimilar fashion, error, in any epistemological domain, might be assigned the philosophic status of an 'unfortunate' cognitive accident or a deception. In and of itself error would represent a foreign body embedded in any given epistemology – something that could be eventually resolved by careful scrutiny of our epistemic grid. In this way, the problem of those most complex, deep-seated links between error and our humanity (hominization in general and self-creation in particular) is ultimately never addressed: it is almost as if a resounding silence falls over us whenever it is a question of taking a closer look at the vicissitudes involving the *genesis* of human knowledge and ignorance. That 'silence' may be traced back to a tendency to flee from the unfamiliar areas of our symbolic origins which is perhaps similar to the tendency betokened by the desire to avoid error (or avoid being 'wrong') at *all* costs.

There is no doubt that the tendency to avoid error expresses a human wish to minimize risk and maximize utility. But humans may also attempt to avoid error by recourse to anti-philosophic and, ultimately, anti-developmental means, such as taking refuge in a theoretical domain designed to be totally impervious to error. Any such system of cognition and representation, even when this means language itself, thus becomes unassailable and for this reason tends to keep buttressing itself in an escalating process of self-justification. An 'omnipotent' system of this kind may have its origins in earlier, fruitless efforts to handle the cleavages between our fragile, developing 'ego' and the complexity of what is other than the self, of what has already happened, of what is possible. And when the subject gives up hope of being able to cross the gap, or distinction-creating distance, involving constant labours of reconstruction, he may try to limit his 'knowledge' – which 'ceases' to be such – to only one side of that philosophic space which is so hard to traverse. The negation of relational facts may be conducive to the invention of two different but 'equivalent' notions of our mind: a knowing ego which is immune from error or an ego which may only be assailed by errors emanating from conditions *external* to it.

The attempt to place oneself in a stronghold of philosophic validity (dignity, purity, and so on), therefore, has the effect of weakening the more highly evolved features of our human condition, namely those qualities by means of which we may identify our deeper propensities and thus mobilize our potential for self-criticism and creativity. Inasmuch as we can rely upon our own capacity for self-criticism, we are no longer as interested in 'truth' as we are in our potential ability to discover errors and treasure such discoveries with a view to developing more illuminating symbolizations of reality in the making. As Popper remarks:

> Truth is not the only important property of our conjectural theories; for we are not particularly interested in proposing trivialities or tautologies. 'All tables are tables' is certainly true – it is more certainly true than Newton's and Einstein's theories of gravitation – but it is intellectually unexciting.... In other words, we are not simply looking for truth, we are after interesting and enlightening truths, after theories which can offer solutions to *interesting problems*.[19]

5

On the Interaction of
Language and Thought

The 'Normative' Role of Language and
Orthodoxy of Thought

If an attempt is to be made to highlight the live complexity of language, it may serve our purpose to invoke the epistemic development of psychiatric and psychoanalytic culture: this may be regarded as a cluster of basic means for trying to come to terms, both as individuals and socially, with all that is obscure, disturbing and enigmatic in the relational expressions of humans. Such lines of reflection may lead us to realize how provisional, or even precarious, is the position of any 'science' of psychopathology in so far as it is inextricably interwoven with ever inadequate conceptualizations of the 'disturbances' affecting thought and language. A possible, complementary approach would thus be to focus on the iterative reprocessing of knowledge by community consensus as well as on the assumptions (or basic paradigms) operating in any field of discourse regarding the human condition.

In this respect Wittgenstein seems to suggest that many of our beliefs in fact constitute the 'unmoving foundation'[1] of our linguistic games, as well as the mutually agreed infrastructure of a great share of our inquiries and certainties. Such rock-bottom, interpersonal beliefs cannot be subjected to intelligible doubt, since people in general are reluctant or even recalcitrant to this sort of questioning: 'The difficulty is to realize the groundlessness of our believing,' remarks Wittgenstein.[2] But things could not really be in such-and-such a way, nor could a belief really become 'fixed', unless what is believed is condensed into symbolic expressions which determine and stabilize certain assumptions. Quine in fact suggests that 'Linguistically, and hence conceptually, the things in sharpest focus are the things that are public enough to be talked of publicly, common and conspicuous enough to be talked of often.'[3]

Any community of speakers might fruitfully be regarded as a community of believers, in the sense that, if a number of beliefs were not shared by the speakers, communication could neither begin nor endure. If experience is to occur, there 'must' be things which are taken for granted before they come to be 'tested'; and if learning does not derive from experience alone – 'The child learns by believing the adult. Doubt comes *after* belief'[4] – we may say that the knowing individual will only gradually and laboriously learn to identify those specific areas of knowledge where it may be *legitimate* to express doubt.

Wittgenstein points out that 'there are cases such that if someone gives signs of doubt where we do not doubt, we cannot confidently understand his signs as signs of doubt.'[5] For if the prevailing climate is such that we may not ourselves doubt, nor think that others doubt a given 'notion' (for instance, that we see with our eyes), any expression of dissent of this nature becomes the demonstration of a 'defect', for the simple reason that it is almost inevitably assumed that the person who seems to doubt such an assumption is really lying, joking or cognitively defective' – a case of madness. Once again, it is enlightening to look at Wittgenstein's thinking on the matter: 'If someone said to me that he doubted whether he had a body I should take him to be a half-wit. But I shouldn't know what it would mean to try to convince him that he had one. And if I had said something, and that had removed his doubt, I should not know how and why.'[6]

Thus it seems to be the authority of communal consensus which establishes the credentials of what is to be believed, and this is so inasmuch as fundamental relational and cognitive paradigms are raised to the status of cognitive fixity. Authority thus seems to derive from the dominant authorship of any micro- or macro-culture. We can then recognize that in this perspective even knowledge itself comes to be supported by pre-cognitive assumptions. In Wittgenstein's words: 'Knowledge is in the end based on acknowledgement.'[7]

The influence of language, however, ought to be viewed as hierarchized at different levels of authority and abstraction. In the interpersonal dynamics of any community of 'believers', in fact, we also have at work the function of non-verbal language, namely an array of expressive factors such as mimicry, tones, etc. In order to be properly meaningful any interpersonal situation is also built around some system of expressive signs: it is not by means of verbal language *alone* that one communicates, but by means of one's whole behavioural involvement. Any subject whose experiences inhibit his development, or who even goes so far as to adopt a way of life which excludes him from the paths to maturation, is probably acting in a detrimental collusion with messages emanating from different hierarchic levels within his culture. In this light, we can appreciate that a non-verbal system of signs contributes in a complementary fashion to language, consolidating patterns of liveable interaction as well as styles of pathology. In the area of personal language, in fact, it is those non-linguistic modes of expression accompanying language which make possible not only meaningful behaviour but also the falsification of a message, and even the injunction not to see the falsification. Such falsifications, however, do not reach extreme levels in the interpersonal context, inasmuch as 'false' messages tend to be weakened by the discrepancy between the linguistic message and the significance expressed in non-verbal form.

On the contrary, when the elaboration of concepts at the 'community' level is addressed, purely verbal language appears to be the essential and decisive factor, inasmuch as it is responsible for the formulation of the general cultural scheme (vocabulary, epistemology, ideology) outside of which one lapses into 'absurdity' and in the dreaded exile from meaningfulness. At that level, moreover, even though non-verbal signs are still present in the system alongside language, they are no longer essential for the purpose of propounding the epistemological vocabulary which sustains community beliefs. Hence, we may posit the existence of an array of 'pathogenous' interactions extending from 'existential' programming, or self-creation projects in the personal sphere, all the way up to the most influential community levels generating systematic 'ideological' claims.

At the one-to-one (or small group) interpersonal level, labels of insanity, or heresy, are transmitted by means of a verbal language that is linked with ulterior modes of expression (gestures, proxenetes, etc.), which allow the labels to be used more flexibly. On the other hand, as we approach a standard vocabulary or 'epistemology' (towards the opposite end of the scale, where we are dealing with a codification which is essentially verbal in nature), it seems to be so much easier to 'offend' the standard general beliefs of the community itself and slip into 'sins of faith', 'heresies' so to speak, ultimately becoming ostracized by the epistemic community to which we none the less belong. In Davidson's language: 'Reality itself is relative to a scheme: what counts as real in one system may not in another.'[8]

And yet, in our opinion, it is not correct to perceive the authority of a culture as something beyond participants and somehow descending from above – an occult power – and members as passively performing its dictates. What may be likely is that each of us contributes, at the interpersonal level, in vouching for and corroborating societal authority. In other words, it is individuals who uphold authority and not authority (alone) which upholds itself through individuals. *Authority*, then, is inevitably linked with the accepted authorship of the standard vocabulary of ratiocination. However, the fact that the patterns of meaningfulness are manmade does not imply that we can control them at our own discretion and replace them with other structures, for indeed they are produced, not arbitrarily, but through disparate forms of mutual agreement. Such remarks in turn do not rule out an ongoing interactive relationship with a prevailing consensus. For the processes which transform symbolic paradigms rest upon our irrepressible potential to question dominant vocabulary and even to believe (think, intuit, conjecture) theses which others deem wholly untenable for one or more reasons: because the majority does not view the grounds supporting a given intuition as sufficiently valid; because it does not seem possible to accept a given intuition on the basis of the specific reasons intended to uphold it; because there are 'good' or 'reasonable' motives for believing exactly the opposite. And yet, whenever such emerging intuitions come to have an impact on basic paradigms, our thinking is then faced with the likelihood, or perhaps the need, of tolerating more than one account or even of opting for one in preference to another. In Whorf's view, 'one of the important coming steps for Western knowledge is a re-examination of the linguistic background of its thinking, and for that matter of all thinking.'[9]

Normative Functions of Language and the 'Risks' of Dialogue

We shall now attempt to explore ways in which it is possible to use a paradigm more as a point of departure than as a point of arrival. As we know, in linguistic communities problems are often couched in the form of a question which implies certain types of meaning, so that it may well come about that each and every problematic issue is articulated using expressions which in and of themselves both determine and foreshadow the 'quality' and 'level' of the answer. The 'formulation' of the basic assumptions underlying communal life is often encoded at the level where prevalently verbal language holds sway – a language which is freed from any of the non-verbal modes of expression and thus all the more stipulative, intended to formalize the cognitive agreements which sustain the community and the 'questions' which enliven its rational pursuits.

A glance at the conceptual history of psychiatry or psychoanalysis, for instance, may enable us to identify a number of doctrinal clusters which are produced not so much by their 'objective', clinical content, as by the *way* in which the 'phenomenon' under observation is approached. Consequently, the manner in which a problem is expressed ultimately emerges as the most significant aspect of research. The 'dialectic' technique used to formalize any given problem may also be traced back to (cultural and cognitive) factors which are not readily obvious inasmuch as they both underlie language itself and develop together with the most diversified modes of expression.

With Gadamer we can remark that the methodology whereby we generally seek to address a problem often takes its first expression in the form of a *question*.[10] However, the form in which a question is articulated both constrains and influences the nature, or level, of any reply which one might try to work out – be it pertinent or misleading.[11]

Were we to ask ourselves, for instance, 'What is in the brain of this man who has gone mad?', we might think up replies referring to likely traumas, poisons or genetic defects. But if we question the type of query itself so that the answer becomes 'Perhaps there is no illness in the brain as such', in reality it will turn out that what we have done is to discard the question together with the cultural and cognitive frame from which it emanates. Yet we might still persist and pose our question in different terms, such as 'Well, then, how did he happen to go mad?' If our 'answer', however, is 'Perhaps he never *went* mad', or 'One does not *become* mad', we then see that a certain type of answer is tantamount to evading the interrogative framework of a given type of discourse, *together with* the basic assumptions directing the thrust thereof.

To the extent that languages function in an unwitting fashion and that we calmly feel that we have the 'right' to pose questions and to employ a given vocabulary, we may at times overlook the fact that our (non-listening) languages rest upon fundamental assumptions which are regarded as both indisputable and unassailable, precisely because, as a rule, they are not sufficiently brought to light.[12] Although such assumptions are not stated, they find expression in the *form of questions*. A question is really an ambiguous proposition; the answer is its determination. There can be only a certain number of alternatives that will complete its sense. In this way the intellectual treatment of any datum, any experience, any subject, is determined by the nature of our questions, and only carried out in the answers. In philosophy this disposition of problems is ... the 'genius' of a great philosopher; in its light, systems arise and rule and die.[13]

The development of the human sciences may then be regarded more as the outcome of the formulation of the essential questions than the result of the solutions worked out in response to *those* questions. While it is quite true that replies are the material with which the edifice is built, it is the nature of the question which determines the structure of the building – at least in those instances where the reply collapses into the question and produces everything that the latter might elicit, but nothing more. Nevertheless, there is always the possibility that a reply will in fact elude the question's constraints. Whenever we wonder, for example, 'Why does this individual want to do things that harm him?', we are already taking it for granted that the individual *wants* to do them and that they *harm him*. But when we reply that 'Perhaps he *does not want* to do certain things at all' and, moreover, that 'Perhaps, rather than *harm* him at all, they actually enable him to survive', at that point we shall have truly neutralized that type of question. And if we were then to wonder 'Why is it that this individual is projecting his mental world on to us?' and receive the reply that '*Our* mind sees only certain projections and not others' and that, indeed, 'It is our very mental approach which elicits certain projective dynamics and even this sort of query', once again the constraints of our questioning language are to some extent eluded.

Towards a Renewable Epistemology of Mental Illness

While it is a generally accepted assumption that there is a valid, cognitive discriminant which distinguishes a simple description (or testimony) of human events from investigations of a 'scientific' nature, it might none the less prove illuminating to reflect on what the nature of the 'scientific' description of mental pathology might be, once it has been previously singled out as a *category* of human phenomena. The names or 'labels' of the pathologies which we encounter when we try to look at human events in a philosophic perspective prove to be the tip of the iceberg of a vast amount of culturally organized activity, all of which has contributed to the production of the names in question.[14] The very propensity to regard and accept the tip of the iceberg (or finished products in the form of linguistically ascribed pathologies) as the starting-point for probing into pre-existing situations ultimately amounts to ignoring the 'social', interpersonal dimension of the naming process – the very dimension which generates paradigms of social cohesion and exclusion.

Research conducted within the human disciplines for the purpose of identifying the degree of pathology expressed in a sample of human expressions may well have the effect of perpetuating the illusion that there really exists a healthy language from which a 'sick language' may be clearly distinguished as an isolable feature, which 'professionals' have a special, ineffable ability to grasp.

Although the 'category' of mental illness commonly referred to as a disturbance (or disorder or perturbation) of thought processes is not strictly speaking a part of the technical jargon, as are terms such as delusion and phobias, it may still be used in cases where the disquieting nature of a relational situation (of any human expression which cannot easily be linked with the mutually agreed rules issuing from an underlying paradigm) comes to be named, and controlled, by means of a (pseudo-)symbolization. Such a 'category' of mental illness may thus become entrenched as a symbolic form which serves to denote an underlying mental condition; the latter, in turn, is thought to explain the deviant forms of communication, recognizable in certain individuals, in a fashion erroneously assimilated to physical events in neuropathology. Given the depth or the enigmatic nature of human communications, the notion of 'disturbances of thought processes' not only provides a reassuring opportunity to transform a lack of understanding into an assessment (which of itself involves depreciation inasmuch as it assumes a judgemental role) but may even be used as an explanation. In other words, the difficulties affecting linguistic expression are placed in a causal relationship *vis-à-vis* the disturbance of the thought processes which allegedly constitutes the specific causal factor behind 'pathological' language. When 'facts' are thus arranged, that is when messages which are hard to listen to (or interpret) are named in such a way as to indicate an illness, the way is open for those 'facts' to be put to further pseudosymbolic uses. For the enunciations in question allow it to be 'argued' that a person may suffer from latent disturbances of thought processes and that such hidden pathology may be revealed or highlighted by means of 'proper' questioning and other techniques of investigation, emanating from the assumption that 'disturbances of thought processes' constitute a condition which might even 'exist' independently of a person's linguistic behaviour.

The indiscriminate, mechanical use of linguistic paradigms illustrates how difficult it is to make an accurate assessment of the distinction between relational behaviour in which an individual applies a mutually agreed rule and, on the other hand, different behaviour in which the subject goes by a rule *of his own*. Such an undiscriminative attitude has the effect of perpetuating the illusion whereby it is believed that the 'mentally ill' are using *our* rules to produce *their* behaviour and language. In other words, we have the illusion that the set of rules underlying phatic communities are suitable for all purposes of expression, and that they are thus both necessary and sufficient for the survival of the symbolic animal.[15]

In our opinion, it is not a matter either of placing a 'language' out of bounds, isolating it in the realm of pathology, or even of bringing it back within the 'normal' symbolic system at all costs by finding it some sort of niche within a mutually agreed normality. The issue, rather, is to recognize the necessity of an 'impossible' dialogue, the 'impossiblity' of which constitutes a challenge that validates the authenticity and *quality* of that dialogue which defies being reduced either to a tautological exchange (conducted within commensurable symbolic circuits) or to *victory* over the other's 'illogical' language. A 'validating' challenge may then originate from attempting a dialogue between 'alien' epistemologies. When a message proves hardly interpretable ('impossible') it is all too often relegated automatically into the a-normal domain, though not in the neutral sense of a message which is non-classifiable within the purview of prevailing metaphors, but rather in a degrading, pejorative sense. It might be more illuminating, on the contrary, to treat such a message as an exception which calls for new approaches such as are no longer (or not yet) connected to the symbolization in one's possession (a standard epistemology used like an arsenal or stock-in-trade), but which depend upon each individual's potential for creativity and symbol generation.

On the Pathology of Ordinary Language

The tacit assumption on the basis of which it is believed possible to make a valid discrimination between functional languages and 'sick' languages stands out more clearly – as resting upon insufficient ground – when we juxtapose two different attitudes underlying the way in which we think of linguistic transactions: an approach which highlights the functional aspects and one which stresses the mystifying, confusing aspects of ordinary language.

Some lines of thought, then, view ordinary language as being basically reliable, that is to say a signally physiological instrument, suitable for representing the interpersonal world of a culture. And the outlook which stresses the functional aspects of linguistic games may be traced back to an aspect of the thinking of the later Wittgenstein. It might prove illuminating to compare this approach with a different way of looking at linguistic transactions brought to light by the study of relational dynamics. The investigation of such intricate exchanges brings out the equivocity and lack of transparency inherent in most linguistic games. Berne, for example, has the following remark:

> For certain fortunate people there is something which transcends all classifications of behaviour, and that is spontaneity; and something that is more rewarding than games, and that is intimacy. But all three of these may be frightening and even perilous to the unprepared. Perhaps they are better off as they are, seeking their solutions in popular techniques of social action, such as 'togetherness'.[16]

There is no doubt that the latter outlook offers a rather different perspective – a more problematic one – yet it is potentially more fertile inasmuch as it does not turn a blind eye to the possibility that mystifying disfunctions may be at work even in healthy and consensual linguistic transactions. Indeed, linguistic games emanating from our forms of life may turn out to be forms of death.

In this perspective, language – which Morris defined as 'a wonderful instrument at the service of life'[17] – is less and less to be perceived as a 'tame' instrument; it may tyrannize us,[18] imperceptibly influencing our way of thinking, giving body to the most powerful perceptual Gestalts and to the most 'sophisticated' relational paradigms.

A philosophical attitude based upon the criteria of meaningfulness inherent in ordinary language may come to regard its own work as a therapeutic analysis of the linguistic illnesses giving rise to traditional philosophy. The (analytic) philosopher might be thought of as someone who treats an issue as a linguistic embarrassment, a dis-ease, and who proposes a certain type of clarifying cure. According to this view, however, the concepts of health and therapy might be perplexingly reabsorbed within a unified conceptual field of 'functional adaption' to linguistic games expressing certain forms of life within a central tradition. In effect, it would come down to transposing the tangles of traditional philosophy on to a 'physiological' plane, that is within the domain of 'current' language and customs. But the persistent obscurity and unfairness present in everyday linguistic games, all of them mediated by consensual language, are always there to testify how easy it is to be misled by ordinary language when it is regarded either as something properly functional (that 'wonderful instrument at the service of life'), or as a public consensus to which one must refer back in order to clear up the confusing situations accumulating in philosophic discourse.

As to the 'deep-down', unwitting (and therefore potentially pathological) choice of the game-paradigms underlying a linguistic community, it may be enlightening to note that Wittgenstein can be regarded as sensitive to proposals for a radical investigation of ordinary language in its diachronic, ontogenetic sense. This openness may be noted in his investigations: 'The problems arising through a misinterpretation of our forms of language have the character of *depth*. They are deep disquietudes; their roots are as deep in us as the forms of our language and their significance is as great as the importance of our language.'[19]

The illusoriness of any attempt to 'treat philosophic diseases' (namely the derivatives of traditional philosophy) by elucidating the linguistic tangles in which they are couched and by re-establishing contact with the supposed functionality and healthiness of ordinary language games strikes home the more clearly if we can go along with Berne's suggestion that 'Procedures may be successful, rituals effective, and pastimes profitable, but all of them are by definition candid; they may involve contest, but not conflict, and the ending may be sensational, but it is not dramatic. Every game, on the other hand, is basically dishonest, and the outcome has a dramatic, as distinct from merely exciting, quality.'[20] It follows that it is not justifiable to accept tacitly at the outset that linguistic games represent forms of healthy life, since in our opinion, they equally determine forms of madness and extinction. By looking to mutually agreed interactions among humans as terms of comparison and points of departure, one runs the risk – paradoxically – of using what is archaic and confusional as if it were a criterion of ultimate functionality.

6

The Symbolic Function and the Development of Inner Time

The Development of Inner Time

Our insight into the integrative function of symbolization could be improved if – over and above a spatialized idea of our inner life – we attempt to appreciate the cognitive worth of the diachronic integration of the 'past', namely the ability to establish meaningful connections throughout prior experiences, from the obscure and 'unconscious' ones to those of which we are more readily aware. As a diachronic perspective gradually emerges, the individual becomes able to dip into the past and, hence, insert his affective and cognitive history into better-developed structures of relational organization.

In the perspective of symbol formation, Segal points out that 'one of the important tasks performed by the ego is that of dealing not with depressive anxieties alone, but also with unresolved earlier conflicts.... Anxieties, which could not be dealt with earlier on, because of the extreme concreteness, of the experience, ... can gradually be dealt with by the more integrated ego by symbolization, and in that way they can be integrated.'[1] In other words, the utilization of symbolic elements as means for containing anxieties is invoked, above all, in dealing with the earliest maturational stages of our ontogeny. The fears which could not be faced in the initial vicissitudes, because of the overwhelmingly 'concrete' nature of situations (brought about by the 'symbolic equation' that is a primal lack of distinction between reality and fantasy, impressions and ideas), may subsequently be redirected to more flexible parts of the mind, capable of translating primal issues into an articulate language. As the strengthening of the mind's integrating function progresses to the point where it is capable of dealing with the archaic fears, a share of our previous experiences may be symbolically worked at a higher level of awareness. The recovery of the historic depth of past experiences thus becomes possible and may consequently function as a potential source of self-knowledge.

The primal vicissitudes of loss, separation or longing, construed as the absence of a gratifying object, cannot take place only in the space dimension. Tolerance of frustration implies not only an awareness of the presence or absence of the desired object within the spatial location of desires; the ability to tolerate frustration seems to also require the onset of a temporal extension, such as may usher in the creation of a time dimension wherein events can follow (and derive from) one another, and wherein a perspective encompassing what went before and what may occur in future also consistently develops. Thus a framework is established within which remembering and planning may unfold. It is only by means of symbolic tools that one can get back in touch with – or 'long for' and thus try to recover – something lost which is 'now' missed and which, as a result, comes to be a part of one's prior history. And precisely because it is mediated by symbols, the ability to create historicity advances hand-in-hand with the ability to envisage prospects and make plans. Wittgenstein significantly asks: ' "Hope is directed to the future" – but is there a feeling, identical with hope, but directed to the present or to the past? The same mental movement, so to speak, but with a different object?"[2]

Processes of splitting and denial, as well as other forms of selective blindness ('contraries' of symbolization), come into play when the inchoate person is forced to sacrifice his propensity for cognitive integration (as well as for temporal continuity) in order to protect himself from explosions of uncontainable fears. Denial, splitting and isolation are thus ways of *coping* with unbearable conditions. In the process of self-formation one might even opt for an 'inadequate' level of integration so as to avoid the certainty of fearsome situations which could result in chaos, or else one might even forgo establishing a personal temporal continuity in the attempt to circumscribe the threat of destructive events: 'If I do not exist there is nothing to be destroyed.' While an identity of one's own is precious and desirable, as well as being to some degree attainable, disintegration into chaos, on the other hand, is the ultimate danger to be warded off by any available means.

When the subject becomes sufficiently capable of using symbolic tools, however, there are alternatives to such detrimental outcomes: it is then that the subject's earliest, most impoverishing conflicts may, to some extent, be recovered and actively 'rearranged', that is to say *actively* taken charge of by the ability to organize inner life (symbolically and metabolically). Such an ability to reconsider old conflicts is due, in turn, to the cognitive faculty of 'remembering' or of using a mental element which *points to* an earlier vicissitude, thereby establishing a relational distance between two different points of reference, which are thus kept *distinct and linked* by virtue of a developing temporal dimension. The dynamics of memory, therefore, take on a richer, *vital meaning*, a proper evolutionary significance. Cassirer observes:

> In order to remember a content, consciousness must previously have possessed itself of that content in a way differing from mere sensation or perception. The mere repetition of the given at another time does not suffice; in this repetition a new kind of conception and formation must be manifested. For every 'reproduction' of a content embodies a new level of 'reflection'. By the mere fact that it no longer takes this content as something simply present, but confronts it in imagination as something past and yet not vanished, consciousness, by its changed *relation* to the content, gives both to itself and the content a changed ideal *meaning*. And this occurs more and more precisely and abundantly as the world of representations stemming from the 'I' becomes differentiated. The 'I' now exercises an original formative activity all the while developing a deeper understanding.[3]

I believe that there is a turning-point at which the 'necessity' to repeat becomes radically differentiated from the *capacity* to repeat (evoke or revivify), and that turning-point coincides with the onset of the ability to function symbolically, to *point* to something not only in outer space but in inner time. It is by means of this ability, then, that the developing subject is able to detach himself to some extent from a personal event and place it at a temporal distance with the help of an element capable of indicating something ulterior.The development of a temporal dimension which allows one to dip into the past permits one also to break free of passive, automatic reiterations of the 'past'. Psychoanalytic theories, for example, are based not only on the hypothesis that people's lives are influenced by infantile experiences, but also, and perhaps foremost, upon conjectures regarding the extent to which individual vicissitudes are the result of the *specific ways* in which early experiences are 'repeated' and appraised in adult life. Early experiences in one's ontogenetic history may in fact be reiterated almost mechanically; the opportunity to 'rehabilitate' and 'transform' early experiences by means of symbolic connections offers an alternative to allowing them to crowd in almost through inertia. A possibility is thus offered to incorporate early affective and cognitive conglomerations into novel, different patterns. Symbolic instruments of awareness allow one's ontogeny to be retrieved, and its contents mastered, without 'eliminating' what is either unthinkable or inexpressible, that is, without deriving cohesive force from mechanisms of denial. The process of retrieval of one's personal history is sustained, then, by the developing ability to utilize even obscure, past experiences for metabolic purposes.

Not unlike the awareness of time, the mental construction of space rests upon laborious processes of individuation and critical detachment. In phylogenetic terms, according to Neumann,[4] there are no *abstract* spatial elements: originally every component of space is endowed with a magical reference to the human body and is in some way connected with divinities, colours, meanings. It is only by degrees, as self-consciousness emerges, that things and places are distinguished one from the other and become organized into an abstract system which is qualitatively different from the primal state wherein space and objects merge into a continuum.

Yet the temporal dimension in which our linguisticity may unfold seems to be far more consequential than our construction of space. Kant's celebrated remarks on the cognitive value of time seem to converge with the cognitive value of the sort of symbolization which allows us to create a sense of our *inner* historicity. Kantian thought, in fact, attributes cognitive priority to 'time' as being an indispensable (direct) condition for the knowledge of inner phenomena and a preliminary indirect condition for grasping external facts.

> Time is the formal *a priori* condition of all appearances whatsoever. Space, as the pure form of all *outer* intuition, is so far limited; it serves as the *a priori* condition only of outer appearances. But since all representations, whether they have for their objects outer things or not, belong, in themselves, as determinations of the mind, to our inner state; and since this inner state stands under the formal condition of inner intuition, and so belongs to time, time is an *a priori* condition of all appearances whatsoever. It is the immediate condition of inner appearances (of our souls), and thereby the mediate condition of outer appearances. Just as I can say *a priori* that all outer appearances are in space, I can also say, from the principle of inner sense, that all appearances whatsoever, that is, all objects of the senses, are in time, and necessarily stand in time-relations.[5]

Even for the neo-Kantian Cassirer it appears to be 'easier' to co-ordinate spatial features than it is to 'construct' a unified sense of inner time.

For 'here' and 'there' can be subsumed much more simply and immediately in an intuitive unity than is the case with the *temporal* factors 'now', 'earlier', and 'later'. What characterizes these factors as *temporal* is precisely that they are never, like things of objective intuition, given to the consciousness simultaneously. The units, the parts, which in spatial intuition seem to *combine* of themselves into a whole, here exclude one another: the existence of one specification signifies the nonexistence of the others and vice versa. Accordingly, the whole fact of the representation of time is never contained in immediate intuition; differentiation and combination, analytical and synthetic thought consequently play a larger part than in spatial representation. Since the elements of time exist as such only because consciousness 'runs through' them and in so doing differentiates them, this act of running through, this *'discursus'* enters into the characteristic form of the concept of time itself.[6]

Although our sense of time may be regarded as a necessary condition for possible experience, in our approach it is of interest more as the *result* of a process of maturation than as the immutable, a priori coefficient of knowledge. According to Popper, for example, it is hard to accept the Kantian notion of a single type of pure intuition, a common denominator, universal in nature and, hence, shared by all, 'For *after* having trained ourselves in discursive thought, our intuitive grasp becomes utterly different from what it was *before* [and] all this applies to our intuition of time.'[7] If we can agree that a theory is a symbolic construct suitable for negotiating with reality, we shall also be in a position to appreciate the dependence of our intuition of time upon the development of the symbolic function. As maturation in the potential for symbolization is reached, namely with the development of discursive thought, even our capacity for inner listening is significantly transformed. And it is precisely the onset of symbolization, by means of which the most diverse modes of cognition are constructed, which explains what happens between this *before* and *after*.

In a well-known work inquiring into the world view of the Hopi Indians, Whorf convincingly describes a peculiar intuition of time – an intuition far removed from any of our own ways of construing or averting time. Yet, even if Whorf's description were 'incorrect', which Popper thinks unlikely, it none the less shows 'possibilities which neither Kant nor Brower ever considered. Should Whorf be right, then our intuitive grasp of time – the way in which we "see" temporal relations – would partly depend on our language and the theories and myths incorporated in it: *our own European intuition of* time would owe much to the Greek origins of our civilization, with its emphasis on discursive thought.'[8]

It is possible that in archaic cultures 'repetition' might not appear so much as a memory of which there is an awareness, or as the retrieval of past usable events, but rather as a non-critical re-duplication or reproduction of the cultural heritage, in the form of an unavoidable repetitive behaviour devoid of a sense of history. Within such a perspective, or rather such a primal *lack* of perspective, the diachronic life of mental processes may not, ultimately, emerge as the sort of cognition which can be directed both towards remembering the past and towards shaping the future.

Cassirer holds the view that, in ancient cultures, a firm boundary divides the empirical present from mythical origins in such a way that 'present' and 'past' are not interchangeable.[9] And mythical origins might well 'correspond' to that obscure share of our ontogenetic history – obscure inasmuch as it is out of reach and linguistically unutterable – with which the empirical present cannot establish meaningful contact. If we admit that nothing may be eliminated 'by magic', then even archaic vicissitudes somehow coexist in our present (life or culture); to the extent that there are shortcomings in the symbolic equipment which keeps the 'empirical present' in touch with the 'mythical past', we are faced with a split which devitalizes our cognitive life. What we could have, ultimately, is a present without a history and a 'historic' heritage which cannot be used because it is out of reach.[10]

According to Cassirer, in the primitive forms of temporal intuition, 'the whole of consciousness and its contents falls, as it were, into two spheres: a bright sphere, illuminated by the light of the "present", and another, dark sphere; and between these two basic levels, there is as yet no mediation or transition, no shading or degrees.'[11] He goes on to say that 'The fully developed consciousness, particularly the consciousness of scientific *cognition*, does not content itself with this simple opposition of "now" and "not-now" but raises it to its richest logical development.'[12] That 'logical development' in the linking of present with past seems to be feasible solely by means of a level of symbolization which is not only suitable for pointing to and establishing external *objects* but also capable of creating those (inner) *relations* that express the connections, or links, between such diverse elements of one's inner world as 'inside' and 'outside', 'present' and 'past'. That humans need to make a specific commitment to working out modes of symbolization pertaining to the temporal dimension may be appreciated if we trace this effort back to our early Western history. With regard to the vital task of remembering, Vernant points out:

> The Greek pantheon includes a deity who bears the name of a psychological function: Mnemosyne (Memory). No doubt this is not the only example of such a deity. Greek gods often represent passions and feelings, Eros, Aidos, Phobos.... Many phenomena which we would term psychological can thus be the object of a cult. In the context of religious thought they take the form of sacred forces that are greater than man and beyond his power even when he experiences them within himself. However, Mnemosyne seems to be *a special case*. Memory is a very complicated function which is related to important psychological categories such as *time and identity*. It brings into play a whole collection of complex mental operations with all the effort, training and exercise that are needed to master them. The power of recall is, as we have pointed out, a conquest.[13]

Whereas Eros overwhelms humans, almost without their awareness, Mnemosyne, on the other hand, seems to receive active assistance in carrying out her divine mission from those symbolic processes laboriously developed in the *effort* to emerge from the timelessness of unconscious life.

Symbol and Interaction in Knowledge-Claims

One of the common ways of conceptualizing time is rooted in the notion of an inner *sequence* of events or of the succession of experiential acts. Simply talking about a series of 'mental states', though, does not do justice to the aforesaid 'sequence'. In my opinion, we are dealing, not so much with a string, but with the *derivation* of one state from another, in the sense of a *mental event* which does not just 'follow' but also derives from a previous condition, with which it is related according to specific modes of interaction expressible through symbolic links. In this view, the vividly concrete quality of time sustains the *relationship* between 'present' and 'past', in such a way that it abrogates the conception of time as a succession of moments, or states.[14] The latter conception may be, moreover, conducive to a misleading abstraction inasmuch as it cannot be relinked with the share of irreversible relations which constitute our life of the mind.

In order to provide a better insight into the specific properties of temporal relations, Cassirer closely compares them to spatial relations:

> Spatial 'here' and 'there' stand to one another in a simple relation of distance; two points in space are merely differentiated and there is in general no preferred direction in the passage from one to the other. As spatial factors, the two points are 'potentially co-existent' and in a sense equivalent; a simple movement can transform 'there' into 'here', and 'here', after ceasing to be such, can be restored to its previous form by the reverse movement. Time, however, reveals, in addition to the distinction and distance between its elements, a unique and irreversible 'sense' in which it proceeds.[15]

A purely sequential model is, thus, hardly a viable proposal, since we are constantly confronted with a variety of paradigms which characterize the *ways* in which various elements follow one another. In fact, if we examine the relational aspects in the sequence of events, we can see that pure 'sequence' is a term equally as abstract as the simple 'flow' of time: it seems that with these terms we may constantly look at it, never quite seeing through.

One might point out a connection between the idea of *repetition* of events and the 'discovery' by psychoanalysis of psychic motivations, whereby behaviour otherwise imputed to situational difficulties, 'chance' or cognizant choices comes to be interpreted as the behavioural outcome of previous, unconscious vicissitudes. My purpose, however, is oriented not so much towards discussing unconscious motivations as towards exploring the potential to retrieve such motivations as meaningful elements by means of a symbolic-metabolic apparatus capable of 'moving through' time, of reclaiming the past and addressing the future. As a result of the increasing distance from 'classical science', contemporary research comes to be marked by a tendency not to think in terms of isolated units and linear, one-way chains of causation. In fact, the general notions of 'interaction', 'organization', 'ecosystem', 'holism' and 'Gestalt'. increasingly prevail in all branches of knowledge: taken together, these notions point to the need for thinking in terms of systems and elements which interact both synchronically and diachronically.

This approach to the connection between one's sense of time and one's level of symbolization could possibly not be the emanation of a comprehensive epistemology based on the commensurability of thoughts and issues. The outlook demands instead that we develop a capacity to 'travel' more freely from one epistemology to another and to look at things hermeneutically when we cannot do so epistemologically. Investigating projects of self-creation conducive to one's history and language, we can see that even the 'causal' connections between prior and subsequent events are dependent upon the 'future' significance which such connections will assume for us – a constantly evolving significance, moreover. Causal connections are also linked with the ever-changing human environment, not only for the sake of what it is, but also for what it is expected or desired to be. As Cassirer suggests:

> The developed consciousness of time creates entirely new means of apprehending a temporal 'whole'. Time is not so much 'a substantial aggregate' pieced together from distinct moments, but is apprehended as a functional and dynamic whole: as a unity of relation and causality. The intuition of the temporal unity of action encompasses both the subject of the action and the aim toward which it is directed. The two factors are situated on entirely different planes; but the synthetic force of the concept of time consists precisely in its ability to transform their opposition into a reciprocal relation.[16]

Outlooks which often influence psychoanalytic culture and philosophic investigation seem to draw their 'validity' from a rather limited view of time, conceived as a mere sequence of individual events. However, it would be imprudent to ignore their confusing potential and regard such views as derivatives of a 'mere' linguistic inaccuracy occurring within the context of a discourse, wherein time is non-critically and 'naturally' defined in terms of a succession of events. The adoption of such a loosely framed definition could, in itself, sanction a selective blindness which could ultimately prove seriously misleading for inquiry. The end result would be to ignore the *complexity* of inner time: inasmuch as it is inextricably bound up with human beliefs and desires, such complexity runs the risk of being all too easily left out of the investigation.

The uncertain continuity of our mental life (as a relational dynamics) is vulnerable not only to obscurity but also to the 'everyday' risk of illness. A lack of symbolic life is in fact a barrier to living in the indivisible continuity of time. True, there is a vague 'sensation' of one's own duration and of the continuity of experience – a sensation which springs from our deep, inner being. But just as we may not live on good dialogic terms with our inner depths, neither do we live in authentic temporal continuity, but make do, instead, with that vague, albeit insistent, 'sensation' which sustains and guarantees what would otherwise prove an inexplicable flow lacking in cohesiveness. There do exist, however, specific situations in which the individual, almost by his own spontaneous volition, seems to put himself through radical changes of habit and painful adaptations, in the attempt to avoid, more or less consciously, the dangers of involution.[17] A person may expose himself to new interactions or laboriously learn 'different vocabularies', apparently looking for a break, or interval, in the regular course of cognitive life, or for some sort of 'distraction', as the saying goes; he may instead be seeking to break new ground and renovate everyday language – the constant uniformity of customary cognitive transactions which involves the risk of irreversible blunting and benumbing.

Symbol and Perspective in Knowledge-Claims

Popper tangentially addresses the speciousness, or at least the problematic nature, of the 'present moment' as he highlights the distinction between two different outlooks of research.

> The role of time in particle physics differs from that in the physics of continua, especially optics. While particle physics suggests a razor-like unextended instant, a *'punctum temporis'* which divides the past from the future, and thus a time co-ordinate consisting of (a continuum of) unextended instants, and a world whose 'state' may be given for any such unextended instant, the situation in optics is very different. Just as there are spatially extended grids in optics whose parts co-operate over a considerable distance of space, so there are temporally extended events (waves possessing frequencies) whose parts co-operate over a considerable distance of time. Thus, owing to optics, *there cannot be in physics a state of the world at an instant of time.* This argument should, and does, make a great difference to our intuition: what has been called the specious present of psychology is neither specious nor confined to psychology, but is genuine and occurs already in physics.[18]

It is the contrast between the 'speciousness' of the non-related present – an abstract point in time to be supposedly identified within the process of knowing – and the profound significance of diachronic relational connections which lies at the root of the latent *pathos* of the human condition. This contrast makes it possible for us to reflect upon errors and to see things in a temporal perspective. As a consequence of these possibilities it may become easier for us to distance ourselves from a standard epistemic vocabulary. Some sundials bear the inscription *pereunt et imputantur*, which may be translated as 'The hours fall and are taken into account', or 'The hours pass away, but they also count'. Presumably *pereunt* refers to the transient immediacy while *imputantur* stresses the linkage, and 'weight' of relational connections.

It has been observed that events which either individually or historically 'follow' one another can be interpreted differently, in accordance with the conceptual model which underlies any human discourse. For instance, when the typically planar, or mechanistic, models of the nineteenth century are employed, whereby 'progress' is measured at the crest of the advancing wave, quite obviously it will be the last word proclaimed which will epistemologically prevail. However, when self-creation is patterned along such lines, we run the risk of being incapable of cognitive renovation, inasmuch as we are locked in the conceptual grip of the equation 'new equals true': the latest verdict of public consensus will be what 'decrees' the establishment of (more or less successful) paradigms of any epistemology. The development of an inner diachronic dimension, then, allows one not only to break free of the timelessness of the unconscious but also, and above all, to shrug off the non-related solipsism of the present moment; we may thus create the logical space in which to formulate the alternative idea that being the 'latest novelty' in vocabulary does not necessarily constitute a criterion of cognitive validity.

When there is no living thread spanning the inner diachronic dimension, cognitive processes are without roots. And even though the life of the mind partakes of culture and history the 'symbolic animal' not only keeps in tune with prevailing epistemic vocabularies but also, and above all, is able to depart from the public consensus, at least for a few significant moments, in order to discover the strength of his own silence and voice.

In situations of serious crisis, as well as in certain forms of pathology, a subject may sink in feelings of timelessness which are all the more difficult to endure as they are accompanied by a poor diachronic organization of the mind's life. With his relational life deprived of its temporal dimension and thus devoid of any intentional planning, the individual is no longer capable, of his own accord, of framing far-reaching questions and of seeking appropriate answers. In illusory fashion, he also clutches at each and every subsequent external response and tries to make his own both the answers which others give, and their interpretations and outlooks. His inner babel of pseudo-replies, taken in without any conscious evaluation – almost as if in a desperate hurry to mimic others' attitudes and replies – creates a harmful spiral opposing the survival of inner, diachronic continuity. Also, symbolizations which are acquired for defensive purposes seem unsuitable for creating communications within the person: they actually interfere with the temporal continuity on which personal identity is rooted. The individual who is somehow 'aware' of the scant value of such discourses is also induced to make the worst use of such material, there being no reason for not wasting words which are worthless for his inner life. The ability to sustain a planned approach to the future is itself dependent upon that very same ability to use symbols which can be employed for retrieving and integrating the past. Just as we come to realize that the symbolic dimension allows us to leaf through time and somehow *overcome* the incommensurable nature of our obscure, mythical past, we may likewise posit that symbolization provides the tools for the exercise of the subject's intentionality *vis-à-vis* the future. Thus we envisage extremes between which extends a gradient of cognitive attitudes, ranging from one of total passivity (which *submits* to the future as an impending 'catastrophe') all the way to one of laboriously projecting and following through events.

The integration of 'time' into a process which combines continuity with change proves to be instrumental in maintaining our inner equilibrium: it allows us to acquire some perspectival view of the past whereby prior experiences, while they come through with a lesser intensity than current ones, yet retain a sufficient resonance to provide a sense of continuing identity. Unfortunately, the notion of a perspectival view can also prove deceiving if one becomes tied to the spatial metaphor in which the concept itself is framed. For it is not a question of erecting an inner control tower charged with supervising the mental terrain; the purpose is, rather, to develop means for creating symbolic links capable of fostering better-organized inner communications. All that is being said here may be brought into sharper focus if we take into account the 'richness' of the diachronic domain inasmuch as it is the 'dimension' from which the future unfolds. When a spatialized outlook prevails, the future is mechanically placed 'beyond' the present like a mass of events which have no links with our present commitments.

Just as awareness cannot be separated from the symbolic tools by means of which inner communication is made possible, intentional planning through which 'future events' are addressed rests likewise upon the use of symbols which are constantly launched to enable us to envisage and articulate our cognitive pursuits. Jaspers seems to offer a synoptic view of time that may complement the conception of our temporal dimension as inextricably interwoven with symbolic maturation. He suggests that, although the future is not accessible to research,

> Yet the future lies concealed in the past and in the present; we see it and think it out in real possibilities. In fact we are at all times sustained by a consciousness of the future ... the present itself becomes the origin and goal of historical consciousness as well. But it is crucially necessary to look at the present from the viewpoint of the future as from that of the past. The ideas that we have of the future guide the manner in which we look into the past and the present.[19]

Awareness of Death and Creative Thinking

The issue of our awareness of death assumes particular relevance as the myths of a linear, unstoppable (scientific) progress are being questioned – a progress supposedly stemming out of human beings' successful 'cohabitation' with science and technology. And yet a cultural climate marked by a propensity to disenchantment may labour to bring forth different ways of viewing our human condition – which is of course contained between the experiences of birth and death.

There is, obviously, a tenacious inclination to use denial as a defensive measure. Still, if we assume that anything that is denied, or glossed over, will re-emerge in distorted form, we shall be motivated to explore those mental coefficients which do not foster cognition, but possibly reinforce the pseudo-symbolic spiral which threatens our cultural thinking. It is increasingly difficult to ignore that, whatever our socio-biological well-being, there is an active 'search for death' which is expressed through disparate styles of violence (both individual and in groups) as well as through self-destructive behaviour, not to mention addictions to altered states of consciousness and the insatiable consumption of 'cultural' products revolving about the theme of death – or, rather, hinging on the pornographic distortion of dying. Just as in the last century selective blindness and denial produced the taboos surrounding 'Eros' (which reappeared in various forms of so-called pathology), in like fashion our century is witnessing an even more pervasive tendency to make a taboo out of death itself. Although often denied, our concern with death continually wells up in a deafening way throughout our culture, which 'denies' death, while it goes on feeding insatiably on a motley assortment of mis-representations of death. An interest in the experience of death as a 'natural' human concern appears as unseemly as an interest in sexuality might have once seemed, which is to say that there do not exist sufficient logical spaces in our culture, or inner affective capacities, suitable for *containing* and rendering thinkable that which is generally presented as un-thinkable. Possibly, one way of defending oneself against the counterfeit pornography of death may be found in the demystifying processes whereby one may create a logical space in which to attempt cognitive pursuits such as the 'work of mourning', the experience of loss, and thus basically establish a philosophical space in which ignorance, error, absence and absurdity may be 'confronted'. A vivid awareness of one's own inevitable end is in fact a remarkable step forward, for all that it remains difficult to entertain thoughts of this kind. One may even wonder if so evanescent an idea of our finite condition is worth keeping, and thus we are tempted to cast it into oblivion by avoiding the effort to symbolize it in some way. If it is true that a pseudo-symbolic attitude precludes partaking of reality, we may attempt to invoke that same hypothesis for an investigation into our conception of human life as a development which includes the awareness of its own end. Cognitive maturation along these lines focuses upon the core of the human condition, namely that of a mortal being who is unable to *say* how he fits within a finite temporal frame and, not being able to construe this symbolically, is forced all the more to deny, ignore and deafen himself. If an authentic notion of life must, of necessity, include its termination, we cannot but notice the variety of pseudosymbolic references to death, ranging from massive silence on the topic to every shade of taboo regarding this essential aspect of our condition. Indeed, if we view death as an essential part of life, it follows that any cognitive attitude which in pseudosymbolic fashion colludes with the multitude of ways in which death is denied will even hinder and falsify the experiences of our 'philosophical' life.

As we know, one of the main functions of our symbolic apparatus consists in dealing with enigmatic, disquieting aspects of reality, a case in point being the 'passage' of time and the closing of a life-cycle. Inasmuch as such aspects of life are un-thinkable, the result is not only a delusional denial of death but also a withdrawal from the potential full 'use' of life. Conversely, to the extent that death is an event somehow 'utterable, thinkable, expressible', the individual will gain the ability to make use of what would, otherwise, disappear into unfathomable fearfulness. Jung's thinking would seem to provide support for such an approach: 'The negation of life's fulfilment is synonymous with the refusal to accept its ending. Both mean not wanting to live, and not wanting to live is identical with not wanting to die.... Whenever possible our consciousness refuses to accommodate itself to this undeniable truth.'[20] He then goes on to remark:

> We straggle behind our years, hugging our childhood as if we could not tear ourselves away. We stop the hands of the clock and imagine that time will stand still. When after some delay we finally reach the summit, there again, psychologically, we settle down to rest and although we can see ourselves sliding down the other side, we cling, if only with longing backward glances, to the peak once attained. Just as, earlier, fear was a deterrent to life, so now it stands in the way of death. We may even admit that fear of life held us back on the upward slope, but just because of this delay we claim all the more right to hold fast to the summit we have now reached. Though it may be obvious that in spite of all our resistances ... life has reasserted itself, yet we pay no attention and keep on trying to make it stand still.[21]

It does not seem out of place, at this point, to call attention to the manner in which that supreme illusion, namely the idea of 'immortality', which perverts our image of the *animal symbolicum* (a living creature which in some way *knows* that he is going to live for a limited period), is suggested through the literary use of a telling paradox. The 'hero' of de Beauvoir's novel *All Men Are Mortal*[22] is an emblematic case in this regard: with the passing of centuries this man, who has been granted the 'gift' of immortality, progressively loses his ability to see, feel, enjoy and seek – capacities which are essential to any creative process. His time-frame is no longer human, fading, as it does, into an undefined blur, so that his life undergoes a numbing transformation which makes it look ever more bleak and monotonous. He is a man alone, and all his efforts to graft his own life on to that of others – the mortals – collapse into mutual envy, for the revelation of his secret is powerless to elicit either compassion or shared sentiments. Thus the supreme illusion leads to exclusion from every form of linguistic communication with other living beings. The denial of death seems to erase the universe of symbolization and to be ultimately conducive to the curse of immortality – the destruction of the diachronic and symbolic dimensions of human life. As it turns out, the destiny held in store for the immortal character of this literary work bears not a few similarities to certain traits of the schizoid mentality of our age which unwittingly, yet obstinately, attempts to elude, or deny, the reality of our temporary time.

As an alternative to the foregoing type of alienating outlook, we could glimpse a way of escape precisely in the awareness of our own end as something intimately linked with the vicissitudes of creativity. The intellectual need to keep all relational forms locked within the grid of the better-known and easily accessible epistemologies and the desire always to 'know' (control) what is going on – even at the risk of falsifying knowledge – both stand in the way not only of any labour of loss (or death) but also of the travail of authentic creativity. Should a climate of symbolic coercion prevail at the epistemic level (involving either the individual or the phatic community), it may induce a cognitive paralysis which impedes the life of thought and even prevents humans from *living* their own deaths. In that way, the experience of death takes on the conventional appearance of an absurd future mishap, never to be mentioned for any reason. The mental muteness which enforces a stereotyped set of blind spots not only obscures the awareness of death in each of us but also and above all, impedes authentic creativity. Whereas the knowing subject will always balk at 'letting' himself die, 'dying' cognitively amounts to giving up the more customary vocabulary in order to tap inner sources, no longer relying upon 'resources' mirrored from leading epistemologies. Quite frequently, in fact, impulses which tend to 'acquire' the creative processes turn out to be futile attempts at manipulation or else thefts of something supposedly capable of providing inspiration. A vocabulary prevails in which 'having' can be passed off as 'being'. Leaving aside questions of linguistic usage, it is not possible to 'have', or acquire, inspiration imitatively; one can only 'be' in an inspired state. And the labour of creation does not tread well-worn linguistic paths: it travels instead on a language springing from the knowing acceptance of the experiences of death and birth. As the only form of life capable of living in the awareness of time and of knowing about death, the human being who does not attain sufficient symbolic maturation has to pretend not to know and then pretend that he is not pretending, and so forth. Caught in such a spiral of fictions, one may even come to deny the reality of one's own death (while disclaiming that one denies it) and, by the same token, risk missing out on any opportunity to achieve creative experiences. It is almost as if the (illusory) denial of death also denied, in effect, creative life.

The creative process, in fact, appears to be the result of the ability to set in motion vicissitudes which are, at the same time, contrasting and complementary: activeness and passivity, orientation and bewilderment. A glance at the 'phases' of creative (artistic and scientific) thought appears to confirm the interactive, interdependent nature of such antithetic human propensities. We might tentatively posit that there is a connection between human creativity and another paradoxical human ability: the capacity both to use one's own cognitive frame and to relinquish it. At some point in the creative process, the ability to set aside the use of our intellectual functions appears to become downright indispensable, almost as if facing the risk of not knowing, and of no longer managing to maintain intellectual control, were an obligatory stage in the course of creative thinking. And yet the ability to relinquish certain intellectual functions, virtually a capacity to let oneself die mentally, to plummet out of the interstices of a grid of intelligibility, is a capacity which is in some way provided by one's inner symbolic organization. For it would not be easy for an individual to silence the epistemological chorus in which his intellect takes part if this meant running the risk of disintegrating inwardly. It is the guide-rope of a vital capacity for symbolization which allows one to let go and come out beyond the constricted spaces of what is consensually knowable and let new thoughts be born.

7

Pseudosymbolic Language

Pseudosymbols: Introductory Notes

Among the unsatisfactory uses of the symbolic function are a variety of 'dialogic' forms which seem to lack authenticity. With a view to gaining a clearer perspective of such 'linguistic' forms, we shall now attempt to explore an elusive and risky topic which we may tentatively label 'pseudosymbolization'.

We shall take as a point of departure the assumption that one of the conditions necessary for the symbol-mutation (the salient aspect of the process of hominization) to pass from a potential to an actualized state within individual ontogenies is the sequence of exchanges carried on with the (parental) environment. It is also appropriate to point out in this connection that linguisticity itself, which provides us with a freer mode of survival, may nevertheless be submitted to the more primitive and repetitive mechanisms of our cognitive structure, so as to become isolated from formative processes and relegated to the production of a most impoverished language – verbal noise.

The manifestation of our tendency to repeat, moreover, appears to be linked with our earliest experiences: though useful for the purpose of reaching a sufficient degree of autonomy, it may take on too great a momentum within the context of our inner life, and thus even prove one of the obstacles to maturation and growth. It is known, in fact, that certain forms of pathological defence mechanisms arise precisely out of the tendency, or compulsion, to repetitive behaviour. As a second-level instrument – in other words, as a capacity for controlling other instruments – the symbolic function exhibits a tendency to become automatic, namely to operate according to rules of its own, with the result that any perturbation, instead of producing a regressive slippage towards instinctual modes, leads to repetitive fixations (or to the automation) of the acquired symbolic competence. The tendency to become automatic is, perhaps, part and parcel of the evolution of the mind itself, for without a certain degree of mental automation the advantages of the symbol-mutation would not have prevailed and the evolutionary 'bet' would have been lost. And yet, even though the processes of symbolization may be regarded as constituting essential, and not accidental, aspects of human life (which the mind cannot shake off), they may still be put to use in a pseudosymbolic fashion.

The symbolism brought into play when one's inner organization has settled into a 'false self' can be of no maturational use: in such cases, 'symbols' are not formed as products of the ability to redirect frustrations into development, and such symbolization is a mimicry of linguisticity. Being pseudosymbols, therefore, they cannot be used for the purpose of progressively creating objects, as they have nothing in common with the high affective cost involved in producing inner transformations of the symbol-generating type.

Winnicott, for instance, reminds us that, by means of a false self, the subject builds himself a whole set of false relations, and, as a result of introjection, the whole conglomeration of falsities assumes the aspect of reality.[1] In fact, the ability to symbolize may even deteriorate into a process which amounts to the negation of the intrinsic constructive purpose of symbolization; the ability may even be used for pre-eminently defensive purposes, such as the solipsistic development of consistent systems of 'explanation' which, precisely because they lack relatedness, prove to be basically unassailable. As a relational style which is observable in personality disorders, as well as in 'cultural' behaviour, the habit of using imitations with oneself and others may be traced to the unconscious memory of the decisive value of symbols for the purpose of creating reality. Symbolization is thus often used as an all-powerful (and, hence, false) means of faking the world and, therefore, of simply 'extracting' reality out of the subject, instead of laboriously coming to recognize it in persons and nature.

Freud observes that in 'neurotic' persons

we meet with the mental phenomenon which we describe as a belief in the 'omnipotence of thoughts'. In our judgement this lies in an over-estimation of the influence which our mental (in this case, intellectual) acts can exercise in altering the external world.... The 'omnipotence of thoughts' was, we suppose, an expression of the pride of mankind in the development of speech, which resulted in such an extraordinary advancement of intellectual activities.[2]

The 'neurotic' capitalizes on his dominion over verbal thought (the 'pride of mankind in the development of speech'). He exploits it – and is exploited by it – to the utmost, in an illusory attempt to manipulate reality for narcissistic purposes. The widespread human tendency to 'lie' to oneself and others, and thus rely upon imitative language when transacting communications, amounts to an omnipotent way of utilizing the tools of symbolization, so that the latter, rather than being used to construct reality, are actually employed to distort it: the subject acts under the illusion that something will be forthcoming as the magical correlate of what is imitatively asserted. As is known, paranoid, persecutory defences are hardened through the 'support' of symbolization, used in omnipotent-magical fashion, and are thus rendered inexhaustible. Whenever some measure of linguistic development is attained, it is no longer enough to manage our mental life in such a way as to perceive threats as originating from without; it also becomes mandatory to assert, demonstrate and justify one's cognitive account of the 'facts'. Such defensive constructs, however, do not obviously constitute a symbolic product in its full sense. A pseudosymbolic process which has the appearance of symbolism but is not conducive to dialogic interactions is 'diabolic' in the etymological sense of the word – the Greek term *diaballo* being a compound of the word *dia* ('across') and *ballo* ('I throw'). Hence a 'diabol' could be something that flings things across, and as a consequence jumbles them up. To be closer to the vital complexities of language we could suggest that communication is symbolic when we have activities that lead to richer interactions and that, insofar as this is achieved, the activity is also a truly metabolic one, a vital one. Pseudosymbols are diabolic in the sense that they cannot possibly be metabolic. Especially in the early phases of mentation the symbol is a necessary metabol, inasmuch as the 'energy' involved in uniting an expectation with a negative realization (when 'something goes wrong') is channelled by means of the symbol towards the formation of inner and outer reality. Thus no vicissitude is neutral in respect of growth – the time-honoured philosophical *Bildung*, (self-)formation – because any event is intensively for or against maturation.

Briefly, even though the tendency to repeat may be understood as constituting one of the more basic and neutral of human propensities underlying all growth processes, that 'growth' may yet manifest itself in pathological forms, for instance in a symbolic activity used exclusively for omnipotent purposes. Where this is the case, symbolization has nothing to do with the construction of reality, since all that is being practised is verbal magic, which ultimately turns out to be the making of 'noise'. It follows that any progress made in symbol-generation, by working through vicissitudes of loss, may be subsequently used for either defensive-regressive or developmental purposes, which is to say that it may be used either 'diabolically' or 'metabolically'. And surely whenever the symbolic function is imitatively and narcissistically put to use, the 'object', rather than being enriched, is impoverished, for the dynamics involved is, in fact, an end unto itself. It may perhaps be appropriate to recall once again that the 'world of objects' could be regarded as a construct, which reflects the symbolic modes by means of which it was developed, and also that the richness of that world is dependent upon the quality and degree of such development. When an object is either not formed or else distorted by the use of a non-symbolic language, the ultimate result is that the object is not usable and we cannot properly interact with it; symbols which are bound up with narcissistic dynamics will thus be incapable of operating developmentally or, in other words, metabolically.

But if our pseudosymbols, or diabols, serve not to construct but to confound reality, undermining interchange and utilizability, one may well ask why they are, nevertheless, products of our mentation.

With this question in mind, we may note that at the onset of our mentation the mere act of *actively* generating anything, even if only confusing noise, is nevertheless something that involves an activity on the part of the subject, by far preferable to passivity, and such that it may defend him against dissolving into a relational field perceived as a corrosive rather than as a catalyst. Winnicott perhaps argues to similar effect when he remarks:

> The term disintegration is used to describe a sophisticated *defence*, a defence that is an active production of chaos in defence against unintegration in the absence of maternal ego-support, that is against the unthinkable or archaic anxiety that results from failure of holding in the stage of absolute dependence. The chaos of disintegration may be as 'bad' as the unreliability of the environment, but it has the advantage of being produced by the baby and therefore of being non-environmental. It is within the area of the baby's omnipotence. In terms of psycho-analysis, it is analysable, whereas the unthinkable anxieties are not.[3]

When the subject is not able to produce real symbols, but only imitation ones, or pseudosymbols, the relationship between such pseudosymbols (falsehoods or diabols) and the mind will be of a parasitic nature. Bion suggests that whether true thoughts 'are entertained or not is of significance to the thinker but not to the truth. If entertained they are conducive to mental health; if not they initiate disturbance. The lie depends on the thinker and gains significance through him. It is the link between host and parasite in the parasitic relationship.'[4] And yet we might go so far as to say that falsehoods are indestructible, in the sense that they already are, of themselves, unreal; and, although unreal, falsehoods are fully capable of destroying a thinker.[5] The point I am trying to highlight may be summed up as follows: the symbolic system is the result of an authentic maturational process, namely a growth which is directed towards progressive inner structuring; however, when difficulties of whatever nature cannot be overcome in favour of development, one falls back upon the mimicry of symbolic forms and sinks into using pseudosymbols acquired by faking and not through laborious maturation. Such symbols are mere shams of the true symbolic function; for even when mixed and fitted into a variety of patterns they add nothing to the depth and productiveness of interpersonal relationships.

The very same dangers of wandering off the path of development and allowing oneself to be sidetracked into imitative compensations are recognizable along the journey of hominization. The point at issue is a compensation which comes to be dominated by the proliferation of precepts and injunctions producing a centrifugal pattern, with the result that the very capacity for inner growth comes to be threatened. In other words, the problem of coping with fears related to our primal condition is falsely resolved through a hasty, impatient attempt to 'engineer' human conduct, by indefinitely multiplying rules, precepts and injunctions in which refuge could be taken. It is that state of impatience and discomfort which may give rise to the danger of trying to avoid all maturational travail through the pre-emptive exploitation of the earliest symbolic tools which may have been acquired. Opportunities to develop further are thus hindered and human anxiety is 'reduced' through an ever more intricate definition of what is and is not appropriate.

Freud had shown that he was aware of how attempts to elude an element of reality which could not, as yet, be construed or contained – being too disturbing – may sometimes be thought out through a system of pseudosymbolic operations. He states:

> whereas the new, imaginary external world of a psychosis attempts to put itself in the place of external reality, that of a neurosis, on the contrary, is apt, like the play of children, to attach itself to a piece of

reality – a different piece from the one against which it has to defend itself – and to lend that piece a special importance and a secret meaning which we (not always quite appropriately) call a *symbolic* one. Thus we see that both in neurosis and psychosis there comes into consideration the question not only of a *loss of reality* but also of a *substitute for reality*.[6]

In fact, by incessantly assigning 'secret meanings', we can continue to conjure up ways of manipulating reality under the domination of our least developed mental structures. Such substitutes of mental life and reality are staged by means of symbolizations which Freud already recognized as inappropriate. There is cause for reflection in the fact that the term 'symbolic' is printed in italics in the *Standard Edition*, with the probable intention of denoting a certain degree of reserve as to the appropriateness of the term itself. In other words, the symbolic function may be used in order to construct reality, as well as abused in order to construct a 'neurotic' substitute for reality. Furthermore, it is well known that pathological 'secrets' may also be matters of vast public consensus, with the result that subjects are in a position to support each other in the massive defensive distortions which they produce to compensate for an impossibility to develop. As communication uses different channels, certain modes are kept away from codification and are thus more easily disavowable. Since verbal symbolizations are eminently suited to convey what happened rather than *how* it happened, the verbal message is the part of communication for which we are more easily held responsible. As a consequence of this unavoidable gap between that for which we are responsible and that which is open to recantation, whatever can be denied with others becomes increasingly open to denial with ourselves. Another diverse, and potentially pathogenic, consequence is the inclination to create an ever wider gap between *what* is formally said (for which we accept responsibility) and *how* we say something; in this way words may actually become a cover or a disguise for what we mean.

When listening and understanding are affected by the public-consensus type of pseudosymbolic degradation, they appear to confine their attention only to the saying of discourse: the message puts across nothing about the relationship with the object being spoken of, since the sole concern is with the expressiveness of discourse. As Heidegger suggests:

> The fact that talking is going on is a matter of consequence. The Being-said, the *dictum*, the pronouncement … – all these now stand …

for the genuineness of the discourse and of the understanding which belongs to it, and for its appropriateness to the facts. And because this discoursing has lost its primary relationship-of-Being towards the entity talked about, or else has never achieved such a relationship, it does not communicate in such a way as to let this entity be appropriated in a primordial manner, but communicates rather by following the route of *gossip* and *passing the word along*. What is said-in-the-talk as such, spreads in wider circles and takes on an authoritative character. Things are so because one says so. Idle talk is constituted by just such gossiping and passing the word along – a process by which its initial lack of grounds to stand on becomes aggravated to complete groundlessness.[7]

The staging and display of fictitious relations are inevitably associated with lifeless, invasive language which may only function as a filler. In parallel fashion, the pseudosymbolic process producing such 'language' is easily amenable to a high measure of manipulation, even suited to determine a 'cognitive' space which is free of conflicts only in appearance and is moreover charged with the task of nullifying all vital relations. Any misrepresentation of reality, such as is implied whenever there is a groundless appeal to the reality of facts, forces the speakers into a progressive distortion of the symbolic function, with the result that it becomes tangled into precisely that kind of deadening perversion which is the most public and most concealed of all. When the denial of, or indeed blindness to, our permanent state of loss, longing or precariousness is coped with through the activity of pseudosymbolic structures, there is a risk that symbolizations originally indicating the lost, or longed-for, conditions will be used for the absurd purpose of denying all loss, longing or precariousness. As Heidegger remarks:

> Idle talk controls even the ways in which one may be curious. It says what one 'must' have read and seen. In being everywhere and nowhere, curiosity is delivered over to idle talk. These two everyday modes of Being for discourse and sight are not just present-at-hand side by side in their tendency to uproot, but *either* of these ways-to-be drags the *other* one with it. Curiosity, for which nothing is closed off, and idle talk, for which there is nothing that is not understood, provide themselves ... with the guarantee of a 'life' which, supposedly, is genuinely 'lively'.[8]

Thus the function of a symbol comes to be split and multiplied in an inconclusive fashion, as a result of inertia, repetition or vaguely manic propensities. As Leclaire suggests,[9] words that have been illusively freed from the burdening complexity of interactive bonds only contribute to the organization of a vast, global delusion. The constant concern with links, affects and conflicts still runs the risk of frustrating our aspirations to an easy freedom which consists in saying and doing almost anything as long as we can break free from the life of world and persons, thus producing a 'culture' in which we only interact with the more successfully advertised symbolic representations. Such 'cultural' styles may become the standard practice.

Philosophy of Dialogue and Pseudosymbolic Falsification

In addressing the question of how it is that the symbolic function can ever be used to destroy and confound, to the point of enmeshing the most disparate forms of human expression in a spiral of falsification – which appears unassailable – we may begin with Bion's remark that 'The human animal has not ceased to be persecuted by his mind and the thoughts usually associated with it – whatever their origin may be.'[10] Humans may doubtless find refuge – Bion goes on to say – in mindlessness, in the eroticization of falsehood, in acting out, as well as in various degrees of stupor. If certain 'doctrinal' differences are surpassed, Wittgenstein's celebrated remark, 'Philosophy is a battle against the bewitchment of our intelligence by means of language',[11] may cast light on the concerns that I am trying to pursue.

Just like the maieutics of Socrates – who raised the art of mid-wifery to the level of philosophy – Wittgenstein's inquiries are also concerned with the interlocutor's disorientation and confusion, the latter being regarded sometimes as adversary, sometimes as ally, or sometimes even as the confirmation that interactive discourse is occurring. The basic aim which brings the two outlooks together is evident in the 'analytic' work that relentlessly strives to break the spell of the 'linguistic bewitchment' which, in various subtle guises, truly prevents the birth of the symbolic modes which are most apt to lead to evolution in the life of thought.

These methodological outlooks are probably rooted in the awareness that any philosophical search for clarity is something eminently maieutic and therapeutic. The need for midwifery and 'therapy' in philosophy can be seen as deriving from our capacity to suspect the constant threat of pseudosymbolic linguisticity. 'There is not *a* philosophical method, though there are indeed methods, like different therapies,' remarks Wittgenstein.[12]

Sharing this outlook, we suggest that one of the preliminary connotations of 'false self' may be that it lacks a vital sense of identity. For modern man, even though he is not ill according to any taxonomy of mental illness based on symptoms, is still shrouded in and coerced by compensations for his lack of authenticity. And when the aspiration to evolve manages, none the less, to 'vex' him, it does so only in a numb, obscure fashion: the latent kernels of the more authentic self have no way of speaking out as they are inserted in a 'mental field' overburdened by pseudosymbols and thus prevented from undergoing enough symbolic maturation. When the interlocutor who is committed to authentic listening in a maieutic dialogue keeps attentively silent, it is often in order to 'auscultate' that part of the other's self which cannot, or cannot yet, speak; and his silence may serve equally to avoid his becoming enmeshed in those highly expressive manifestations of the false self which, virtually without end, are composing and unravelling verbal messages.

Reflection regarding psychoanalytic dialogue in general exhibits a clear-cut theoretical relevance in that it transforms our customary understanding of the way in which we develop a measure of self-awareness. In fact, even though, as philosophers, we always move along with the orientation rooted in the Socratic 'know thyself', the element which strikes us as innovative is the fact that self-knowledge is to be gained, not through unrelated introspection, but solely within the confines of a bipersonal field wherein somebody other than ourselves listens, interprets and responds to what we say.

But that same philosophical 'battle against the bewitchment of our intelligence by means of language' may in turn degenerate, and even energize the cognitive derivatives of destructive narcissism, whenever in the 'battle' we lose the maieutic root of our *philo*-sophical work. It is the maieutic attitude, that is the midwifery of our thinking, which provides us with the key (or compass) for a creative project to be found even beneath the linguistic inconsistencies which we try to identify and elucidate. It is a part of the maieutic task to engage in monitoring the diabols of pseudosymbolic language. Wittgenstein remarks: 'Socrates keeps reducing the sophist to silence, – but does he have *right* on his side when he does this? Well, it is true that the sophist does not know what he thinks he knows; but that is no triumph for Socrates. It can't be a case of "You see! You don't know it!" – nor yet, triumphantly, of "So none of us knows anything!" '13 In detecting the non-metabolic (anti-vital, dia-bolic) quality of pseudosymbolic language we also run the risk of failing to listen to the truly metabolic message mixed with it, or even shrouded by it, and ultimately restrict philosophy to a censorious, scarcely *philo*-sophical practice. A derivative of some such attitude might even be seen in the following remark: 'My aim is: to teach you to pass from a piece of disguised nonsense to something that is patent nonsense.' [14]

The general lines of Wittgenstein's 'therapeutic' programme can be juxtaposed to one of the questions running through Ricœur's work, namely whether revelation and concealment (in psycho-analysis) always disclose or disguise desires or whether they could sometimes be manifestations or revelations of a creative blueprint. The basic question tends to underscore the recognition that different levels of 'hermeneutic' approach are involved, and that conflicts among diverse levels of interpretation are a possibility. We have in fact, on the one hand, philosophical 'interpretations' of language which primarily demystify and, on the other, interpretative outlooks which are revealing inasmuch as they focus on the effort to extri-cate from either disguised or patent nonsense a project of personal development.

It is well to bear in mind, however, that in certain settings, for instance in the process of psychoanalysis, it is impossible to separate entirely efforts towards demystification from efforts towards con-structive revelation, for the two mutually imply and sustain each other. Assuming that symbolic distortions which confound reality, or mystifications in general, are without doubt among the sources of pathology, it will follow that in the analytic 'dialogue' attention is laboriously released from mystifying traps (the 'bewitchment by means of language'), for the purpose of redirecting it in such a way as to energize processes of growth or individuation. Within a thera-peutic relation, the unravelling of absurdities through interpretation leads to more complex, higher-order interpersonal relationships, in the sense that the subject is helped to engage in richer levels of dialogue quite different from the mere denunciation or unmasking of disguised nonsense.

The speaking subject is perennially at grips with his own oscil-lation between the search for truth and the search for states of (emotional) certainty. If we bear this in mind we shall be in a position to posit that, in certain 'contingencies' of our mental life, the conflict between the need to 'know' and the need to 'deny' (in order to safeguard certainty) becomes so acute that it triggers defensive moves aimed at perverting the goals of symbolization together with the logical connections which are responsible for self-awareness. In a report concerning a narcissistic person with whom it was not easy to work analytically, Khan stresses the patient's highly expressive, articulate, incisive style of speaking and even goes so far as to remark: 'She was perpetually ... "acting into" language, which is then not symbolic discourse.'[15]

Taken together, pseudosymbolic attitudes can accumulate and, as a result of an inexorable run of staged acts, may even acquire an outright dominion which leads to a possibly irreversible pathological style. And this amounts to consolidating and sanctioning the false self's control over the whole relational pattern. When pseudosymbolization is preponderant,

> Everyone is acquainted with what is up for discussion and what occurs, and everyone discusses it; but everyone also knows already how to talk about what has to happen first – about what is not yet up for discussion but 'really' must be done. Already everybody has surmised and scented out in advance what Others have also surmised and scented out. This Being-on-the-scent is of course based upon hearsay, for if anyone is genuinely 'on the scent' of anything, he does not speak about it; and this is the most entangling way in which ambiguity presents *Dasein* possibilities so that they will already be stifled in their power.[16]

Awareness of the danger that all cognition may be flawed draws attention to the need to identify possible pseudosymbolic absurdities in the conceptualization of any therapeutic approach. For this reason, it is well not to lose sight of the need to review constantly any notion of 'therapy'. The absurd, inexplicable aspect of psychic suffering finds partial expression in symptoms, regarded as defences raised against an 'unthinkable' interactive condition which then becomes 'mentally' impossible. Symptoms, moreover, in all their expressive shadings, make critical, ironic and aggressive allusions to the entire interactive set-up: any relational condition which is felt to be undefinable or unthinkable by the same token comes to be felt as unbearable. To the extent, then, that attention is focused on the symptom, there is the danger of a naïve verbal realism which twists the very foundations of maieutic or therapeutic dialogue into an abstract game. And the one taking up the 'maieutic' role *vis-à-vis* his interlocutor's disorientation, with a view to coaxing a more vital way of speaking out of the other's inner travail, can never eliminate the risk of falling into the sterile indifference of irony. In fact, the term 'irony' is linked etymologically to the Greek word *eiron*, meaning 'the questioner'. If we are concerned with our own questions about symptoms, as emerging against the background of an underlying epistemology, we may end up with more questions and ultimately avoid the challenge of authentically listening to someone and thus allowing the birth of his own thinking. Symptoms could be viewed, rather, as being part and parcel of that 'impossible discourse', namely maieutics, and certainly not as a foreign body to be removed without even attempting to resymbolize the overall condition. Similarly, detecting nonsense, rather than being considered an end in itself, could be viewed as paving the way for a project of development emanating from that very 'nonsense'.

Resymbolizing a Dialogic Condition

Symbolic falsification might also affect the whole 'therapeutic' relationship when it is propagated by playing imitative 'as if' games which enmesh the 'therapist' together with the patient, in the sense that both become entangled in pseudosymbolic falsifications detached from the complexity of life. We might join with Hillman in calling to mind that the persons involved in the 'therapeutic' relationship may even come to believe that the desire to be freed from an illness might coincide with a return to what one was before; when both doctor and patient collude in the 'hope' of re-establishing a previous condition of health, they both illusively move against the flux of time, the process of ageing and the reality of death.[17] There is collusion between the two in denying the complexity of life by means of a missymbolization of the therapeutic relationship, which removes the likelihood that the vital labours of the processes of maturation will come to be unveiled and appreciated. In other words, they share in the same pseudosymbolizations, which cannot possibly perform a metabolic role and thus cannot be focused into a developmental dynamics.

The conception of life as a 'biological condition', which is not a function of anything else and, at the same time, is the measure of itself, is a notion which may be sufficient and correct for the practice of medicine, but unsatisfactory from a 'philosophic' point of view, inasmuch as life is regarded as a process involving 'quality' and not as mere survival. For, obviously, if it were only a question of surviving, any pathological style whatsoever might well do.

A major temptation running counter to development is that of borrowing a set of symbols from the medical tradition and applying them to the inner world of mental life. Such terms may be employed outside the context wherein they are meaningful only at the cost of seriously mystifying a relationship. When this is done, the symbolic apparatus of the relationship becomes devitalized, which is to say that its metabolic role is denied, thus rendering the interaction disordered and 'diabolic'. In the symbology of medical ethics, in fact, 'saving life' means, first and foremost, postponing death in a manner which can be assessed by measuring time intervals. 'Saving life' also means promising to provide a greater 'quantity' of life, which may be construed in terms of conventional measurements. But the temptation to believe that saving life in a biological sense is, in and of itself, tantamount to saving the person is a sign of inauthentic symbolic use, given that often medicine responds to the demand for more life and not to the request for an improved or transformed quality of life.[18]

A more profound significance of the goals of medicine may, perhaps, be seen in the effort to combat illness and delay death not only in order to gain more life – as if it were a 'good' valued according to definite criteria – but also in order to achieve a different experience of approaching death, so that the event can receive some degree of conscious elaboration.

When attempting a psychoanalytic 'dialogue', one faces the risk of having to abandon a customary symbolic terrain, and faces the need to undergo deep mourning of an epistemic nature. In fact, the subject usually confronts the 'helper' with a type of request which, though different in content, is yet similar to the one expressed to the 'physician', namely to prolong the type of life the subject knows, or to extend the past; but what is requested above all is to have some disturbing component removed as quickly as possible, so as to be able to return, undisturbed, to the way things previously were. In extreme cases, what is asked for is a sort of 'scientific' intervention capable of denying and eliminating – the sooner the better – the annoying ailment which has jolted our customary way of surviving.

In the area of psychoanalytic dialogue, on the other hand, the idea of treatment often needs to be transformed and resymbolized, primarily in the sense that symptoms, as the immediate cause of suffering, may not constitute the target of the treatment, but can be used as 'gauges' of the shortcomings of inner organization which lead to the onset of symptoms. Viewed thus, the very meaning of 'therapy' comes to be resymbolized inasmuch as there is a realization that a disturbance has a meaning which can be deduced only from the individual's relational life as a whole and that it would be misleading to cling to a classical concept of treatment as relief from a symptom or elimination of the 'pathogenic agent'. There is an attempt to come to terms with the nagging requests for effective treatment by construing that the very request is part of the 'illness' itself and is thus rooted in hindered maturation of the person's inner structure; for it is the latter which may be regarded as the source of both the symptom and the magical expectations of a therapeutic resolution.

To return, now, to the 'enigma' of a discourse which is symbolic in appearance only, we may notice that at times one is astonished by the vivid eloquence and precision with which persons weave the most extraordinary descriptions of their mental states. And we are even more dismayed to discover that they cannot use this ability to dredge up an authentic inner life. Paradoxically, it seems that the symbols involved are 'blind' and 'mute'. The subject appears to be 'possessed' by his own pseudosymbolic language, as well as by a deployment of mental activity forming a barrier against any relationship with the outside. Further pseudosymbols, or diabols, emerge to throw up a 'noise' screen between the self and others, thereby pre-empting all likelihood of a relationship. Consequently, outside 'objects' can neither be affectively invested nor provide relief. Almost as if it were an infestation of diabols, pseudosymbolic language takes on a virulence possessed of autocratic control, with the result that instead of being in a position to know oneself or use others, one becomes virtually enslaved to that power as if it were a form of addiction. Some truly disconcerting situations may arise as a result of the indefinite propagation of pseudosymbols. For an extraordinary self-'knowledge', in the form of the ability to articulate one's own emotional and cognitive states, may go hand in hand with the inability to conceive making any use of that knowledge. One is, so to speak, possessed by a diabolic, life-suppressing language, with the result that it is impossible to establish relationships based upon use or exchange, for all the subject can do is vex others with impossible 'dialogic' demands.

We may suppose that this acting of one's 'illness' into language may have been useful as a defensive strategy for protecting an inchoate real self during some stage of development. But when 'acting into language' persistently continues and becomes a compulsion, it may, as such, turn into a stifling, pathological habit which makes the mind's life impossible. And if a relational system is based on pseudosymbols, or diabols, it cannot metabolize and develop, and the subjects are forced to suffer constant mental 'hunger'. This same system may also be used in order to hurt with words, thus averting any 'danger' of having to accept relief and depend upon others. As may happen in cases of addiction, the subject barely hangs on to life, locked as he is in the grip of his pseudosymbolic system, which, despite all appearances, tilts the scale of cognitive-affective life towards degradation, or at best towards a drastically reduced functionality.

One of the ways of looking at the enigma of self-destructive behaviour is to regard it as a desire to tear down an unusable structure in a desperate effort, perhaps, to get a chance to start anew, almost as if, paradoxically, one had to plunge blindly into disruption in order to come out with one's framework rebuilt. In our opinion, however, attempts at, and 'threats' of, self-destruction can be seen as forms of acting out, aimed at destroying the person without even slightly modifying the pseudosymbolic (and hence diabolic) structure itself, which was what made life 'impossible' in the first place. In such cases, the analyst faces a tough, drastic confrontation when he asks that life, which he 'embraces' at the outset, be spared, so that he can attempt the 'mad' enterprise of eliminating instead the parasitic, despotic incrustation, which has taken over and damaged the subject's inner life.

The 'Energy Sources' of Pseudosymbols

As we have seen, structural systems which are more pseudosymbolic than properly symbolic may come to be formed within our cognitive apparatus. With a view to striving for a more accurate understanding of such pseudosymbolic constructions, it may be useful to recall a piece of advice coming from the area of semiology, namely that one should guard against the danger of confusing the bearer, or vehicle, of meaning with meaning itself.

Starting out with what is considered as a common error (the failure to distinguish between signifier and signified), and using it as a valuable heuristic tool, we may trace back to the origins of the question of pseudosymbolic construction. We shall thus be in a better position to address the issue of how such pseudosymbolic formations can acquire their undeniable power and establish their totalitarian sway over the individual's inner structure. The question posed, in other words, is how it may be possible that a pseudolanguage can

spoliate and enmesh the whole 'personality'. In this same perspective, we can examine the reasons for the disturbing nature, both
stubborn and unassailable, of mental formations of the pseudosymbolic kind.

We may then wonder whether the pervasiveness of such symbolic
'error' might not depend upon the virtually incalculable importance
assumed by the bearers of meaning,[19] precisely when the individual
is beginning to make headway with building his reality. These
bearers, or supports, of meaning are so intimately interwoven with
the situations to which they belong that it is difficult to separate
them conceptually from the early relations wherein the subject takes
his first steps towards the symbolic dimension. Thus a bearer of
meaning tends to absorb the thoughts, emotions, desires and even
the objects that actually belong to the situation which creates the
conditions of meaningfulness. In other words, at the outset, the
carrier of meaning is such a necessary, even decisive, factor that it is
all too easy for the subject to make the 'error', so to speak, of mistak-
ing it for both the meaning itself and for the interpersonal reality
from which the meaning derives. We are now in a position also to ask
in what way the early condition of dependence and need may come
to underpin the formation of pseudosymbolic trends.

Departing from the basic assumption that needs are objective
before they become subjective, one should recognize that they are
gradually processed and expressed by the individual as the suffering
for something missing. To the extent that such a condition is experienced as dissatisfaction, and to the extent that the perception of an
object capable of satisfying the need is also developed, it may be said
that a need is being processed, in the sense of attempting to gain
access to, or create, a mental – no longer just biological – dimension
in which the inchoate subject constructs his interactive reality. While
the process of transforming a need into a desire marks the transition
from a biological state to the onset of self-awareness, it is precisely
in the course of this crucial developmental transition that there is
the greatest likelihood of serious distortions affecting our incipient
mentation.

In the course of such early vicissitudes the roots of 'false needs'
may in fact take hold. Their extent will depend largely upon the
flaws in the symbolic organization of the desires through which the
underlying need finds expression at some level of awareness. But
once again: if it is a (biological) need, how can it be 'false'? In my
view, the 'falsity' of certain illusory cognitive approaches may be
traced back to the inadequately constructed forms taken by both the

need-expressed-as-desire and the framing of the response to that desire.

Nevertheless, the question which most concerns us is the stubbornness of the symbolic structures involved. In a developmental view, we may suppose that the tenacity of pseudosymbolic formations corresponds to the force of our primal needs in the process of self-creation and may thus be ascribed to their being linked with the subject's instinctual resources. In this way, both the expression of a state of need and the response to that need may be 'true' or 'false' or, in other words, symbolic or pseudosymbolic, without it being implied that they are detached from the instinctual roots of the need. But let us once again ask how the primal condition of need is woven into the making of pseudosymbolic structures so as to support the latter.

The most disconcerting dynamics of all is the one whereby a pseudosymbolization of desire – that is the formation of a symbolic construct which has a distorted connection with a primal need – comes to function as the mental equivalent of an actual need, comparable to the actual needs related to the maintenance of a vital equilibrium. The pseudosymbols through which the desire is laid down can be seen as parasites which usurp the full force and urgency of the primal need. And inasmuch as the pseudosymbolization of a desire fits within a model of unrelatedness and omnipotence uprooted from reality, it will by no means support interactions such as knowledge, utilization, satisfaction of a desire, growth through absorption and gratitude for what has been received. Lacking a proper link with interactive reality, pseudosymbolic forms of desire are unable to take part in relations involving exchanges of recognition and may ultimately lead to the pathogenic treadmill of insatiability.

Assuming some sort of equivalence between the notion of a pseudosymbolic language and the ubiquitous need for rumour (gossip, hearsay), we may agree with Heidegger that idle talk 'discloses everything and anything, yet in such a way that Being-in is everywhere and nowhere'.[20]

According to Bion:

> The idea that is nourished by love develops from matrix to function in Language of Achievement; from which it can be transformed into achievement. But if the idea is subjected to splitting, it may split again repeatedly, each split growing and having to be split again. Thus one gets not development but division and multiplication – cancerous, not qualitative, increase.[21]

In such cases, rather than there being any development of symbolic thought, there is an indefinite, disordered reduplication, fragmentation, which is more like a rise in the noise level than an improvement in quality. Bion goes on to say:

> There appears to be a great increase in ideation, but there is not, because all the ideas turn out, on inspection, to be the same one. The emotional matrix from which this springs is not envy and gratitude, but envy and greed. The idea is split over and over again and is felt to produce a quantity of splits…. Envy and gratitude, on the other hand, stimulate a desire for gain, but enable the individual to establish a good relation between what has been gained and that which has enabled him to gain it.[22]

Hence, a pseudosymbolization of desire cannot be metabolic; it can only act as a parasite, feeding off the 'psychic energy' of the primal vicissitudes of need. In addition, the otherwise feasible ramifications of authentic language tend to decay, inasmuch as the opportunities to put them to genuine use become ever more rare.

With the expansion of our world view and with the ever-increasing complexity of needs, compared with primary ones, there is an opportunity for disruptions and compensations to develop in the space between primal needs and ensuing ways of articulating the awareness of such needs. The risk of disordered outcomes is especially high when our inchoate modes of awareness of needs are being worked out. For pseudosymbols are illusory ways of representing a need and, as such, do not correspond to factors of development. Pseudosymbolic constructs of desires are not built of metabolic language, but of diabols, in the sense that already at the beginning, with the very onset of awareness, diabolic and non-metabolic pseudosymbols are inducing an illusory state which tends towards an omniscience of the magical variety, as if words could directly control the world. As a result, the missymbolization of desires is mistaken for a state of need and the subject swathes himself in a solipsistic certainty which gives the illusion of catering to one of the subject's real needs, and may thus parasitically feed on it.

The 'Sophist' Within

In order to gain a better understanding of the divergence between symbolic and pseudosymbolic languages, we might explore the figure of the 'sophist', as viewed in its traditional, emblematic sense, namely as the opposite (at least in some aspects) of the 'philosopher'. We are not, however, casting the 'sophist' as a character taking part in interpersonal dialogue; his role is, rather, that of standing for an aspect, or state, in human vicissitudes of self-creation. In short, 'philosopher' and 'sophist' may symbolize a conflict within a single individual.

To highlight the fact that pseudosymbolic outcomes are always possible with language, we shall invoke certain incisive passages in Jaspers's work where he tries to 'diagnose' the insidious, pervasive features of our falsifying, pseudosymbolic language.[23] Any attempt to define the pseudosymbolic side of our linguisticity in terms of a mere 'perversion', or 'form' of pathology, would amount to a rash simplification of the problem, in that the perversity of pseudosymbolic language is a general problem of constant concern. The danger of degradation and involution in language, moreover, seems to be inversely proportional to the distance covered in the process of hominization. In fact, the very instant that some such 'perversion' is identified, it has already begun to change its camouflage once again.

Jaspers goes so far as to believe that space is found for the sophistication of language in culture so that it may perform the functon of a 'nameless warning'.[24] In the face of such an appalling danger – 'nameless', in fact – (which, in my opinion, may be interpreted as the danger of degradation and involution in human linguisticity) it is almost as if measures were demanded for more vigilant monitoring of the symbolic processes.

The 'nameless warning' is perhaps the most accurate expression for stressing the potential threat of a linguistic involution (far more relevant than the danger of ethological-ecological imbalances) which might go so far as to jeopardize the development of a meaningful relation between nature and culture, between world and language, deforming the relationship itself into a parasitic, destructive pattern. Just a few decades ago the notion of ecology was rarely invoked, while our fashionable language now resounds with worrisome expressions related to the degradation of the planet we biologically inhabit; and yet there is hardly any concern for the potential degradation of our linguisticity, our symbolic habitat, our transpersonal cultural home. Even though we do not have conceptual instruments that can adequately monitor any such degradation, there is no way of excluding such a trend, which may be all the more pervasive because we cannot properly articulate it – as dangerous as it is capable of concealment.

The need sometimes arises to step outside a conventional scheme and risk a leap into the void, in order to escape the invasion of the sophist within, who conditions and constrains almost as strictly as do the signals of our animal nature. The hereditary load of programmes which, by means of countless drives and reflexes, rigorously determine our responses to the environment seems to assume a secondary position in the face of the even greater pressure of a pseudosymbolic system which, instead, responds to nothing but to itself. It is like an endless echo, relayed from one member of the community to another, reverberating and rebounding through empty discourses – taking delight, as it were, in degrading man's symbolic habitat.

Our linguistic potential may be suppressed by the despotic influence of a falsifying cultural 'normality' as well as by the requirements imposed so that 'normality' may prevail. One might even surmise that linguistic normality is linked with a latent pathology, involving as much falsification as consensus, and ultimately deafening the mind to those inner dynamics which run counter to the prevailing illusory normality.

The degradation of language can be conceptualized only in terms of a ubiquitous, never-ending perversion. As soon as there is an attempt to describe the cultural profile of the sophist (construed as the mystifying potential within each of us), his outline comes into such sharp focus that it is misleading. Our sophist, in fact, is never there to be recognized in any ostensive way: ever versatile, he can assume radically different attitudes from one moment to the next. Jaspers's unmasking of the endemic sophist continues as follows:

> When everything turns against him, he can cringe and crawl, to resume a ... defiant posture as soon as the atmosphere grows less threatening. He is able to find an advantageous route even when the prospect is most unfavourable. He enters into relations everywhere, on the assumption that he must necessarily be welcome and that everyone will delight in furthering his wishes. He is pliable when vigorously resisted; brutal and disloyal when he has the upper hand; pathetic when it costs him nothing; sentimental when his will is crossed.... He is characterless without being malicious, simultaneously good-humoured and rancorous, at one and the same time obliging and ruthless, and is utterly devoid of sincerity ... he is not a consistent devil.[25]

However, what is most pertinent, philosophically speaking, to the investigation of the pseudosymbolic degradation of language is the habitat of the sophistic attitude. According to Jaspers, the sophist finds that the best setting for his ubiquitous virulence is, in fact, intellectualism:

> There he feels comfortable, for there only can he really fulfil his task of persistently conceiving the stream of thought as something other than it is. He metamorphoses everything. From lack of selfhood, he can never make science his own; and, according as the situation varies, he vacillates between the superstition of science and the superstition that makes war against science.... He has a passion for discussion.... But, whatever happens, he would rather be annihilated than make no appearance on the stage at all or attract attention.[26]

The sophist, according to Jaspers's profile of him, attaches great importance to ensuring that everything be treated 'rationally'.

> He accepts modes of thought, categories, and methods without exception, but only as forms of speech, not as embodying the substantial movement of cognition.... His thoughts have a syllogistic consistency, so that, by the use of the logical instrument with which every thinker is familiar, he can achieve a momentary success. He makes use of dialectic so that he may transform whatever is said into ingenious antitheses; and he riots in intuitions and examples, without ever getting to the root of a matter; luxuriates in crude rationality, since he always talks for effect, and has no concern for true insight. He reckons upon the forgetfulness of those with whom he converses. The emotionalism of his rhetorical professions of resoluteness enables him to slip away like an eel from any resolve which it might trouble him to fulfil.... Nothing grows out of his words, for they are empty chatter. Those who have anything to do with him are merely wasting their time and their energy.[27]

Jaspers's conclusion is as follows: 'Such descriptions might be continued interminably. They circle round a nameless power which in secret might gain the mastery over all, either in order to transform us into itself, or else in order to exclude us from life.'[28]

The danger of a latent degradation of human linguisticity is far more threatening than any form of deterioration in the biological domain inasmuch as it may escape monitoring and even constitute the initial motivation for the manifold ecological devastations which we observe and clamour about. But we only remark on danger when it returns to us as a result of interventions operated by our logocratic power. Since we inhabit language, we might do well to develop a concern for the ecology of human linguisticity.

Possibly, the vigorous appeals from such 'continental' voices as Jaspers and Heidegger, the exhortations of a Wittgenstein to seek a cure for the bewitchment of our intelligence perpetrated by language, and the lucid exactitude of the contributions of analytic philosophers, may indicate not only a wish to enrich the domain of a time-honoured and prestigious discipline – philosophy – but also concern, respect and care for the liveability of the language we inhabit.

One way of being excluded from life is to find it difficult to hear and read its events. Alongside the symbolic activity which enables us to construe and read reality, another kind of 'symbolic' activity is at work. Benumbing and defensive, the gushy world of chatter tends to produce deaf spots in all kinds of interactions. Heidegger observes:

> Idle talk is the possibility of understanding everything without pre-viously making the thing one's own. If this were done, idle talk would founder; and it already guards against such a danger. Idle talk is something which anyone can make up; it not only releases one from the task of genuinely understanding, but develops an undifferentiated kind of intelligibility, for which nothing is closed off any longer.[29]

He continues:

> Idle talk does not have the kind of being which belongs to *consciously passing off* something as something else. The fact that something has been said groundlessly, and then gets passed along in further retelling, amounts to perverting the act of disclosing into an act of closing off. For what is said is always understood proximally as 'saying' something – that is, as uncovering something. Thus, by its very nature, idle talk is a closing-off, since to go back to the ground of what is talked about is something which it *leaves undone*. This closing-off is aggravated afresh by the fact that an understanding of what is talked about is supposedly reached in idle talk. Because of this, idle talk discourages any new inquiry and any disputation, and in a peculiar way suppresses them and holds them back.[30]

One alternative, though, which might increase the chances of avoid-ing such degradation, is to adopt the rare approach of authentic listening, wherein both parties involved find it possible to break free of certain parasitic sophisms.

Conflicts between opposite tendencies such as narcissistic om-niscience, on the one hand, and the labours of inquiry on the other, are issues of constant concern at varying levels of awareness. And surprisingly enough it is not easy to sustain a recognition that motives are not causes and thus accept a transition from the causation of knowledge to the justification of our cognitive claims. When the torments of inquiry become too much to bear, the 'knowing' subject may convince himself and others of the validity of a causal sequence whereby he 'explains' even the most tenuous constructs. Numerous arguments are mobilized in order to gain the interlocutor's assent. And even though it is dimly realized that the interlocutor does not have an alternative causal sequence of his own to propose, the important – essential – thing is that the 'explanation' be valid enough not to elicit further investigation. 'The insidious thing about the causal point of view is that it leads us to say: "Of course, it had to happen like that". Whereas we ought to think: it may have happened *like that* – and also in many other ways.'[31]

Inasmuch as the labours involved in the search for 'truth' are too much to bear, a mirage is conjured up, beckoning the subject to the quest for certainty. In this regard, we might point out that any experience is 'truthful' if a subject is in a position to recognize therein some sort of meaningful message. For there are no 'bad' experiences, but only events which elicit reactions that are so far removed from our range of comprehension that they remain mute and opaque, like 'evil' itself. It is under such circumstances that the inner sophist may grow despotic, indeed usurp the attention of the knowing subject, to the exclusion of every other way of construing the continuation of dialogue or research. When a sophistic, pseudosymbolic model prevails, it ultimately prevents the use of pleasure and suffering as instruments of cognition. Conversely, the inner sophist may be eluded if the subject, rather than being either stricken by suffering or gratified by pleasure, uses these very experiences instead as instruments that are cognitively *necessary* to the interaction (previously unthinkable) with that which elicits them.

The self-propagating power of languages which have crystallized into finished epistemologies (in other words, which are no longer organized for development) turns into a force which, in extreme cases, makes it impossible for us to advance to the level of being speaking individuals and confines us instead to being spoken subjects – in the sense that it is 'language' which speaks through us. The process whereby the producers of language are transformed into consumers of language begins right from the origin. Sophistic language seems to possess a robotic autonomy of its own, such that it spreads and grows, without links with the dynamics lying at the affective and cognitive roots of relational life. Such language stiffens into a 'symbolic' universe which is of little use inasmuch as it is too detached from the subjects' inchoate efforts at self-creation. Hence the danger of linguistic involution or degradation takes on a diachronic as well synchronic extension, an epistemic dimension which truly justifies Jaspers's notion of 'nameless warning'.[32]

Pseudosymbols and the Philosophy of Education

To address the problems of affectual and cognitive maturation, viewed as the genesis of an experiential organization endowed with the ability to develop, we may easily recognize that content, or information, is relatively less important than the development of inner structures capable of utilizing the individual's potential for maturation – structures suitable for the projects of self-creation.

One often wonders what more illusory mystification could be perpetrated than to impose profusions of notions unrelated to the 'struggle to grow'. The contents of such 'educational' policies have no contact with the subject's life of the mind while increasingly occupying his cognitive system, with the result that only a minimal part of mentation in the making is available for attempting a development of its own. This amounts to enforcing notions (or symbolizations) which have been neither developed personally by the individual nor acquired through mimicry for survival purposes, but actually 'swallowed' reluctantly – and ready to be quickly forgotten.

Should one forget notional contents, one may be left with neither culture, education nor maturity, but only with an experiential void accompanied by a memory of inner pain deriving from the abuse of the cognitive framework, which is forced to expand and twist in order to accommodate contingents of pseudosymbolic derivatives of standard epistemology. 'Education' at times almost seems to favour a subtle, yet massive, falsification of the epistemic dimension itself, as if the intention were to impart a 'rich education', provided it is of no use for constructive purposes. In the pedagogic act itself of *imparting* an education, what is provided is something which the recipient cannot learn to produce on his own, so that 'symbolic contents' are ultimately being imposed upon the student. Bombarded by information, one has not only to pretend to grow but also to watch oneself being impoverished by the tangle of linguistic games in which one is hooked and which one is unable to stop playing, precisely because those games are meant to coincide with a way of living.

As a person's sociocultural reality as well as his biological circumstances are subject to transformation, a cognitive framework which is not organized so as to permit development, in the sense of independent maturation, can only lead to a string of falsifications and other ways of concealing the overall picture. The fact is that any static adaptation very soon turns, of necessity, into counterfeit pseudo-adaption, which must then be accompanied by distortions in the relation with 'reality'. This can easily be seen in everyday life: 'adults' with infantile behaviour patterns attempting to manage human coexistence by coercion; 'adults' voicing the sterile complaint that culture has *excessively* changed. Any philosophy of education which fails to enhance means for independent maturation is abetting, *de facto*, the perpetuation of the primitive, stunted conditions that it purports to overcome in appearance only.

Acceptance of an educational message does not constitute sufficient proof of its formative validity. Affective shortcomings in an individual's ontogenetic history may induce an attitude of 'cognitive passivity' wherein any human message (be it sadistic, contradictory, undecipherable) carries a positive sign, inasmuch as it is at least a message, a bit of relationship (or, better, of contact). Were there no messages whatsoever, no structure would be produced and degradation would ensue. Infants tend to take in all messages, initially for survival purposes and, later, as a consequence of the automatisms of experience. The confusing pain brought on by the forced coexistence of incompatible messages is aggravated by the initial prevalence of symbolic equations, namely the lack of distinction between sensations and ideas, fantasy and reality, self and not-self. Although interpersonal contact is essential during early infancy, such contact may – if backed by static schemes – induce a symbolic passivity devoid of critical ability, with the result that a poorly constructed (or distorted) relation with reality is hardly likely to be remodelled. Since our eagerness to soak up messages rests upon biological and affective bases, any 'educational' system will all too easily be in a position to point to its 'enormous successes' as well as to the 'interest' with which subjects in the making will absorb it. In extreme cases, that is when facing the prospect of symbolic extinction, the inchoate self may soak up just about anything with no regard for its formative value.

The fundamental cast that a child first gives to his own ability to construct reality therefore exerts a decisive influence over his subsequent educational experiences, in the sense that the sociocultural heritage, upon which the subject draws, can only strengthen the interactive system already laid down, but may be unable to correct it should it prove inadequate. Consequently, it is hard to expect that relevant changes of a qualitative-structural nature will come about of their own accord. It might be recognized that, if we are to include in the aims of a philosophy of education the development of the individual's relational and creative abilities (*Bildung*), then a better appreciation of the genesis of the symbolic function will be more meaningful and enlightening than any segmented or sectorial concern.

When the interlocutor who has greater responsibility within a bipersonal educational field – the roles being defined by mutual agreement – is not sufficiently aware of how difficult it is to make contact with the depths of his own self, the relationship will be steered by the 'educator' in such a way as not to risk the danger of attempting unexpected symbolic links and connections; the 'education' will only take the pathways which are already well known and present no threat to the epistemology he inhabits. Within such a relationship, disapproval and threats, however expressed (even, for example, by withholding all articulation or by swaddling in protective benevolence), are forms of reprisal aimed at the child's disturbing epistemophily. Without implying any cognizant strategy on the part of the 'parent', 'educator', 'therapist' or 'author', such policies could paralyse any creative impulse. Recognizing a child's natural thirst for knowledge, and sharing in it, implies a continous struggle for inner renewal which one is not always able to sustain.

On the assumption that there could never be any such thing as a new-born infant in the abstract, but only an individual in a relationship with a (parental) environment, we can see the issue of adult language as something eminently formative or potentially stifling. In this light, we may see how certain manifestations of the pseudosymbolic type can disrupt the metabolic process of growth and even affect the mental perception of one's body. We might mention as an example the way in which the pseudosymbolization of any part of the body for which allusive terms are used can lead one to regard certain parts of the inner model of one's bodily self as isolated, or marked by taboos; there ensues a fragmentation of what is in reality an organism and, therefore, naturally whole and undivided. Pseudosymbolization may actually split an organism. In cases such as this, disordered pseudosymbols are 'diabolic', inasmuch as they fragment even the individual's basic organic unity and influence his experiential patterns while these are in the making. This case is a specific instance of the way in which pseudosymbols act as factors pitted against life itself (inasmuch as they disrupt metabolic processes).

The confusing terminology alluding to the genital regions, for instance, amounts to a pathogenic repository for persecutory or idealized parts of the bodily self which have been segregated as well as 'stories' fabricated about the generative process. We are facing an attitude of permanent mystification, deployed against the processes of integration. When we then consider dialogue as essential for the life of thinking processes, pseudosymbolism turns out to be a pseudonutrient: a poison, that is. One wonders, in the end, how an individual could possibly live in harmony with any functions so fearsome that even the 'grown-up' masters of language cannot utter their name.[33]

The alienation of certain functions or questions may also be accomplished by use of the most deadly of all languages, namely selective silence, which virtually forces the developing person to let himself be carried away by his own archaic fantasies. Yet the word 'silence' seems a quite inappropriate term for this type of muteness, since the absence of audible, or mentally usable, messages does not result in silence at all: on the contrary, it unleashes outbursts of primal fantasies. When the learner meets the language of 'silence' he can only respond by falling into a deafening hush, with a whirlwind of mute, unutterable 'thoughts' inside. As we can see, the educator does not really 'silence' anything. Paradoxically, he creates situations in which words may be used as a kind of defence against such silence. The 'discourse' which ensues functions like a verbal smokescreen that the subject uses to protect himself from the din of his own muteness.

Pseudosymbolization versus Creative Thinking

If the deep-seated aspirations of the parental environment come to act virtually as cognitive guides, from the very beginning the developing subject will be induced to strive to please the numerous, and often contradictory, expectations of the epistemology underlying the culture to which he belongs. Even if some aspects of these expectations seem intended to safeguard the subject's life, they do little to develop his ability to generate symbols. Though the individual will doubtless manage to set out in life, he can hardly come to function as a self-creating person. He may begin, imperceptibly, to respond to cultural signals, namely to act out 'his' part, ever more ably, through an increasing detachment from any propensity to develop a thinking life of his own.[34]

The developing subject may thus embark upon a series of compensatory manoeuvres, the outcomes of which, all foregone conclusions, are actually preordained. Talking himself into what he is not, in the sense that his own potentials never have an opportunity to unfold, he does everything possible to find a compensatory 'affection' (meant to repay the loss), although he is incapable of knowing what that could be, since he has never experienced enough of the affects which allow one to be oneself. Certain experiences are privileged because they are amenable to expression through the pseudosymbolization which prevails, at the cost of inducing an ever greater discrepancy with the experiences deriving from a silenced, concealed, truer part of the self. At the level of verbalization a situation is created whereby language may be recruited to endorse a potentially increasing gap between a private true self and a social false self; to the extent that the false self is amenable to verbalization by means of dialogic responses it will increasingly establish its dominance. Pseudosymbols may acquire the stability of semantic constructions *stating* who one is and should be. If we can look at pseudosymbols, however pervasive and massive, as instruments which have made it possible for the inchoate self to share experiences of being *with* others, of *sharing* (whatever) life, then we can gain a freer approach to the most challenging and threatening forms of linguisticity. It may be that only through pseudosymbolizations can a nascent personality attain emotional recognition or a validation of his knowledge, for it may, sadly, be the case that whenever authentic symbolization is expressed the global cultural environment may react with no reaction and thus function as if the developing individual were non-existent. In this sense we could say that a non-listening attitude is the most damaging approach and conversely we could maintain that a listening propensity is the sole condition for any dialogic interaction. Klein has thrown light on the perils of recognizing the falsity of certain ideas whose truth has been sanctioned by standard epistemologies, as well as the danger of maintaining that certain issues which have been ignored or rejected really do matter: the subject is induced systematically to avoid delving more deeply into his doubts and, in general, to retreat from deep thinking. Klein believes that in such cases development has been influenced by 'injury to the *instinct for knowledge*, and hence also to the development of the reality sense, due to repression in the depth dimension'.[35]

Thus relevant issues are systematically glossed over, so as to deny contact with other experiences which are at odds with the established patterns of knowledge. Also, as a primary precautionary measure, one is led to ignore the very existence of an inhibitory dynamics, since the awareness that there are defensive processes of selective blindness and deafness can be far more dangerous than being aware of the specific facts and issues which are being ignored. A subject can afford to commit a factual breach of the 'prohibition', provided he does not attempt an epistemological violation of the statute itself, by questioning the relational framework itself in order to reveal the unutterable cognitive vetoes which underlie linguistic culture. As Klein remarks:

> We are apt to lay stress on the 'courage' of the thinker who, in opposition to usage and authority, succeeds in carrying out entirely original researches. It would not require so much 'courage' if it were not that children would need a quite peculiar spirit to think out for themselves, in opposition to the highest authorities, the ticklish subjects which are in part denied, in part forbidden.[36]

A few extracts from one of Schopenhauer's letters to Goethe may serve to illustrate the foregoing reflections:

> Every work has its origin in a happy thought, and the latter gives the joy of conception; the birth, however, the carrying out, is, in my own case at least, not without pain; for then I stand before my own soul, like an inexorable judge before a prisoner ... and make it answer until there is nothing left to ask. Almost all the errors and unutterable follies of which doctrines and philosophies are so full seem to me to spring from a lack of this probity. The truth was not found, not because it was unsought, but because the intention always was to find again instead some preconceived opinion or other, or at least not to wound some favourite idea, and with this aim in view subterfuges had to be employed against both other people and the thinker himself. It is the courage of making a clean breast of it in face of every question that makes the philosopher. He must be like Sophocles' Oedipus who, seeking enlightenment concerning his terrible fate, pursues his indefatigable enquiry, even when he divines that appalling horror awaits him in the answer. But most of us carry in our hearts the Jocasta, who begs Oedipus for God's sake not to enquire further; and we give way to her, and that is the reason why philosophy stands where it does.... This philosophical courage, however, is the same thing as the sincerity and probity of investigation.[37]

8

A Philosophy of Listening

Listening as Philosophical Midwifery

A significant aspect of listening may be perceived whenever cognitive prospects are opened, not by a 'frontal' breakthrough, so to speak, but as a result of a disposition to listen properly. It is as if our tentative, ignorant approaches, sustained by a determination to heed, almost to *auscultate* something obscure which 'seems' devoid of meaning, were precisely the factors which open the road, thus perhaps reversing trends in the impending degradation of any particular form of linguisticity; in fact, what is not listened to remains inaudible and consequently 'unheard of' – susceptible to degradation.

Ricoeur, for instance, makes the following remark on philosophical 'ausculation': 'For my part, I have encountered the problem of symbolism in the semantic study I made of the avowal of evil. I noticed that there exists no direct discourse of avowal. Evil – whether the evil one suffers or the evil one commits – is always confessed by means of *indirect expressions* that are taken from the sphere of everyday experience.'[1] Frequently vulnerable to obscurity, such 'indirect expressions' may only be identified in authentic listening experiences. What Ricoeur's work stresses is not the productiveness of a particular class of symbols, but those functions of symbolization which may be revealed through attentive heeding: the point is not so much the problem of 'evil' as the role performed by language in the investigation of the issue. And of course we mean a 'real' language, capable of both saying and listening.

Whereas the language of suffering often inclines towards the opaqueness of solipsism (a 'sick' language), it is precisely the listening function which allows a subject to transform his despairing and exasperating linguisticity into viable forms of communication. If listening is assigned the function of a midwifery of thought (maieutics), it might follow that a philosophy of listening is concerned with the efforts to allow a new life of thinking to come forth; and the birth of the mind cannot be induced but only facilitated from the outside. As we know, in the early vicissitudes of mentation the soundness of a relationship largely depends upon the readiness with which the nascent person is welcomed and respected – no conceptual reference being possible to any 'educational' process. Heeding exhibits a radical difference from other forms of participation inasmuch as it shuns providing (or imposing?) any advice, exhortation or means of compensation. The purpose is not only different but divergent, as it strives to let the inchoate speaker go over his developmental experiences and work out ulterior symbolic tools such as permit him to initiate communications with himself as well as with others. An individual can speak only when he is being listened to, rather than when there is something he might say that someone would subsequently attend to 'by means of' listening.

Listening may be conceived of as the basic tool for coming to share in the speaker's vicissitudes: hitherto excluded from the process of communication and thus mainly expressible through pathological or compensatory manifestations, his inner history is 'attracted' on to the level of meaningful and usable articulations. Listening aims to capture precisely those elements which are normally left out of messages and which none the less (possibly for that very reason) act as domineering constraints in linguistic interactions. Listening tends to tune in with 'obscure' attitudes so as potentially to integrate and transform whatever seems to have been banished from the realm of thoughts into something amenable to articulation. In a broader philosophical perspective, Lugarini argues that individual consciousness inclines to its own benumbment as a result of persistent oversights and denials; when what has been forgotten seeks a way to the surface, that which has been neglected from the start of our inchoate mental life 'demands' that it should come to light.[2]

Language is not only a way of communicating synchronically, but also a way of creating symbols that can be used to cope anew with antecedent problems (and even future prospects) so as to 'rearrange' them in the light of any attained maturity. Our varying levels of linguisticity do in fact enable us to narrate and reinterpret our own story – the sort of history which has priority for us. Any such opportunity is linked with an actual or potential listening reciprocity and with the chance of modifying one's self-perception. No narratives would exist without some disposition to listen. Inextricably interwoven with listening experiences, the propensity to narrate may appear as something profoundly different from the intellectual activities of description or solving problems. A narrative propensity may be a necessity for regaining a sense of our own history and the continuity of life; in fact our own history may be ultimately construed as being as ancient as life itself. The urge to create narratives might even represent a 'universal' inclination and thus a potential source of models for construing the vicissitudes of mentation. Yet no narratives could be conceivable in the absence of some listening disposition. Concern for human linguisticity might thus be approached through two diverse but complementary ways: a synchronic outlook conducive to an appreciation of structures, and a diachronic view aiming to regain a sense of our historicity, narratability and finite condition. It may be that in the ontogenesis of linguisticity the standard symbolization of an experience becomes the dominant version of it while the more personal experience recedes into concealed areas only to reappear under different circumstances which may counterbalance the dominance of 'normal' symbolizations. Therapeutic, poetic, educational language may occasionally serve the purpose of retrieving the significance of full experiences through successful evocation. And yet it is our standard words that split and reduce experience, or push it into concealment, whenever we cannot listen to it; we thus transform the experience into something unheard of. Under such circumstances a language only capable of expression becomes a constant violation of our personal life. To gain access to a world of standard 'dialogic' interactions (people talking *at* one another, thus perpetuating dialogic delusions) we may have to forsake the strength and fullness of primal experiences; the cultivation of a listening language may possibly salvage such early vicissitudes.

According to Ricoeur, the problem of symbols, in certain developmental aspects, comes to coincide with the related problem of language and listening, throughout both human history and individual ontogeny.

There is no symbolism prior to man who speaks, even though the power of symbols is rooted more deeply, in the expressiveness of the cosmos, in what desire wants to say, in the varied image-contents that men have. But in each case it is in language that the cosmos, desire, and the imaginary achieve speech.... There must always be a word to take up the world and turn it into hierophany. Likewise the dreamer, in his private dream, is closed to all; he begins to instruct us only when he recounts his dream.[3]

The dream is unknown to us; it is accessible only through the account of the waking hours. However, an account is possible only if there is someone who *can* heed, even if this were the same person who originated the dream. Dream-life and listening are vitally inter-woven and cannot be detached.

In a human relational situation (potentially conducive to mental development and not amounting to animal husbandry), the decisive condition is not so much the opportunity to receive something – even an overabundance of gratification – but rather the opportunity to express a need and gain the experience of being understood and listened to, despite the shortcomings of whatever inchoate, rudimen-tary language is used. As Heidegger points out, 'We can make clear the connection of discourse with understanding and intelligibility by considering a ... possibility which belongs to talking itself – hearing. If we have not heard "aright", it is not by accident that we say we have not "understood". *Hearing is constitutive for discourse.... Being-with develops in listening to one another.*'[4]

Inasmuch as being listened to originally creates an opportunity to begin to differentiate the level of thinking from the domain of (sensory and affectual) states, its philosophical relevance stands out all the more clearly: if, in fact, listening is sufficiently accurate (devoted, precise, unrelenting) as to discern a consistent sequence of thoughts developing in the midst of apparent fragmentation, it will then turn into a maieutic (birth) process which lets the individual produce structure even within conditions of chaos and stagnation. That emergent consistency into which fragments seem to organize in meaningful sequences can be regarded as embryonic thinking which begins to separate out from the flux of sensory and emotional life. Vice versa, when 'listening' is not supported by a maieutic dispo-sition, the only outcome can be a pleasurable or displeasing impact. The most demanding listening situations may ultimately be experi-enced as a mere shock, or insult, capable of dissipating the remnants of any as yet insufficiently developed maieutic ability in the listener. Such situations also imply the inhibition of the speaker's propensity for symbolic thought, inasmuch as the potential consistency running through the various parts of his complex message is not noticed, and its parts are perceived as merely isolated emotional signals. The development of a thinking sequence is denied. The philo-sophical interaction of listening unfolds in grasping thought in the making, thus surpassing the level of mere reaction to the *impact* of a message.

In order to grasp more clearly the philosophical significance of listening, it might be useful to invoke the model of a therapeutic dialogue, viewed as a limit-condition wherein messages stream in, demanding to be made meaningful and reinstated within some interactive language. In certain obscure vicissitudes, which are experienced as a malignant condition but are not, as yet, truly suffered, one may encounter a prevalence of 'concrete thought', namely an inability to distinguish between feeling and thinking, words and objects.

When we are unable to differentiate among thoughts, words and feelings, the fact that we expel air as we speak may even induce the conviction that the actual significance of expressions can be expelled in the same way; the mind is thus experienced as a device for getting rid of unliveable experiences rather than as the locus for generating vital thoughts.[5] Bion suggests that such a situation is comparable to the condition of the stammerer, whose words seem to contain rather than communicate meaning. Alternatively, the meaning is too powerful for the verbal formulation; the expression is lost in an 'explosion' in which the verbal formulation is destroyed.[6] The listening problem is that of coping with the percussive impact in such a way as to allow a clear understanding of the comprehensive interaction. A person who listens attentively to the verbal utterances of someone who uses words as if they were tangible things may steer the situation towards maieutic listening: he may bear witness to the speaker that the concreteness of expressions does not altogether overwhelm him. He may thus demonstrate that it is possible to identify a cluster of meaningful connections which do not coincide with the emitted expressions but actually stand out as a further dimension indicating an inchoate line of thinking. These thoughts, moreover, can be returned in the form of an interpretation, thus creating the awareness of a line of thinking that *can* be shared.

In a maieutic dialogue, the expressive propensity may become heightened as a result of the effort to communicate as much as possible and thus demand a good quality of listening. Conversely, the maieutic listener tunes in to the other's effort to express a vital line of thinking even through the mutest and most opaque of utterances. 'Saying' and proper 'hearing' thus imply and sustain each other as inseparable partners in a unified development.

In extreme cases, as when a person appears sunk in a stupor (in tumultuous stillness), one may suspect the presence of conflicts that are as yet incapable of any expression and thus ultimately unthinkable and paralysing.

The Interaction of Listening

The challenge of paying heed reveals the close attachments it creates whenever we respond to 'obscure', non-literal invitations to do something that an explicit message might equally well invite us to do. The personal link originates from justifiably presupposing a shareable attitude in the interlocutor. If the speaker's expressions were cogently explicit, no closeness generating work would be involved. The extent to which an implicit invitation is worked out by the listener could be viewed as a measure of the attachment, as it is revealed by any generally 'metaphoric' utterance. In the dynamics of listening, attachments are created through the personal absorption of new metaphors which a speaker offers; such linkages would just not emerge from the understanding of a possible 'digital' conversion of the message.

Appreciation of a sub-epistemic (or non-literal) message demands the recognition of an inner attitude in the speaker; conversely, if we could systematically translate a metaphoric message into its literal paraphrase we would lose sight of the listening tension required by such appreciation. A sequential development of metaphors rests on the prerequisites of a listening disposition inasmuch as inchoate messages presuppose and reinforce the closeness of interactions. Listening can thus be viewed as the other side of language: an area in which offers *can* be made and *can* be accepted.

Proper hearing constitutes a response to a request for some measure of reconceptualization. As Kittay suggests, the detour through a semantic field that normally applies to another domain 'is the perspectival shift in which the projection of the structure of the vehicle field onto the topic domain can *force* a reconceptualization of the referent ... of the metaphor'.[7] Although this is only tangentially connected, one may envisage cases in which such a request of perspectival shift is not accepted, or not even acknowledged. Significantly, Kittay's discussion hinges on an account of a two-year-old child who suffers from earache and who approaches a parental figure saying, 'An elephant stepped on my ear.' As can happen, such a message may not be properly listened to and, although the entire episode is resolved, the symbolo-poietic injury induced by a mistrust in one's own metaphoric efforts may be irreversible. In this perspective, then, the challenge of listening reveals itself as an approach radically diverging from the muteness of indifference and unrelatedness.

The effort to identify any evanescent thread of consistency running through an obscure, enigmatic (or too painful) history is perhaps the key element for extracting the basic meanings involved. The more the listener exposes himself to the force of the other's emergent thinking and silences the knowledge-claims of his own ('well-founded') parameters of interpretation, the more the other's history will become capable of speaking out. But the subject's message only acquires symbolic value if there is a relationship wherein the listener comes to enter into the speaker's symbolic dimension. Yet anyone who tries to listen may 'enter' that dimension only in a manner which is as paradoxical as it is demanding, namely by exiting, stepping aside and making room. Perhaps the kind of understanding which turns into a mutative event is expressed by a few lines from Rilke, which may be thus freely translated: 'If you want to get a tree to live, surround it with the inner space that is in you.... It is only within your renunciation that it can take shape and really become a tree.'[8]

The sort of understanding which actually turns into a mutative event might be highlighted by 'comparing' it to the common procedures of curiosity; their illusory similarity may strengthen a differentiation. In Heidegger's inimitable words: 'The loudest idle talk and the most ingenious curiosity keep "things moving" – illusively, of course. He also suggests that such 'being-with-one-another ... is by no means an indifferent side-by-sideness ... but rather an ambiguous watching of one another, a secret and reciprocal listening-in. Under the mark of "for-one-another", an "against-one-another" is at play.'[9] And again:

> When curiosity has become free, however, it concerns itself with seeing, not in order to understand what is seen ... but *just* in order to see. It seeks novelty only in order to leap from it anew to another novelty. In this kind of seeing, that which is an issue for care does not lie in grasping something and being knowingly in the truth; it lies rather in its possibilities of abandoning itself to the world. Therefore curiosity is characterized by a specific way of *not* tarrying alongside what is closest. Consequently it does not seek the leisure of tarrying observantly, but rather seeks restlessness and the excitement of continual novelty and changing encounters. In not tarrying, curiosity is concerned with the constant possibility of *distraction*. Curiosity has nothing to do with observing entities and marvelling at them.... To be amazed to the point of not understanding is something in which it has no interest. Rather it concerns itself with a kind of knowing, but just in order to have known.[10]

The experience of being lost amid the everyday contradictions of dialogue is qualitatively different from the 'restlessness' of curiosity and seems almost to constitute the very basis of proper relational approaches. For if the aim of the understanding-event is to seek out something meaningful, and thus necessarily open to development, one must recognize the necessity of working out interpretations which the interpreter may soon after relinquish. If interpretation is the instrument by means of which a meaning may show and make itself felt, it must also be ready to move aside in order to make way for any subsequent developments.

The work of interpretation is a dialogic process not so much because the various fragments of discourse become clearer and gradually form a whole, but rather because the word which interprets, welcomes and grasps the unutterable upsurge within (irrepressible but not yet thinkable) allows deep-seated potentials to be expressed and thereby permits 'functioning' thoughts to emerge from a multiplicity of shapeless elements. It is thus that one gains direct experience of those levels of understanding which constitute a maturational event.

If we seek the internal consistency of a message in order to allow its underlying thought to come forth, we may invoke the procedural model of psychoanalytic dialogue as a prototype setting in which an effort is made to free the mind of its constraints and let a new life of thought take hold. The analytic setting, moreover, may prove enlightening as regards the constant effort to make room for the other – the patient. If too much room is made for the analyst and his reality, he may become 'too' alive and real (for the analysand) with the result that he cannot be used as a cognitive space in which one's inner world can be projected. Even though the analyst is the source of interpretative strength, any 'existential' dominance on his part would ultimately defeat the very purpose of maieutic dialogue, as he would absorb the lion's share of the attention and any new stirrings in the analysand would thus be nipped in the bud. When the analyst's cognitive resources prevail, for the suffering individual he may even become a person just like all the others, that is largely a construct of his fantasy: his projections interfere with his interactions and he cannot *see* them inasmuch as there is primarily an analyst to be seen. When the listening task is conceived along such lines we can better appreciate the 'strategic' necessity of committing oneself to an interpretation only to let it go, refusing to hold on to it possessively.

The distortion of, or the deafness to, meaning goes against our symbolizing potential inasmuch as it reduces a large share of the message to the status of noise. Symbolic language develops instead wherever the multiplicity of meanings in linguistic expression encounters a measure of interpretive-listening work. And what originates such work is the recognition of some (inchoate) intentional structure.

In Ricoeur's view,

> A symbol exists ... where the linguistic expression lends itself by its double or multiple meanings to a work of interpretation. What gives rise to this work is an intentional structure which consists not in the relation of meaning to thing but in an architecture of meaning, in a relation of meaning to meaning, of second meaning to first meaning, regardless of whether that relation be one of analogy or not, or whether the first meaning disguises or reveals the second meaning. This texture is what makes interpretation possible, although the texture itself is made evident only through the actual movement of interpretation.[11]

The interpretative attitude, therefore, is not external to the symbol, nor is it superimposed on it. It is, rather, an intimate participation in the other's symbol-generating activity, which is activated by making room, stepping aside and listening.

9

Epistemophily and Knowledge

Introductory Notes

'Originally the mere existence of a presentation was a guarantee of the reality of what was presented. The antithesis between subjective and objective does not exist from the first,' remarks Freud.[1] Invoking this proposition, we could say that inchoate humans are not able to distinguish between their inner world and outside events, with the consequence that in an individual's early experience his fantasy manipulations of the environment may coincide with the real actions to which the nascent personality is subjected. In other words, a primal self is not capable of differentiating between what is actually happening and what he is imagining. An additional difficulty could be seen in the inability to 'localize' affects inasmuch as a cluster of 'ego functions' is as yet unformed, with the result that, in early experiences, the developing person does not know whether he is the subject or the object of the events he is experiencing. We are led to suppose that, during this period, an infant's life is an undifferentiated world of events, so that he is not in a position to distinguish between what he is actually experiencing, at a given moment, and the array of images which might refer to either past experience or future possibilities: his time dimension, in fact, has not yet taken shape. The peculiar emotions of early vicissitudes occur in a 'non-dualistic' context, in which there is no awareness of an ego, or of any proper boundary between an inner (personal) world and any set of external realities. In regard to such early stages, we could invoke a relational model emanating from the myth of Narcissus, although it would perhaps be more appropriate to suggest that this is, after all, a narcissism without a Narcissus, in the sense that, rather than there being any knowledge centred around an incipient ego, there is, instead, an unwitting concentration of events corresponding to the nascent state of mentation.

We might think that in a primal state such as this an inchoate person's images do not *mean* or *indicate* anything other than themselves. Throughout early phases of experience, images cannot be (clearly) distinguished from reality and the young self is a 'prisoner' to an illusory, timeless present, out of which he can emerge only by labouring through vicissitudes of loss and restoration.

There is no point in arguing that whatever 'food' may be formed in the infant's hallucinations is just not nourishing, that it leaves him hungry in the long run and that consequently such an image has to be expelled. In fact there is not sufficient distinction from real food which does nourish, since the infant possibly makes a fantasy of the latter too, regarding it as the fruit of his own fervent instinctual desire.

Such a 'correspondence' between fantasy and reality, desire and satisfaction, almost in the form of an equivalence, constitutes the general meaning of the term 'symbolic equation'.[2] An equation (or equivalence) is involved inasmuch as sensations are experienced as the 'same' as a memory or a fantasy of the actual sensations, there not yet being inner structures capable of creating such a distinction. As such structures seem to be as yet lacking and as inner experiences of the past refer to nothing but themselves, it is appropriate to point out that the term 'symbolic' is given a rather improper meaning here, solely through the lack of a better expression.

Taking our cue from the concept of 'concrete thought', we may suppose that, for the nascent mind, an idea (or image, or fantasy) comes to have a concrete feel, like a sensory impression. In simple terms, the main source of difficulty along the arduous trail of human knowledge is the fact that, while a sensory impression (namely, the object perceived) may well be concrete, the impression itself (and hence the object perceived) cannot be permanent until symbolic instruments (in other words, non-concrete thinking) has sufficiently developed to be in a position to refer to the object perceived and, then, to retain it (permanently) when it is sensorily absent.

The absence of any distinction between reciprocal (symmetrical) relations and non-reciprocal (asymmetrical) relations is a further cause of the precarious pre-symbolic state from which the subject in the making strives to emerge, in the sense that at this stage it is not possible, strictly speaking, to talk about a relationship, since this concept involves the complex notion of asymmetric relations. It would in fact be an uninteractive world if only symmetries existed. Although the subject is originally immersed in a state of non-distinction between the source of food and the oral cavity, a feeding presence is really in the position of a dispenser *vis-à-vis* someone who is a receiver and who is not a dispenser for the person who offers a nutrient. According to Matte Blanco:

> It is impossible to consider mental life without asymmetrical relations. ... It seems that we must first try to understand this fundamental question of the relationships between symmetrical and asymmetrical relations in mental life before we can proceed with our studies. For we are confronted here by a most extraordinary fact, namely that there are central aspects in men which are completely alien to the notion of asymmetrical relations. This fact, as far as I know, is unique in nature. It is for this main reason that, if we wish to know something about the intimate being of man, we must try to understand the meaning of this fact, its extent, its projections and all that it entails.[3]

Given the situation outlined above, it is understandable that an infant may often feel that he is in danger of plunging into non-existence. According to Matte Blanco, in fact, the only unity used in the (symmetrical) unconscious system is the class, or set, in which all elements belonging to it are included; the unconscious cannot, therefore, deal with parts except by treating them as whole classes or sets. In our unconscious life we do not deal with 'objects', whether they be total or partial, but with the total class of that sort of thing. Our inchoate mental life, therefore, 'attributes to the object the maximum of potentialities that are implicit in the propositional function of the class. In other words, the unconscious follows the law of either positive or negative infinite sets: either it does have an object, in which case it has in it full (infinite) positive potentialities as a class; or it does not have it, in which case its absence is taken to mean that this object has maximum (infinite) negative powers.'[4]

The salient point about the vicissitudes of our early ontogenetic history is that fantasy objects, actions or events are experienced in terms of infinity, thus saturating one's inner world. There is, hence, an infinite life force in maternal derivatives and in any introjection of them there is an infinite capacity to keep the subject alive and to infuse inner organization. And of course there is a similarly saturating power in primitive destructive fantasies or experiences.[5]

According to this line of thought, it seems clear that a single indication of persecution may completely permeate an individual, creating a uniform inner mood in him, with the result that everything becomes fearsome and terrifying, to the extent that every minute detail of perception is experienced as yet another means by which the persecutory atmosphere is extended. It is almost as if the element which acts as the random cause of a flare-up of anxiety could induce a saturating feeling which may be considered as a set comprising an infinite number of negative qualities.

With regard to the ontogenetic dimension of knowledge, we may suggest that the onset of our thinking implies some kind of relation with the emergence of the 'co-ordinates' of space and time. What emerges, in fact, is a cognitive dimension in which one thing comes after another in conformity with relations not dissimilar to temporal 'succession' or to the construction of physical reality in space. In this sense we may suggest that 'rational' processes (or relational thought, broadly speaking) are closely associated with the incipient development of space–time proportions, measures, differences. In 'symmetrical thinking', by contrast, none of this holds good, 'for each element (as seen from an asymmetrical vantage point, because otherwise there can be no elements) occupies the whole "space" of the class; neither is each element distinguished temporally from the others or from the class, even in a symbolical way or any other which could be compared to time.'[6] An inexhaustible source of examples of such deep human dynamics may be derived from the individual's oneiric life as well as from diversified cultural manifestations.

The problems involved in becoming human recur in every individual who faces life, in that each ontogenetic history exhibits its own peculiar difficulties which affect the maturational process, thereby creating the conditions which lead to such widely diversified paths of experience and levels of awareness. This work attempts to look for a better conceptual framework for the early experiences in ontogenetic history so as to focus on the inchoate relational processes which originate cognitive and linguistic development.

Whereas in the early stages of subjective solipsism the possibility exists of a unique point of view – a 'sympathetic absolute'[7] – in which the inchoate self lives in symbiotic union with the (parental) environment, during later phases a type of perception takes over which strives towards the acceptance of hiatuses, distances or gaps that are amenable to being processed symbolically, and ultimately leading to the relativity of points of view and to the multiplicity of outlooks. As is the case with the early labours of maturation, the visualizing element, with all its overtones of detachment and distance, is once again given pride of place during subsequent stages in the construction of reality. Perhaps this may to some extent link with the mirror imagery and visual paradigms which prevail in our 'scientific' vocabularies: in the language of Rorty, 'the story of the domination of the mind of the West by ocular metaphors'.[8] Until one's distance from any element has been established, one cannot make it an object in realistic terms, inasmuch as it is shrouded in one's own most archaic, pre-symbolic and possibly disruptive dynamics. The earliest object accretions may almost be regarded as proto-symbolic systems, which serve to establish centres of interest, the latter serving, in turn, to connect and subdivide our early sensory multiplicity.

As we are trying to explore possible correlations between the symbolic function and the development of object relations, it seems appropriate to point out that inquiries into language and research in the area of object relations have often been conducted independently of each other. Such a state of affairs seems to be based upon a tacit assumption that is rooted in some essentialistic outlook implying that there is a mind (and a world) organized according to laws to which philosophers might have some privileged access so as to even render them 'isomorphic' and commensurable. On the basis of such an assumption, we speak about something (which may be within our mind or outside it) while assuming that language plays no role of any importance in the shaping and processing of that something.

In Cassirer's view, indeed, it is only what is relevant to our hopes, desires and actions that receives the 'seal' of verbal meaning. In his inimitable language:

> As philosophy brought a new breadth and depth to the concept of 'subjectivity'; as this concept gave rise ... to a truly universal view of the *spontaneity* of the spirit, which proved to be as much a *spontaneity* of feeling and will as of cognition – it became necessary to stress a new factor in the achievement of language. For when we seek to follow language back to its earliest beginnings, it seems to be not merely a representative sign for ideas, but also an emotional sign for sensuous drives.... The ancients knew this derivation of language from emotion, from the pathos of sensation, pleasure and pain.[9]

'Symbolic' Equations and Symbol Generation

Invoking Kleinian hypotheses, we could assume that early vicissitudes related to oral drives profoundly influence every aspect of maturation. Klein suggests, in fact, that:

> Side by side with the libidinal interest, it is anxiety ... which sets going the mechanism of identification. Since the child desires to destroy the organs ... which stand for the objects, he conceives a dread of the

latter. This anxiety contributes to make him equate the organs in question with other things; owing to this equation these in their turn become objects of anxiety, and so he is impelled constantly to make other and new equations, which form the basis of his interest in the new objects and of symbolism.[10]

Recalling that during primal stages of development we may not assume any proper distinction between reason and instinct, awareness and unconsciousness, we ought to conceptualize such early experiences in terms of symmetrical relations, as the only possible mode of functioning. Inasmuch as the primal organization can work only in terms of symmetry, if a subject 'makes' an attack upon the primal object of his desire, he inevitably feels himself to be simultaneously attacked by the object which he wants to destroy. Even Freud left in his theoretical work enough logical space for this sort of approach: 'It may well be that before its sharp cleavage into an ego and an id ... the mental apparatus makes use of *different* methods of defence from those which it employs after it has reached these stages of organization.'[11] In this perspective, Money-Kyrle's suggestions acquire a specific relevance:

If not overwhelming, the anxieties of this period act as a spur in the first steps of intellectual development. For whenever, as is always liable to happen, the good and bad pictures of the breast again become confused, the child is particularly receptive to the perception of similar, but not identical, objects which can take the place of the good one temporarily lost. Moreover, since the same fate of confusion between good and bad can overtake ... he is forced to find still more distant substitutes. In this way, anxiety compels him to notice similarities and differences between perceptions, to widen his interests and to increase the number of distinct objects he can separately perceive. Conversely, it would seem impossible for human beings to take the slightest interest in, or even to perceive, anything not ultimately linked by a series of such displacements with the few primary symbols we are innately predisposed to respond to.[12]

In Klein's view, anxieties deriving from primitive experiences imply dangers of retaliation: as a developing person may desire to attack parts or aspects of parental figures, he conceives a dread of them. This anxiety contributes to make him equate such features with other things: 'Owing to this equation these in their turn become objects of anxiety, and so he is impelled constantly to make other and new equations, which form the basis of his interest in the new objects and of symbolism.'[13]

Viewing the process in this light may enable us to appreciate the inseparable link between humans' epistemophily and the survival of the mind.[14] The implications of such a hypothesis regarding the genesis of cognitive thought open up vast, fertile fields for inquiry which may, perhaps, be indicated by a complex of questions. Might it not be that, in those who meet excessive obstacles in their search for new affectual equations, the interest in new objects and, hence, in the construction of reality is quenched? If the subject in the making has been impeded in the development of his ability to form similes and analogies, is he not perhaps condemned to a symbolic exile which he will not even be in a position to decry, inasmuch as he has been rendered mentally mute? Hobbled in this way, is not the inchoate subject condemned to a relational level dominated by his most primitive fantasies, all too remote from the horizons of awareness?[15] Klein goes on to add:

> The development of the ego and the relation to reality depend on the degree of the ego's capacity at a very early period to tolerate the pressure of the earliest anxiety-situations. And, as usual, it is a question of a certain optimum balance of the factors concerned; a sufficient quantity of anxiety is the necessary basis for an abundance of symbol-formation and of phantasy.[16]

In other words, mental development depends upon the ability to make a number of investments or cathexes, *at any cost*, at first in the sequence of diversified symbolic equations and then, by degrees, in the domain of 'proper' thought processes. Steiner suggests that, rather than conceiving the process in terms of a fixed pattern, we might think of it, expecially in cases of normal development, as a sequence of tensions and transformations, wherein what is past, present and potential is linked together by a dynamic interrelation; and this allows for an 'open' approach to the examination of primal processes of communication.

But let us ask what might be the decisive factor which makes the outcome of such relational displacements successful, to a greater or lesser degree. The 'quantity' of aggressiveness that is directed on to an object which is then reintrojected by identification may be altered (namely, mitigated or reduced) as a result of the impact with the (benevolent) world outside the subject; as a consequence what is reintrojected may prove sufficiently unthreatening for a further attempt to be made at improving the situation. It may be added that reintrojection leads fantasy back into an inner proto-space, so to speak, equipped with proto-symbolic 'wiring', or memory traces, inherited from previous introjections of a maturational type. Such memory traces might be regarded as proto-mental constituents, through which subsequent reintrojections (at varying levels of anxiety) may also flow and circulate. When a reintrojection happens to be the cause of particular anxiety (as it may be laden with an excessive potential of destructiveness), and if it takes root in an inner area devoid of, or poorly supplied with, memory traces (or proto-symbolic 'wiring') to conduct it, we may have an explosive outburst of anxiety. On the contrary, when there are 'cognitive' traces capable of conducting a potentially traumatic fantasy or event, we may take it that the inchoate mind has a good 'ability to tolerate anxiety'. Should any phase in the sequence of symbolic equations become fixed, though, the birth of thinking may veer towards the pathological. Inasmuch as a particularly violent form of aggressiveness becomes extroflected, aggressive parts of the self intrude within objects so as to control them omnipotently and be controlled, in turn, by the objects, so severely that the equations cannot develop any further.[17]

With reference to the foregoing considerations, we may once again ask how it is that the displacement of drives on to substitutive objects can be blocked; in other words, how it is that the process is not enhanced whereby the infant is led to assimilate the object which has been attacked (and which could, therefore, be reintrojected laden with extroflected aggressivity) to further objects, and also how it is that one remains confined in a situation which does not permit displacements of cathexes. I believe that the more the 'ego' is engaged in keeping persecutory contents at bay, the less its feeble structures will be available for perceiving affinities and differences among objects. Conversely, the more an ego in the making is in a position to create substitutive elements, the more it will be shielded from the dangers of an inner paralysis, with the result that it will be ready to make new proto-symbolic achievements. It seems, almost, that the primal dynamics of cognitive expansion and narcissistic contraction constitute the polar opposites between which initial experiences oscillate.

When a reintrojection heightens anxiety, it becomes virtually impossible for a nascent mind to react or make an attempt at displacement of impulses, the reason being that his fragile organization is 'crushed' by the inner persecutory fantasies which he tries to expel (and is forced to reintroject), aggravated by external frustration and by the overall negative result of his efforts. Bearing in mind that such displacements, namely the efforts to assimilate an earlier object to a different one, are the precursors of symbolization, it will be 'seen' that, when such attempts repeatedly end in failure, the experience may even lead to a state of paralysis impeding the development of mentation. To enhance the transition towards further 'symbolic' equivalences and growth of thought, then, there should be a prevalence of gratifying (versus frustrating) experiences in early interactions. Whatever their ultimate structure, symbolization and thinking do not develop automatically, that is irrespectively of the interactive context within which they originate.

It is the prevalence of 'good' over 'bad' experiences which determines the supply of memory traces derived from a sufficiently good relationship between parent and child. Such memory traces allow a missing source of gratification, a no-object (in other words, a frustrating state of loss), to be processed symbolically so that one becomes able to respond to each micro-vicissitude experienced by using a mental trace as a *sign, a pointer*, or as something which stands for something else. In this way, a developing mind may attempt to extricate itself from a space–time continuum which is fused and confused with primal narcissistic fantasies. That a child should have prevalently reassuring experiences is a necessary condition for the mental traces in question to be utilized for the purpose of creating asymmetric relations, as well as for the emergence of the symbolic dimension which underlies the very functions of our thinking.

The ability to tolerate frustration cannot be conceptualized in schematic, static fashion, detached from the time dimension; it should be viewed, rather, as a composite factor and as a constantly evolving ability – in other words, as a process. Such a process is dependent both upon modifications from the *outside*, as a result of contact with the world, and upon the inner modes of coping with (that is organizing) what is absorbed from outside.

In these early stages we are faced with such radically divergent alternatives that we may truly speak of either a pathological, 'vicious' circle or of a 'virtuous' symbol-generating circuit which foreshadows the life of thought. As Klein suggests: 'Upon the degree of success with which the subject passes through this phase will depend the extent to which he can subsequently acquire an external world corresponding to reality.'[18] We may deduce from the foregoing that the key issue is the greater or lesser degree of success encountered in attempting the earliest displacements of projective facts; as a consequence, whenever displacement has not gone well, the subject will *not* be able to 'acquire an external world corresponding to reality'. In summary, when there are too many shortcomings in the primal precursors of symbol generation, the evolving subject will be tragically diverted towards an area of relational and symbolic exile haunted by the most confusing fantasies. Worse still than being 'mutilated', the inchoate person is exiled from the symbolic dimension and, hence, from the pathways to knowledge.

Our Metaphoric Potential

We might point out that some of the constituent factors of human intelligence, such as the capacity to metaphorize, could be conceptualized as exosomatic instruments, 'distinguished' from the more organically rooted functions, and thus possibly more versatile and susceptible to ever new uses. Language itself, inasmuch as it is applicable to an indefinite variety of contexts, is, in its origins, a metaphoric achievement. Without metaphoric language, I believe, the possibility of expressing inner phenomena virtually vanishes.

In Nietzsche's synoptic view:

> The drive towards the formation of metaphors is the fundamental human drive, which one cannot for a single instance dispense with in thought, for one would thereby dispense with man himself. This drive is not truly vanquished and scarcely subdued by the fact that a regular and rigid new world is constructed as its prison from its own ephemeral products, the concepts.... This drive continually confuses the conceptual categories and cells by bringing forward new transferences, metaphors and metonymies. It continually manifests an ardent desire to refashion the world which presents itself to waking man, so that it will be as colourful, irregular, lacking in results and coherence, charming and eternally new as the world of dreams.[19]

To the extent that we ignore a diachronic – ontogenetic – approach to language we inevitably grant cognitive priority to the standard vocabulary of literal language. The metaphoric moves operated by the inchoate self of a nascent personality will appear as a deviant, marginal use of language. The denial of emerging metaphorical language is tantamount to enforcing the imitation of language and arbitrarily decreeing its lack of historicity. An implicit negation of the historicity of language would be an anti-biological attempt to stabilize any current linguistic power and to ignore that past metaphors deriving from the most disparate phatic efforts may constitute current language.

The systematic trend of having to acquire imposed meanings in a context of insufficient negotiation may result in a persistent linguistic caricature of 'parental' symbolizations or, similarly, of a redundant scholasticity in any domain of normal science. That there is an immense literature on the notion of metaphor indicates that diachronic and synchronic approaches can in fact be re-linked and relativized, for whether we characterize an expression as metaphorical or literal may well be dependent on the outlook for which we opt.

Words which designate objects and mediate interactions are often sufficiently vague (or flexible) as to become 'exact' only within the specific contexts and changing structures wherein they are used. As the process of constructing the 'real' takes the form of a step up from (or beyond) the narrow designations typical of early stages, such an original state of indeterminateness does not, to our mind, bespeak either inner shortcomings or mental 'idleness'. Attempts to metaphorize, therefore, appear as the result of efforts to broaden our early, restricted way of seeing things. As symbolic or proto-symbolic elements are not excessively specific, additional and new relations of meaningfulness may be discerned and created. Metaphors, in fact, do not confine the individual in a static context of significance but, on the contrary, actually enhance opportunities for ever new openings: inasmuch as metaphor leads to the creation of new 'worlds' of experience, to which one could not otherwise gain access, an inchoate propensity to metaphorize cannot be reduced to a mere 'transfer' of meanings.

Broadly speaking, we might say that metaphoric thought may be conceived of as a cognitive function which uses the transfer of meaning as a vital mode of operation: from the very beginning the inchoate person is tirelessly trying both to fit the unknown to the known and, at the same time, to transform what he 'knows' in such a way as to be able to accommodate even the unknown in a meaningful fashion.

A measure of effort is indispensable in the process of cognition if the subject is to begin to form hypotheses and develop models, by means of the transposition of the experiential meanings that he has mastered. 'Metaphor' manifests its full relevance for cognition if we bear in mind that every meaningful situation must involve both a bearer of meaning and a context of signification. We might note, furthermore, that any situation in which a meaning appears must be traceable to some element of otherness. If we concede the indispensable function performed by bearers of meaning, the result is to highlight the specific role of the original metaphoric process whereby such supports (bearers, or carriers of meaning) are gradually invented and learned by the knowing subject in the making. It is when we view our learning in relation to the ability to bring a meaning to pivot at a different point, thus making an object of it (through a metaphoric dynamics), that it becomes clear why it is necessary to invent, or acquire, carriers of meaning. On the contrary, were there no such broadening of the horizon of meaning, it would be hard to see why a subject in the making should strive to learn or invent a language, given that reality looks so threadbare and restricted as not to elicit any creative commitment. If nascent thought is unable to endow with inspiring meanings a (possible) surrounding world, that same external world will be unable to 'emit signals' which arouse interest, or cognitive 'wonder', and ultimately demand that dialogue come about, that symbolic interactions begin to function.

If we ask which concepts are at hand to provide a better insight into the maturational efforts directed towards symbolic functioning, we find that the notion of 'imagination' (or fantasy) is essential, inasmuch as it is through imagination that any two dissimilar elements may be assimilated, or made equivalent. As Milner points out, however, the role of imagination is not, paradoxically, specific enough to explain the phenomenon: in her view, 'illusion' is equally required. However imaginary, a relation with an outside object implies, in fact, that there is an 'illusory' fusion whereby a secondary object (which comes into being through the transfer of meaning) comes to be considered as if it were an object of primal gratification.[20] The human capacity for illusion ('self-deception') seems to join forces with our *cognitive* potential, in the sense that the former acts as the metabolic agency for the transition from primal, undifferentiated subjectivity, to the creation of an 'ego' capable of achieving interactions with external reality and persons. As is known, we owe to Winnicott the studies on the intermediate, or transitional, area of cognition which infants work through, and which might be assigned a place midway between the instinctual roots of primal fantasies and prevalently objective perception based upon an examination of reality. Allowing an inconsistency, or 'error', to develop, illusion could be said to provide a necessary prerequisite for a process of 'correction'. One may *infer* that 'error' is necessary for purposes of cognitive development; yet that development is also dependent on the 'behaviour' of the environment which supports the genesis of cognitive processes. Cognition, in fact, is not an 'automatic' biological process, since it only comes to function in association with certain facilitating conditions. Winnicott suggests that when parental adaptation is good enough

> the infant begins to believe in external reality which appears and behaves as by magic (because of the mother's relatively successful adaptation to the infant's gestures and needs), and which acts in a way that does not clash with the infant's omnipotence. On this basis the infant can gradually abrogate omnipotence. The True Self has a spontaneity, and this has been joined up with the world's events. The infant can now begin to enjoy the *illusion* of omnipotently creating and controlling, and then can gradually come to recognize the illusory element, the fact of playing and imagining. Here is the basis for the symbol which at first *is both* the infant's spontaneity or hallucination, *and also* the external object created and ultimately cathected.[21]

As the ability to make use of illusion for developmental purposes is based upon the progressive discovery of similarities that are capable of successfully matching the illusory (yet chaotic and static) experiences associated with a lack of development, this capacity represents the specific maturational effort inherent in the sequence of symbolic equations. We may certainly agree with Winnicott in noting that the study of such stages of transition enables us to think about symbol-formation in terms of the utilization of transitional objects.[22]

The effort to create meanings successfully linked to the external world and hence the pursuit of a relational universe probably constitute the crucial aspects of our laborious process of maturation. At the beginning, in fact, the struggle within each of us to communicate our own 'deep-down view' of the world takes place at levels even comprising our biological experiences of survival. Reasoning along such lines, we might strive to identify those maturational crossroads at which our joint affective and cognitive experiences are far from neutral, in the sense that they can direct development either towards creativity or towards deterioration. Davidson believes that there are extreme suppositions that founder on paradox or contradiction and modest examples that we have no trouble in understanding. 'What determines where we cross from the merely strange or novel to the absurd?'[23] According to Milner, the decisive juncture at which the development of creativity is actually routed towards pathology, or vice versa, is to be pinpointed in the subject's attempts to cope with the customary criteria of objectivity and to defend the legitimacy of his own way of seeing an aspect of reality.

The battle over communicating the private vision, when the battlegound is the evaluation of the body products, has a peculiar poignancy. In challenging the accepted objective view and claiming the right to make others share their vision, there is a danger which is perhaps the sticking point in the development of many who would otherwise be creative people. For to win this battle, when fought on this field, would mean to seduce the world to madness, to denial of the difference between cleanliness and dirt, organization and chaos. Thus in one sense the battle is a very practical one; it is over what is a suitable and convenient stuff for symbols to be made of; but at the same time it is also a battle over the painful recognition that, if the lovely stuff is to convey the lovely feelings, there must be work done on the material.[24]

The work in question revolves upon the search for a symbolization that is well suited to being freely utilized by the developing individual as well as by others.

Situations in which a subject does not know how to *express* a meaning which he already 'possesses' within his inner life are indeed crucial, since they constitute stages in which he is searching for a bearer of meaning which he can eventually share with others for the purpose of developing 'real' consensual meanings. Milner further observes:

> Both the artist and the scientist are more acutely aware than the 'average' man of the inadequacies of what Caudwell calls 'the common ego', the commonly accepted body of knowledge and ways of thinking about and expressing experience, more sensitive to the gap between what can be talked about and the actuality of experience. If this is true then it is also true to say that what is in the beginning only a subjective, private vision can become to future generations, objectivity.[25]

When a symbol-formation model is adopted, it may result in an unexpected convergence of the cognitive processes aimed at objective knowledge and of those creative pursuits which involve the development of paradigms conducive to a new objectivity; in this perspective, then, it does not seem fruitful to maintain a dichotomy between logical and creative processes.

The root problem is how to manage to shape the 'quality' of our cognitive processes in such a way that the apparent breaks with reality (namely those cases in which something is used as if it were something else) make for a more complex, richer structure of an 'object', in the sense that we may thus succeed in holding a more articulated and richer dialogue with it. Such an approach contrasts with the ever-present alternative of restricting and coercing reality as may occur whenever we fall under the sway of unrelated, static, narcissistic trends. The creative process depends on the greater or lesser ability to forgo (freely and knowingly) a perception of things so circumscribed and univocal as to make reality in the making a hide-bound one. In fact, as Milner has it, creative thinking requires a temporary abrogation of discriminative ratiocination.[26] Within such a conceptualization of cognitive growth, a place may be found for the notion of 'regressive adaptation' postulated by Hartmann. In effect, regressive adaptation corresponds substantially to the set of operations by means of which affectual and cognitive investments are shifted on to elements taking the place of *proper* objects, '*referents*' actually invented by means of metaphoric connections whereby one acquires the ability to recognize 'similarity' in that which is different. Inasmuch as such 'regressions' allow symbolic tools to be developed, as well as the ability to discover ever new cognitive dimensions, it is in *appearance* only that such processes may be thought to constitute a withdrawal from reality.

Epistemophily and the Life of Thinking

If the fruition of reality depends upon the discovery and construction of objects, we ought to recognize the vital importance of the shifts in one's affectual investments throughout the succession of symbolic equations. Since such progressive transfers involve 'risk', they seem to bear witness to humans' overwhelming propensity for epistemophily. And this may be associated with the commonly accepted beliefs regarding the child's 'natural curiosity'.

Klein seems to have substantially identified the sense of reality (and hence of its fruition) with an 'impulse for knowledge': 'The fact that thinking ... could not expand in every direction ... prevented the significant intellectual development for which as children they seemed destined. The important causes of injury to the impulse for knowledge and to the reality sense ... set repression in operation by dissociation.'[27] Klein, moreover, raises the problem of inhibition in the genesis of symbols. The analysis of a young child who was unable to speak or play revealed how terrified he was of both his own aggressive fantasies and of their consequences, which were experienced as concrete reality. Given the force of such terrors, the child had established firm defences against them. The result was a para-lysis in the life of fantasy and in the formation of symbols. Not having been in a position to develop a good enough sequence of emotional equations, he had not been able to endow the world about him with any symbolic meaning, with the consequence that he could take no interest in it.[28] Klein thus comes to the conclusion that where symbolization does not occur the whole development of ego-functions is arrested.[29]

If it is legitimate to compare instincts to tropisms in the simpler forms of life, we may see that, in the human condition, instincts become differentiated and organized into desires by means of sym-bolic channelling which permits impulse fantasies to develop into cognitive structures. Whenever shortcomings prevail in the symbolic function, although physiological life may proceed unaltered and instinctual management is possible, the life of thinking may not properly develop. As Money-Kyrle makes clear:

> An impulse represented by a phantasy, or a behaviour pattern, is not strictly speaking *either* instinctive *or* acquired. It is both at once, since the relation of instinct to acquisition is that of genus to species: we have a general instinct to eat and acquire specific eating preferences and habits. All the impulses of men are, therefore, just as much instinctive as the stereotyped tropisms of the simplest form of life. Of course, his instincts at birth are immensurably more plastic; they comprise a vast pyramid of potential development which experience progressively narrows. In highly conventional individuals they may end by becoming almost as rigid.[30]

As we have seen, symbolic representations are needed in order to produce a connection between one set of data and another. Accord-ing to Bion, when the data thus connected are in harmony one experiences a sense of truth.[31] Failure to bring about such a connec-tion between data, or, in other words, failure to generate a consistent experiential point of view, induces a state of consciousness marked by weakness or discomfort, as if the hunger for clarity were in some way assimilable to a hunger for food.

In the Preface to his *Tractatus Logico-Philosophicus*, Wittgenstein remarks that 'Its purpose would be achieved if it gave *pleasure* to one person who read and understood it',[32] almost as if the author were proposing to offer something pleasing and satisfying, or perhaps some form of consolation. The pleasure one could experience might be intimately bound up with philosophical clarity and with clear speaking: at first glance, a highly intellectual pleasure, but one which, none the less, is rooted in our deep self. But in order that clarity be so highly prized, it must be that its antithesis, namely obscurity, generates suffering, confusion, perhaps even anxiety. As Filiasi Carcano suggests,[33] clarity and obscurity have to do with language, that is with the medium in which thoughts and knowledge are formulated, and by means of which messages (whether oral or written) are transmitted; such messages may provide us with all the information we need, through the expression of agreement or dissent, approval or denial. Granted that in the *Tractatus* obscurity and clarity have an obvious *logical* meaning, there is yet no doubt that such terms also have some *affectual* meaning: they are laden with emotion, and, if this were not so, there would be no explaining that sense of *pleasure* to which Wittgenstein makes direct reference in his Preface. One has the impression that the need for clarity plays a central role in the genesis of the *Tractatus*, possibly even more so than the general notion of *truth*. In the closing phrase of the Preface – 'it shows how little is achieved when these problems are solved'[34] – he seems to 'withdraw' the philosophical worth of what he has achieved as a logician. Rather than any abstractly theoretical satisfaction, it seems to be a sense of relief – of liberation associated with clarity – which characterizes the pleasure promised by the book: the chance of releasing intellectual blocks and removing obstacles to communication. Such pleasure may ultimately be a derivative of human episte mo*phily*.

Even the most sophisticated creative games possibly imply the ability to forgo the overall view of a given problem, namely the ability to endure a temporary state of confusion, loss, disorientation in one's 'field' (and a consequent feeling of being lost in a 'forest'). When a subject lacks such ability, which derives from an earlier capacity to make shifts in the sequence of primal equations, he will be unable to give up (creatively) any established cognitive patterns. Such models may thus become increasingly rigid and pervasive (almost a cognitive addiction) so that they tend to impede any progressive reorganization of the symbolic means with which one builds possible worlds. One may thus speak of the mechanisms of splitting and cognitive dissociation, as being equal and opposite to the devlopment of the symbolic function, almost as if they were the terms of an antithetic polarity. It is the cultivated liveliness of one's epistemophily which may ultimately allow us to 'play' with different epistemologies.

10

Genesis of the Symbolic Function

The Experience of Loss

In an ontogenetic perspective, early experiences of loss might be tentatively conceptualized as devastating plunges into the void, in the sense of plummeting beyond any possible frame of reference, beyond the lattice of any supporting network, for all that the latter might be frail. What is characteristic of the primal drama of the experience of loss is the extreme difficulty of eliminating the sense of something missing, there being nothing as pervasive or invasive as that 'shadow of the object' – its absence – which cannot be fitted into the subject's as yet rudimentary 'cognitive' structure.

A missing object which cannot be taken in and processed within some meaningful frame of reference is something that is still present in a persecutory, confusing way, perhaps not unlike the well-known fears associated with 'phantasms' which characterize certain stages of phylogenesis and ontogeny. And it can be hypothesized that many activities of our relational life are derivatives of expedients and rituals intended to exorcize and neutralize the menacing effects of the object's lost presence, that is to say, its pervasively negative presence. More specifically, we may conceptualize the trauma of loss as a break in an inner organization which acts as a rudimentary system of channels for emotional life to run in, or even as a laceration which opens a void so abysmal that an inchoate subject can risk disintegrating into a boundless emptiness. In a desperate search for comfort, the nascent person may readily seize upon any 'thing', in the sense that all he wants to do is grasp whatever he comes across – provided it is in some way recognizable – and cling to it, investing it with full power to neutralize the horror of the void, and to protect him against the flare-up of a 'presence' which is negative and destroying. The potential menace of such vicissitudes may be described as the danger of tumbling out of the fragile net of all existing reference points and plunging into an immensely empty time-space in which the developing individual runs the risk of lapsing into disintegration.

Despite the fact that he is primarily dependent, the subject in the making wants everything in an 'absolute' fashion, while both physical and interpersonal reality come into play as the representatives of an order which rejects symmetrical, absolute, confusing dynamics and generally refuses to acknowledge drives which are not borne, or supported, by mental elements which have been sufficiently metabolized. Furthermore, inasmuch as during the stage of 'subjective monism' the idea of an object and its possession tend to coincide, in the beginning nothing can exist which is not possessed by the inchoate subject. It follows, therefore, that the primal form of 'relationship' will be an attitude involving incorporation and gathering in, for it is only what is 'controlled' that can exist. Consequently, the lack, or loss, of elements which satisfy desires have all the more dramatic impact upon a subject's inner world to the extent that the latter is organized around the dynamics of possession.

During the early phases of an individual's ontogenetic history, as well as during the early stages of hominization, the degree of stability in cognitive values made possible by symbols does not seem to go beyond the preservation of memories, in other words, it does not exceed the function of merely re-producing something. As Cassirer points out:

> At this level the sign seems to add nothing to the content to which it refers, but merely to preserve and repeat it. Even in the history of the psychological development of *art* it has been thought possible to identify a phase of mere 'recollective art', in which all artistic endeavor was directed solely towards stressing certain features of what was perceived by the senses and presenting it to the memory in a man-made image. But the more clearly the particular cultural forms disclose their specific energy, the more evident it becomes that all apparent 'reproduction' presupposes an original and autonomous act of consciousness. The reproducibility of the content is itself bound up with the production of a sign for it, and in producing this sign the consciousness operates freely and independently. The concept of 'memory' thus takes on a richer and deeper meaning. In order to remember a content, consciousness must previously have possessed itself of that content in a way differing from mere sensation or perception.[1]

Faced with the inexorable drama of yearning and loss, the future individual is induced to 'sketch' developmental lines which may bend either towards pathological defences or towards maturational sequences that pave the way for a measure of contractual dialogue, that is to an interactive relationship with reality. Freud himself comes to grips several times with the crucial enigmas surrounding the escape from reality, which he views as lying at the root of all relational pathology. He remarks that both neurosis and psychosis exhibit an analogous tendency to compensate for the loss of the real in an 'autocratic manner, by the creation of a new reality which no longer raises the same objections as the old one that has been given up'.[2] In both ramifications of pathology, one is catering to 'the desire for power of the id, which will not allow itself to be dictated to by reality. Both neurosis and psychosis are thus the expression of a rebellion on the part of the id against the external world, of its unwillingness – or ... incapacity – to adapt itself to the exigencies of reality, to ... necessity.'[3] In any case, there is no getting away from these 'exigencies of reality', which also constitute the crucially important gateway not only to pathological outcomes, but also and above all to new levels of maturation. Retracing the development of psychoanalytic thought, we come to a remark by Klein regarding the early experience of the 'depressive position': 'This position is stimulated and reinforced by the "loss of the loved object" which the baby experiences over and over again when the mother's breast is taken away from it, and this loss reaches its climax during weaning.'[4]

For the nascent person, in fact, weaning is one of the most meaningful initiations into life, precisely because, when he is at the stage of weaning and of the depressive position, the process of symbolic internalization is so rudimentary that his most vital dynamics of survival imply and support one another in a metabolic cycle which is fragile and demanding to the utmost degree. Indeed, it is only by 'working through' the loss that the infant can manage to realize that his desire and the lost object are not the same thing. Conversely, an inchoate mind would not be able to perform any work of mourning if he were totally incapable of using 'something' mental, or psychic, in order to refer to 'something' external which has been lost. As Freud had noted, 'it is evident that a precondition for the setting up of reality-testing is that objects shall have been lost which once brought real satisfaction.'[5] As a consequence the two dynamics, namely the experience of an absence and proto-symbolic internalization support and imply each-other in inseparable fashion in the construction of object relations.

When, on the other hand, the relational climate is permeated by too high a degree of anxiety, mechanisms of splitting which avoid 'bad' qualities of reality are kept active and, as Klein points out, both the ability to form object-relations and the life of fantasy itself come to be inhibited.

Also, the tendency to homeostasis, which is always present alongside the urge to develop, almost never allows a smooth progression between 'stages' to occur, for the simple reason that every new relational mode which comes forth may be perceived as alien and hostile, whereas links with the earlier stages may come to be idealized as 'warm', protective, primal containers of our incipient organization, despite their turning into causes of suffering.

The main impediment to making use of new levels of consciousness is the attachment to what is 'old', to a long-standing relational attitude; by attitude, or position, we mean an inner order which brings about a propensity to act or react selectively in response to certain aspects of reality rather than others. Just as symbolic thought may be established solely through a process of mourning (or working through of loss), so also the changes necessitated by life may be implemented primarily when one achieves the ability to discard something, such as an explicative Gestalt, or a basic cognitive assumption for which an individual may have developed a mental 'addiction'. As a matter of fact, what we often need to do is to give up an explicative hypothesis which is constantly and unwittingly introduced whenever we address a problem with reality, and which makes it impossible to solve the problem. For example, if we interpret the Oedipus complex in this light, we could view it not so much as a psychic occurrence in its own right, but as a conglomerate of defensive fantasies, in the sense that the conflicts deriving from that 'complex', in our opinion, come down to attempts to perpetuate earlier relational attitudes of a symbiotic-fusional type. In this sense, an incestuous relation, rather than being pictured as an interpersonal occurrence, is to be viewed as something truly mental and cognitive; in this same perspective the phylogenetic value of the incest taboo may reside in the emergent human ability to avoid those symbiotic-fusional relations which would keep the labours of creative cognition at bay.

Viewed as a temptation to return to unconscious and pre-symbolic relations, incest permits us to equate relations with a mother-figure to relations with the unconscious world of desires; in this light, then, what incestuous leanings really stand for is the need of the unconscious to be taken into consideration. What it might be useful to sacrifice is the set of early attachments to the parental environment, inasmuch as they are regressive affectual attitudes, while safeguarding the desire for contact with the unconscious layers of the self – the irreplaceable source of mental life. Whenever Klein reflects on the need to endure ever more frequent separations from the mother-figure, the problem is automatically raised as to which inner structures allow a subject to tolerate detachments in such a way that each well-tolerated separation makes the next step away easier to bear.

The inability to tolerate absence is the outcome of a complex condition. When frustration is excessive, an awareness of it would obviously prove unbearable. Thus the subject's rejection of his own conscious processes constitutes a desperate survival measure. At the same time, however, the subject's break with the processes of symbol-formation which generate consciousness further reduces his ability to deal with frustrating situations, creating a vicious circle detrimental to the processes of mentation. When, instead, frustration is tolerated, the experience of an expectation and of its negative realization can initiate the procedures necessary to ensure that the experience of loss be used for the purpose of maturing – basically for self-creation.

We might ponder over the 'deeper' meaning of the difficulty involved in guiding the construction of reality in such a way as to favour our own development; in particular, we might ask why an individual is always insidiously tempted to elude the *awareness* of any loss or absence. In my opinion, the problem is rooted in the extreme difficulty of mentally processing the ways in which we elude any experience of loss; it may be exceedingly difficult to understand, and therefore cope with, the inclination to blunt or benumb oneself for the purpose of continuing to elude, or be selectively blind to the existing loss. When the primal dialogue with parental environment is basically favourable to development, it may also provide verbal tools for mediation and conduction such that the unthinkable, unutterable drama of loss may in some inchoate way be 'spoken' or mentally dealt with; the cognitive elusion of loss may thus begin to be fruitfully overcome.

One could legitimately posit the 'non-necessity' of a dimension of symbolic awareness only within a theoretical 'earthly paradise' setting, never disturbed by imbalances or frustrations; yet such a hypothetical condition may not be construed as obtaining even in the pre-natal state, in the sense that traumas and frustrations could not be ruled out even during that period of our ontogeny.

Klein, at her most pessimistic, viewed pathological greed as an irremovable constitutional trait which is not responsive to maturational processing.[6] And yet it could be illuminating to address the problem of oral greed by regarding it as an expression of resistance to processes of separation, loss and differentiation. We can recognize that the infant's own physiological life provides him with opportunities to live through his first experiences of separation and change: the inexorable return of the state of hunger tells the infant that what he eats will not become his own for ever. Similarly, the psychic voracity exhibited by certain individuals may be interpreted as a desperate attempt to suppress the whole experience of hunger, need and dependence with a view to escaping the fearsome awareness of temporariness, change, separation and dependence. It seems almost as if certain subjects are trying to call attention to the desperate hope that, if only their efforts were to succeed, they would remain for ever in a comfortable state of unconscious union with some re-edition of a maternal environment, conceived of in an affectual and epistemic sense.

It should also be pointed out that an individual who returns to an earlier level of maturation is not in the same condition as one who has never managed to surpass that level. Once it has been attained, a relational attitude leaves its mark even upon those who, for various reasons, find themselves forced to abandon it and regress to an earlier organization. With regard to the ability to make a maturative experience out of living through a loss, we ought to bear in mind the risk of slipping into a surreptitious moralism aimed at exalting the ascetic qualities inherent in 'depressive' modes of processing experience, and at treating these qualities as the 'good' ability to forgo 'bad' symbiotic conditions. Indeed, neither stability nor the ability to effect transformations (these being functional characteristics of the organization of the mind) is either good or bad *per se*: in our inner life, as in any form of life, there can be no achievement of 'stability' without there being an adequate ability to undergo transformation, and no vital changes which do not originate from a sufficiently stable condition.

One might even go so far as to believe, erroneously, that the concept of 'maturation' involves a veiled apology for the renunciation of everything that is pleasing and for an equation between gratification and detriment; in other words, one might believe that this concept of development implies an endorsement of ascetic ways of interaction – all of which is misleading. For the crucial point in the progress of symbol-formation lies at that juncture where the inchoate subject is in a position to make use of any pleasurable experience whatsoever, provided that it is not a case of the experience using him, so to speak, by sidetracking him into repetitive dynamics which hinder maturation and preclude any further broadening of his range of accomplishment. There is no merit whatsoever in any act of renunciation, or painful task, unless it strengthens the subject's relational abilities so that he may, potentially, extend his utilization of the real. Unless one is 'philosophically attracted', so to speak, towards giving up certain modes of seeking satisfaction for the purpose of making innovative 'investments' running contrary to acquired habits, no inner tools for growth will be generated and cognitive progress may be retarded. When affective life is circumscribed and attached to its very earliest of forms, the subject is held at the most archaic levels, wherein he finds himself at the mercy of his own emotional *states*, rather than gradually attempting a dialogic 'mastery' over them and over his expanding world.

What has been suggested as regards the ability to bear the experience of loss may also apply to the capacity to put up with errors. The latter is very likely a derivative of an earlier ability to endure frustration and separation. The tendency to avoid errors is a legitimate human aspiration, whereby we seek to minimize the risks and maximize our attainment of reality. When a subject, however, attempts to avoid errors by 'anti-philosophic' means, his efforts prove ineffective and counter-productive. Indeed, he may well take refuge in a sanctuary which is utterly impervious to error, with the result that his cognitive and explicative system becomes unassailable. Such systems of 'omnipotence' have their origins in earlier, fruitless efforts to handle the cleavages between the fragile, developing ego and the non-self. When we abandon the hope of ever crossing that gap or differentiating distance (between an inchoate self and an expanding world), we may then seek to limit 'knowledge' to one side of that space which is so hard to cross. When there is a rejection of the cleavage between self and world, the unfortunate, but necessary, consequence is that the subject goes so far as to reject reality itself.[7]

Yet a creative propensity for thinking may be experienced as a persecutory limitation inasmuch as it interferes with the 'absolute freedom' of one's own world of fantasy and omnipotence. Paradoxically, almost every new epistemologic space comes to jeopardize the 'natural freedom' to think whatever we want, in the sense that when thought is released from its magical-omnipotent condition (for which humans seem to have a secret nostalgia) it becomes subject to the requirements of consistency, invalidation by experience and interpersonal criticism.

Our primal, omnipotent solipsism may gradually transform itself into cultural attitudes aimed at fostering certain types of cognitive processing suited solely to satisfying a demand for reassuring certainty. Much of our cultural labour thus primarily appears as an effort to cater to a tormenting quest for certainty, for an 'all-encompassing truth', which tends to re-emerge continually under the most varied guises. The point at issue is a philosophical effort not to turn a blind eye – and actually listen to – these derivatives of the various attempts to satisfy archaic quests for certainty.[8] Many cultural contributions possibly derive from a latent need to satisfy such a quest in the sense that many constructs are offered and proposed as harbingers of 'ultimate' methods. According to Danto, philosophical endeavours often suppose themselves to be 'possessed of the answer to a prayer for a logical miracle':

> A concept has been discovered, or a class of concepts has been identified, whose semantical value is uniquely determined by some internal feature of itself, whose contact with reality is guaranted by some internal mark which, having been discovered, renders us both in touch with reality and immune for ever to mistake. We need not traverse that horrendous gap between concept and reality since the concept itself gives us all the reality we require. Philosophers, however otherwise ingenious and astute, are often almost neurotically oblivious to the fact that their projects fit this unfulfillable characterization to perfection.[9]

Even the general notion of linguistic studies as a sound philosophical point of departure could be regarded as sharing in the same misconception pointed out by Danto.

In such a perspective the 'horrendous' relations which constantly reconnect and diversify our biological and cultural dimensions, our analogic and digital processes, could be 'safely' kept at a distance. And our inchoate transition from biological to logical life is by no means automatic, but rather enigmatic, challenging and fateful. The processing of experiences of loss is thus carried out in the transition from a 'biological' to a 'dialogic' level almost as if our developmental progression took the form of a tendency to transform a frustrated expectation into something truly relational.

From a phylogenetic point of view, we may picture the emergence of the symbolic horizon, not so much as bringing to perfection existing capacities for expressing signs, but as constituting, rather, a break or a void, which brings on an irremediable crisis in the system. The evolution of the higher primates is perhaps not to be conceived of as training expressive abilities up to peak performance, but as a 'lapse of memory', as failures in the old habits of signalling. A novel reality is like something that 'does not exist', and one only finds out about a new dimension after the fact. It is almost as if a memory gap suddenly opened within the routine of survival, or as if a branch gave way and left one lost ... in thought. And it is, perhaps, this yet unfocused 'thought' which lights up in the desolation following loss, and which forms the 'crack' through which the new is opened up to us.

It is perhaps that which is to be discovered in our inner life which urges us on, and the resulting pressure could well be the most authentic of philosophic openings. And since it is an urgent need for 'nothing' yet known that motivates us to move on, philosophy is possibly concerned with grasping that celebrated 'experience of nothing'[10] (the focus of any experience of loss as the only thing that matters). If one had the presumption to know about our evolution, one might set about imagining it as continuing the customary cognitive structures blown up to a larger scale.

The Experience of Loss: Surpassing our Biological Level

Nascent minds seem to be intent upon attaining an incipient awareness of identity by striving to insert in our own ontogenetic history evidence that our own identity no longer depends so heavily upon recognition from others. Such evidence, or guarantee, is developed by going through experiences requiring an ability to challenge, lose and risk. The self in the course of formation is on the lookout for those pieces of 'evidence' which can show that so many things, situations or persons increasingly turn out to be vanishing moments, unessential to our own identity. True, in certain optimal settings an infant is regarded as a person – in the full sense of the term. But such one-sided good fortune and benevolence can by no means suffice for the purposes of achieving self-awareness. A self-cognizant identity does not in fact depend solely upon recognition, however authentic and respectful, on the part of others. It is based, rather, upon the symbolic tools by means of which the subject perceives himself; and such tools of self-perception are a truly autonomous and innovative creation, the only one which can provide an awareness of one's own incipient environmental independence and identity.

A dramatically evident feature of early infancy consists in those multifarious and frequent attempts to challenge parental figures, which take the form of extremely tenacious efforts to define one's own identity and uniqueness. The earliest instances in which there is a challenge to a parent-figure or to the environment may truly be described in terms of a 'mortal' challenge on behalf of life. Seen from another point of view, the subject in the making seems really to be engaged in risking his life, inasmuch as he 'despises' it for its excessively 'natural' quality and thus for not being sufficiently individual; he tends to defy 'death' in order to celebrate some sort of detachment from an all too natural kind of life (a mere unexciting biological survival) which seems to hinder the development of a more authentic self-awareness.

Although the challenge in question has nothing to do with the dynamics of self-destruction, it is yet, in its most radical form, a way of challenging death; its goal is certainly not destruction but rather the challenge itself or, more precisely, the radical quality of the confrontation. Death, in its biological naturalness, stands for nothing but the negative side, or reversal, of that same 'excessively natural' life.

There remains, however, a possibility that the dynamics of challenge may deteriorate into pathology, depending upon the degree of symbolic falsifications which may be at work. The urge to defy situations may in fact become perverted, in the sense that what was an effort to achieve a way of life marked by independence and self-awareness may break down into self-destruction. In the process of self-creation, maturational goals are achieved through the 'thrill' of the challenge and certainly not through the 'thud' attending destructive outcomes; in other words, inner growth is enhanced by running 'risks' and certainly not by damaging oneself. But what is it that constitutes the essential discriminant which may be lost sight of and falsified to such an extent as to lead to self-destructiveness rather than to the exciting exercise of negation, challenge and risk? What probably makes it feasible to reach maturation through defying 'death' is the proper orientation of the symbolic function, inasmuch as it may be directed towards searching for inner truth – understood, by no means, as solipsistic omniscience, but as a readiness to form relations with oneself and with reality in the making. Such an orientation does not make it easy to 'cheat' at a game being played with oneself.

Further ways in which a subject's need to make challenges may become degraded and detrimental to development are the disparate, subtle ploys whereby a challenge can be neutralized, rendered banal and innocuous – basically a non-challenge. In such fashion, an individual may keep feigning his challenges, trotting them out over the most stereotyped and impersonal of symbolic circuits, namely those which stand in the way of any awareness or creativity. An individual will smooth out his dynamics of defiance to a gratuitously conventionalized level of game-playing, acted out in an inner collusion, to the detriment of development. In fact, it would seem that a sham challenge, being a habit detrimental to maturation and, as such, only falsely symbolized, could even serve the purpose of warding off any real defiance, that is the risk of any all-out challenge.

It is in the involvement with challenges that it may become clear to the nascent personality that gratifying objects are less important than the efforts to achieve one's own independence from both the gratifying objects and the world. While working through experiences of loss, a primary relational mode is established whereby a symbolic element refers to something absent or lost: an aspect of the symbolic function which has connections with the world outside. But our symbolizing capacity performs another task as well, namely that of making it possible to refer to the relationship (or connection, or correspondence) between some primary symbolic form, on the one hand, and the outside world, on the other. This further mode of symbolization has to do, not with the world, but with the *relation* (made up of a symbolic element and of an external element) between ourselves and the world. These two essential aspects of the symbolic function constitute, respectively, a relational level which is more directly dependent upon external objects (either present or absent) and a further inner relational level which largely ignores objects, inasmuch as its cognitive structure is reaching out for an awareness of the *relations* between subject and object. And, obviously, relations are not as tangible as persons or things.[11] It is at this level that the most disparate forms of questing after challenge and risk come into play in the form of attempts to exercise our ability to break out of (primal) conditions of total dependence. A further perspectival level enhances our capacity to imagine ever new ways of dealing with former conditions and thus of challenging the rules for the creation of new games. Unless this capacity is individually exercised, its use may be permanently surrendered to institutions or myths.

Symbol-Formation

Early experiences of loss tend to coincide with the subject's first attempts at reaching the symbolic level, namely with the vicissitudes in which he tries to avoid the devastating emotional immediacy of absence and strives to create a substitute for the missing object. It is indeed by means of some form of mental surrogation that the subject can *begin* to establish his own 'reality' as real, his own symbolic dimension as independent of the stream of emotional states, and the self as the protagonist of its own experience.[12]

Testimony to the effect that the vicissitudes in question constitute a 'position' or a relational attitude, and not a phase (or stage, or moment, or period) in life which may be considered a matter now gone by and closed, may be found in a subject's fluctuations into reabsorption and confusion. Every culture caters to these unresolved inclinations by offering a variety of opportunities for satisfying them, in ways intended precisely to perpetuate the practice of mentally eluding any awareness of loss or absence by continuously turning out compensatory delusional prostheses. On the other hand, by working through mentally the experiences of loss and absence, gratifying conditions come to be distinguished from their hallucinatory re-evocations, with the result that the objects providing satisfaction begin to be differentiated from the signs or symbols which indicate, at once, both the object and its absence.

Lacan seems to suggest in this connection that in every maturational phase of the person, at all levels of self-creation, we may encounter transitions involving a prior occurrence in which a frustrating experience must be endured and a subsequent development in which the individual 'transcends himself in a norm-creating sublimation'.[13] By virtue of such 'normative sublimation', a nascent self may make his first attempts at distinguishing between 'true' and 'false' so as to progress beyond the sole 'distinction' of which he had formerly been capable, namely separating what is pleasurable from what is frustrating. It would also, perhaps, be appropriate to mention that each stage of a subject's maturation or decline (school, work, emotional attachments, vocations) may involve a major re-elaboration of any previously ascertained distinctions.

We may approach the question of 'signs' by noting first that they are elements that refer to something else which is not immediately available, either because it is absent or because it no longer exists. Communication in fact occurs by using an inner and interpersonal symbolic 'reality' that is present, in order to make a connection with a reality in the making that is in some way absent; this is made possible through our mutually agreed conventions negotiated within a relationship.

The purpose of a close examination of early experiences is to identify the features which characterize a specific aspect of the development: the process of mentation. The inchoate symbolic function, or the emergence of a 'differential signifier', derives from a split (or gap, or hiatus) which differentiates qualitatively the elements of a perceptual nature from elements of a properly psychic or mental nature: inasmuch as the latter are unbound, uninvolved with sensory experience they may be utilized for purposes of recollection, planning, self-reflection. It is only such qualitative detachment from the sensorial level which places the developing person in a position to wield the cognitive tools by means of which he may create a critical distance between himself and his involvement with experience. As a consequence it appears that there is no longer a tangled dynamics of signals but an attempt at cognitive processing implemented by means of independent (or properly 'mental') tools of representation.

As has been pointed out, in the context of symbolic equations, not only is any proto-symbolic substitute viewed as if it really were the object of desire, but the specific qualities of a substitutive psychic, or mental, element are neither admitted nor recognized: they are not yet thinkable. On the other hand, when proper symbols begin to flicker during primal mentation – and to the extent to which they can be actually used for interacting with persons and things – they can be perceived as something which refers to the world in a *representative* manner; such a specific aspect of a symbolic form can thus be recognized and utilized. A proper symbol springs to life when the affects connected with the endurance of absence and loss seem to prevail over a defensive tendency to split and expel; on the other hand, were an individual in a virtually constant condition of contact, presence, fullness, there would be no need to strive for symbolization. Thus symbols may develop when separation from the object, ambivalence and loss may be creatively experienced and tolerated. On the contrary, when situations are unbearable, they may be segregated, or split, from the rest of our inchoate mind and projected on to some external element. Rather than being used in order to deny the experience of loss, symbols are used in order to get over its impact. In fact, one of the ways in which one may successfully defend oneself against the trauma of losing primal objects of gratification is the capacity to mourn, (or long for), where mourning is taken to mean a web of dynamics which are of decisive importance for the development both of the symbolic function and of every subsequent cognitive step. Hence the two dynamics, namely the work of mourning and the formation of symbols, sustain and imply one another in inseparable fashion in shaping the paradigms of subsequent relations.[14]

The painful cleavage between an infant's world of fantasies and reality may be used in order to further maturation to the extent that another gap, or hiatus, opens within his primal inner structure. In other words, some distance must be created within the self, as if it were the outline of a primal symbolic layer which begins to separate out from a world of conditions and states. Such a symbolic margin of an inner hiatus may allow some way of 'visualizing' our own personal, interactive life, that is our subject–object relations; thus on the one hand we have a symbol and on the other the subject–world relation to which the symbol may refer. It is the use of ulterior symbolic levels that ensures that the human infant can gradually obtain an image of himself as *he* relates to the world. This second cleavage, or hiatus, or distance, is the sole means by which an inchoate person can engage in the activities of taking up responsibility and contractual dialogue *vis-á-vis* his reality. The development of the symbolic function thus forms the basis upon which 'is built up the subject's relation to the outside world and to reality in general'.[15] In the words of Cassirer: 'The ... distinction between "I" and "not-I" proves to be an essential and constant function of theoretical thinking, whereas the manner in which this function is *fulfilled*, the boundary between the "subjective" and "objective" contents, varies with the level of cognition.'[16]

The fantasy images corresponding to the hallucination of a desire are not real thoughts, at least in the sense that they are not readily interchangeable. When the working through of our hallucinated expectation leads to the production of a symbol, what is achieved is a quantum leap comparable to the transition from the practice of barter to the use of money, the latter having a symbolic value as well as being immensely more versatile and negotiable. And the symbolic function is not only a tool for experiential activity but also, and above all, an instrument for building experiential hypotheses, which is to say ideas or projects concerning, not so much the world, as the relation between our nascent cognitive apparatus and whatever reality there may be.

When we bear in mind that abandoning an instinctual object may be comparable to losing maternal nourishment (or any of its equivalents), we are in a position to recognize that the work of mourning will be successful only when the unavoidable loss of an object is experienced as 'something of a psychic or pre-cognitive nature (no longer involving mere phantasms), by means of the dynamics of 'inner restoration'.

We shall, perhaps, be in a better position to probe deeply into the complex process of symbol-generation if we regain the full richness of meaning contained in the term 'symbol' itself. The first thing that we notice is that the word 'symbol' is made up of the prefix *syn*, meaning 'together', 'with', 'according to', and *bolon*, meaning 'that which has been thrown' (from the Greek verb *ballo*, 'I throw'). A value equivalent to *syn* is to be assigned to the preposition *meta* which is also employed in ordinary language to mean 'with', 'together', 'beside' or 'beyond'. *Meta* is also used as a prefix and, as such, is combined with the verb *ballo*. On the other hand, when *meta* is in combination with the verb *ballo*, the former takes on meanings referring to the process of transformation and change, in other words, with metabolism. Consequently, it may be supposed that similar meanings are taken on by combinations associating *syn* with *ballo*, which is how the word 'symbol' came about. It is the complexity of the inquiry into the symbolic function which leads us to use the term 'metabols' even where cognitive and emotional matters are concerned. Our position is that only symbols can be metabols and that only vicissitudes which are sufficiently symbolized as growth proceeds may be metabolized into a real process of inner development.

Any pseudosymbolic process which bears a resemblance to symbolism in appearance only, but which leads neither to authentic object-formation nor to a richer use of reality, is 'dia-bolic' in the etymological sense of the term. The Greek verb *diaballo* is a compound of the preposition *dia*, meaning 'across' with the verb *ballo*, 'I throw'; hence, a 'diabol' is something that flings things 'across', mixing them up and confusing them in a way which runs counter to cognition.

In an attempt to find a guide for a better appreciation of the vital complexity of the symbolic function I propose the following as a working hypothesis: communication is symbolic when it is seen to involve mental activities which lead to a fuller appreciation and enjoyment of reality; to the extent that this is the case, such activities will be truly metabolic and, hence, vital. Vice versa, anything that seems to be a symbol but does not lead to such dynamics is nothing more than a dia-bolic phenomenon, in the sense that it cannot possibly be metabolic.

In the early stages of development, symbols are necessary mental metabols, in the sense that the energy used when an expectation meets its negative realization – in other words the experience of loss – is channelled by means of the symbol into the formation of an inner and outer reality. When the outcome of the conjunction of an instinctual desire and an act of renunciation is not the formation of a symbol, the frustration of instincts may trigger a chaotic state of despair such as is capable of jeopardizing whatever symbolic structures might exist at the time. In the very early phases of life, no vicissitude is neutral in relation to inner growth because any event is intensively for or against maturation.

As Bion says: 'The capacity for tolerating frustration enables the psyche to develop a thought as a means by which the frustration that is tolerated is itself made more tolerable.'[17] The question will be asked: what is the nature of this capacity? Granted that there are innate or biological components of this capacity, we must turn to the affectual and cognitive vicissitudes which help to shape that same capacity for tolerating frustration; this is the only part of the problem accessible to our investigation.

Bion further points out that 'omniscience substitutes for the discrimination between true and false a dictatorial affirmation that one thing is morally right and the other wrong.'[18] I would suggest that what an inchoate person's omniscience establishes as morally right cannot be adequately described as a mere 'substitution', since the nascent personality comes to realize intuitively that, whatever the products of his omniscience may be, they are necessary to the defence of his frail ego, and as such they are right and proper. The best that a nascent subject manages to do for his own mental survival is necessarily valuable and therefore can easily be expanded in terms of moral rightness. Under those circumstances the evolving person cannot afford the distinction between truth and untruth. Why is it so?

In order that an adequate ability to endure frustration may develop, enough psychic or mental 'traces' must be available for use in the formation of symbolic vehicles. A sufficiently rich supply of 'traces' may be developed only where there is a sufficiently good relation with the parental environment. Only such traces are capable of functioning as containers for the inner perception of a frustration (or loss, absence, denial). Primal operations such as these can tilt the scale in the direction of dominance by the reality principle rather than towards forms of solipsistic narcissism. With no such 'traces' the incipient subject would only be capable of 'producing' (in the sense of allowing to come about) bad, destructive objects, fit only to be expelled. In fact, a developing individual may hallucinate in an omnipotent way, for instance, food which is not present, but in the long run the 'good' thing in the hallucination offers no nourishment or satisfaction and will eventually turn into something persecutory. The idea of mental or psychic 'traces' may refer both to any memory element grasped by the infant as a result of his contacts with a sufficiently good environment, as well as to anything of a relational nature which may be used in order to neutralize supposedly innate, archaic fears.

In Kleinian thinking the response to frustration is a hallucination which generates a fantasy of an object capable of giving satisfaction. The fantasy produced, however, cannot eliminate the state of need (for example, hunger), with the result that the hallucination crystallizes into an 'object' which persecutes and destroys from within. And the only way to expel such an invasive presence is through a destructive emptying out of the embryonic life of the mind. But how can an individual in the making, or suffering subject, realize that neither the hallucination of a desire nor the expulsion of an 'object' (initially absent, subsequently hallucinated, then unsatisfactory and therefore persecutory) is the answer to his state of need? One wonders which ingredients put one in a position to see a fantasy for what it is, so that one realizes that an unsatisfied need is not something which one may get rid of. How is one to *realize* that needs arise within and refer to something needed from the outside? It would seem to be quite impossible for one to realize anything of the kind, inasmuch as one would be required to differentiate and 'visualize' two 'elements' which either correspond, or do not correspond, to each other, but which in any case form a relationship, or have a relatedness between themselves. One wonders how it is that a nascent individual may reflect upon himself, or 'stretch' in such a way as to gain a position from which to obtain a synchronic view of two relational poles, namely his own self and its relation with the world.[19] One wonders also how a subject can put himself in a position to grasp the relation between an unsatisfied desire and its compensatory hallucination. Unless that relation is somehow perceived, one will be absorbed into a spiral of omnipotent fantasies which are not only something other than reality but are actually at odds with it, inasmuch as they have been generated as substitutes for reality itself. And of course this pre-symbolic paradigm may propagate into innumerable cultural variants.

I cannot see any answer that does not depend upon the presence of symbolic elements which are either developed within the inchoate self or provided for within a dialogic context which enhances the vicissitudes of maturation. The overwhelming power of omnipotent fantasies may be identified and then neutralized with the help of a symbolic support which functions in its place, that is to say, with the help of someone who tells (hints, communicates, explains to) a nascent subject about the relationship between his fantasy and the absent object, between himself and his desires. As soon as the subject is in a position to use a symbolic element capable of establishing a meaningful connection between himself and his desires, between fantasy and reality, he will then become able to 'think' his own fantasies, and thus use them creatively as the germinal onset of his cognitive development. A symbolic element offered in the course of early dialogue allows one to distinguish not only between fantasy and reality but also, and above all, between oneself and one's own desires. A fantasy which, on the contrary, is not supported by symbolic bearers, or channels, tends to lure incipient mentation into an unassailable, narcissistic structure.

We may now turn to one of the basic questions, namely the nature of a sufficiently good parent–child relationship such as will allow the genesis of symbolization. A significant reply to the crucial question of what may be meant by 'sufficiently good' is offered by Winnicott:

> The good-enough mother meets the omnipotence of the infant and to some extent makes sense of it. She does this repeatedly. A true Self begins to have life, through the strength given to the infant's weak ego by the mother's implementation of the infant's omnipotent expressions. The mother who is not good-enough is not able to implement the infant's omnipotence, and so she repeatedly fails to meet the infant's gesture; instead she substitutes her own gesture which is to be given sense by the compliance of the infant.[20]

That which is passively taken in when one has to adapt systematically to the style of the parental environment is certain to lack what is needed for fostering the development of the symbolic function. A psychic 'trace' can have a maturational effect only when it is an element sufficiently endowed with 'vitality', when it can function metabolically, furthering a process of synthesis, that is a conjunction between expectations and frustrations. A pseudolanguage emanating from the parental world, of course, offers no symbolic channels to think one's feelings but only induces further confusion. We may assume that on the basis of early experiences of omnipotence (that is coincidence of desire and satisfaction) an adequate supply of 'traces' is formed with which to face and overcome (with maturational results) the inevitable sequence of instinctual frustrations.

I believe that the nascent self can only transform something into something else and that he cannot transform nothing into something – into a symbol, for instance. Sufficient implementation of the infant's early omnipotence forms the basis for his capacity to tolerate frustration, for his ability to hold together and match an instinctual expectation with its frustration. Only by means of these antecedent experiences can the 'no-satisfaction' inside become a symbol. We now have something transformed into something else (a symbol) instead of nothing (nothing, no gratifying object) becoming a symbol.

A chronicle by Salimbene de Adam of Parma (1221–88) narrates how Frederick II of Sicily wished to discover which had been the first language spoken on earth, wondering whether it had been Hebrew, Greek or Latin. The methodologically inclined sovereign arranged for a number of new-born babies to be kept in isolation, with the injunction that they be seen only for feeding and that no one should ever talk to them. The enlightened monarch had worked out that the language which the secluded babies would spontaneously begin to speak would be the first language that had ever existed on earth. The result of the experiment is unknown, as not one of the children survived. And Salimbene remarks: 'How could they have survived without the cuddles, gestures, smiles and endearments of their nurses.'[21]

11

From Biological Life to Dialogic Relations

Preliminary Notes

In an attempt to outline possible affinities and points of contact between the process of interpretation performed in psychoanalytic 'dialogues' and the development of the symbolic function which takes place in our early interactions, I believe that some of the premises for articulating any such convergence should be specified.

Recent currents in psychoanalytic thinking tend to hold that most forms of pathology can be traced back to our disturbed development of early object-relations. From this point of view, a more accurate examination of the genesis of the symbolic function would seem essential to a better appreciation of the growth of the self and hence of interpersonal relations. Seen in this light, what differentiates psychoanalysis from other forms of therapy is the effort to re-create a process of psychic conception, birth and growth whereby the subject's inhibitory experiences may be re-elaborated so as to regain the path towards maturity.

The fact of having constructed a particular type of object-relation determines subsequent modes of experience, in the sense that the cultural heritage drawn upon by the individual can reinforce the interactive system already instituted, but cannot make major corrections should this prove basically inadequate. Hence, it can hardly be supposed that significant changes of a qualitative-structural nature might occur spontaneously.

The fitness of the basic matrix on which the subject patterns his interactive structure is thus held to be a determining factor. An insight into the basic ways in which the inchoate subject goes about shaping his reality proves incomparably more meaningful and enlightening than the description of diverse shades of disease identifiable in a clinical perspective that is more or less consciously hemmed in by a conventional vocabulary or epistemology of mental illness. A deeper knowledge of the symbolic function is thus essential to any discipline striving to focus on the human condition construed as an *indivisible* unity of both affectual components and culturally determined patterns.

The methodological characteristics of psychoanalytic practice are qualitatively dependent more upon the formulation of its questions than on the solutions proposed for them. The questions posed by the analyst may in fact establish the perspective and the style of his therapeutic endeavour and, consequently, the way in which the analytic relationship is approached. Let us invoke a classical macroscopic example: is transference an unpleasant professional mishap (a kind of sepsis to be brought under control as quickly as possible) or the instrumental medium of therapeutic work? Of course the same issue could be raised with regard to what we call countertransference. In fact, the therapist's ability to effect significant reconstruction is proportional to his ability to listen attentively and thus make interpretations which, in turn, depend on the questions that he can formulate and even more on questions that he lets patients put to him; one certainly cannot hope to see more than he is prepared to see *within*.

We may thus acknowledge that, in analytic work hinging on the processing of relations, attention shifts from the 'disease' to the communications which mediate the expression of suffering, thus focusing not so much on a nosographic entity, on a specific mental 'illness', but rather on what the person, namely the *patient* – in the sense of *patiens*, suffering – is able to get across as regards his inner travail.[1] When analysts are engaged in this type of work, they are dealing with something other than the initial manifestation, or clearly visible expression, of suffering. Yet this 'something other', though considered separately from the 'mental' illness, does not as a result lose contact with pathological vicissitudes. Even though our concentration on the messages that may reach the analyst initially leads us away from the world of pathological events, that same attentiveness to the realm of spontaneous verbal communication offers us a way of making effective use of our tools of inquiry, and thereby of accepting (and exploiting) more than one type of vocabulary or narrative, more than just one mode of absorbing the speaker's meaning.

To the extent that he recognizes the existence of diverse levels and modes of communication, the analyst is more receptive to (conversant with) the lively multiplicity of meanings and dimensions within the message and avoids confining himself to its manifest contents. What ensures the opportunity to appreciate a wider range of the interlocutor's inner potential is thus a measure of detachment from the descriptive content of the message.

Restricting attention to the evidence of pathology may prevent the analyst taking cognizance of the person's symbolic apparatus which could serve as a guide in decoding (apparently absurd) messages, and thus may hinder the creation of authentic interpretative interactions. Such an approach might prove an unwittingly harmful limitation to the subject's development, in that comprehension comes to be circumscribed by the therapist's previous patterns of interpretation; in other words, the less the analyst is aware of his own set of hermeneutic instruments, the greater the risk of narrowing the patient's opportunities for expression and development. If the analyst fails to keep his inner ear open to the most diversified modes of communication, he may in the end only listen to what is in keeping with his own cognitive system.

As can happen in any cognitive approach, one is sometimes inclined to believe that things and persons are there as they are in themselves; all the investigator has to do is 'photograph them', pin them down in some way, so as to grasp them as they really are. This outlook takes into account neither the investigator's peculiar way of processing 'data' nor the process of linguistic uncoding or categorization; yet the way in which so-called 'facts' are identified probably corresponds to the inner or societal apparatus through which objects are constructed at various levels of completeness.

If it is true that in the more serious forms of illness people interact with only partial objects (namely with a small part of the components of another person's life), we cannot avoid asking what a complete or total object could be like. As Cassirer points out, what distinguishes human perception from the animal perceptive process is that man is faced with a 'different' kind of object; the reason for this is that data as such are not what counts, but rather man's peculiar way of representing them to himself with reference to an ideal of objectivity for which no internal limits can be set, thereby producing a never-ending task.[2]

Interactive efforts which strive to correct the utilization of partial objects, that is to remedy impaired ways of life, may indeed constitute such a never-ending project. Winnicott, for instance, remarks that it is '*creative appreciation* more than anything else that makes the individual feel that life is worth living'.[3]

In support of what has been suggested so far, we may quote from

Bion's reflections on the analyst's effort to represent accurately the dynamics of the relationship: 'Formulations can be judged by considering how necessary his existence is to the thoughts he expresses. The more his interpretations can be judged as showing how necessary *his* knowledge, *his* experience, *his* character are to the thoughts formulated, the more reason there is to suppose that the interpretation is psychoanalytically worthless.[4] Such interpretation, in fact, may be focusing on his own way of construing things and not on the vicissitudes his interlocutor is trying to convey.

The Genesis of Symbols and Primal Dialogue

In the early phases of development, symbols act as the essential 'psychic' metabols by means of which the 'energy' involved in uniting an expectation with a negative realization comes to be channelled into the formation of external and inner reality. If an adequate capacity to endure frustration is to arise, we ought to assume, perhaps, the presence of 'psychic traces' which may be employed in order to develop symbolic vehicles. An adequate source of such 'traces' can be acquired only through a sufficiently good parental relationship. Such traces (that is any memory element that comes from a sufficiently good experiential relation) may act as mental vehicles – bearers of affects – for processing frustrations, that is for the inner perception of a lack, or loss, of whatever nature.

As Winnicott suggests, even an instinctual satisfaction may prove a trauma that hinders development if it remains confined outside a dialogic context which joins, or connects, opposite experiences and which thus functions as a precursor of the process of symbol-formation.

> It must be understood that when reference is made to the mother's adaptive capacity this has only a little to do with her ability to satisfy the infant's oral drives, as by giving a satisfactory feed. What is being discussed here runs parallel with such a consideration as this. It is indeed possible to gratify an oral drive and by so doing to *violate* the infant's ego-function, or that which will later on be jealously guarded as the self, the core of the personality. *A feeding satisfaction can be a seduction and can be traumatic if it comes to a baby without coverage by ego-functioning.*[5]

But what is the meaning of this statement, so intensely paradoxical and yet at the same time unambiguous? On this point Winnicott explicitly states that even adequate gratification of oral instincts in the inchoate person may prove harmful to the maturational process. How can this be? The emphasis with which Winnicott imbues this passage – almost as if to enhance the incisiveness of his message – offers itself to several lines of explanation. A first approach might be to suggest that it is precisely during such early vicissitudes that the paths of physiological growth and of affective and cognitive development attained through the symbolic function may part company, with a detrimental effect. To the extent that such paths become detached from one another, the subject will be herded through a sequence of 'maturing' stages possibly describable as animal husbandry directed at the breed *homo sapiens*. Winnicott claims, in fact, that in the absence of sufficiently good relationships (and no reference to shortcomings in catering to physiological needs is intended) 'the infant is not able to get started with ego-maturation, or else ego-development is necessarily distorted in certain vitally important respects.'[6]

However, we are immediately faced with several interwoven questions such as: For what reason may an infant's ego not begin to mature? Why is his development, of necessity, distorted? And which, precisely, are those 'vitally important respects'? The import of such questions is not to be reduced to that of a cue for formulating better definitions; what Winnicott's message does, rather, is to create a valuable theoretical space conducive to improving the *scope* of our work. We believe it may be taken as a preliminary assumption that, in the human condition, the development of the symbolic function may certainly be regarded as a 'vitally important' element.

It is not unreasonable to suppose that most individuals' instinctual needs have received enough satisfaction in the sense that, were this not the case, they would not have reached maturity, having succumbed, instead, to severe physiological imbalances. In most cases, in fact, we may observe ontogenetic histories wherein instinctual needs have been met, at least to the extent that they allow physical development. What may not have gone so well – and may thus have become detached from physiological growth – is the other (inner) developmental paths, namely that of affective and cognitive maturation. Indications of this may be seen in the not infrequent cases of so-called 'optimal' child-rearing conditions which have proved almost irrelevant to the ideal of 'good' cognitive and affectual growth.

Winnicott's message makes it extremely clear that adequate instinctual gratification, although necessary, is by no means sufficient or decisive for the purposes of personal maturation. When an inner structure of awareness fails to develop, the ensuing void will produce an incessant urge for compensatory symbioses formed in accordance with a private or collective pathology, often supported by a variety of cultural legacies. Yet, if the maturing virtues of dependence upon parental care cannot be explained by the satisfaction of needs, what then is the relational factor which actually enhances the potentials for knowledge and creativity?

In reply to the questions posed by Winnicott, we may construe that, as we see it, sufficiently good parental figures are those who know, for instance, how to use frustrations preceding instinctual satisfactions for the purpose of creating *some* dialogue, which is to say that they use a biological fact in a dialogic function. Failure to exploit an infant's biological frustrations for dialogic purposes amounts to adopting the animal-husbandry approach wherein the nascent person is not allowed to generate symbols to a sufficient degree or even attempt establishing a relationship with the adult. Those actions that deliver biological satisfaction but ignore dialogic needs represent crucial points at which both the most damaging form of mutilation and the most radical rejection of the infant may occur. It is a drastic repudiation which may sidetrack the developing individual into the consumption of the myriad affective and cognitive substitutes offered by every culture in response to such unfortunate vicissitudes of self-creation.

According to Spitz:

> only the living can engage in dialogue, take the initiative or respond to it, and by this same token anticipate initiatives. The inanimate neither acts nor reacts, it merely exists, it is there. Any initiative aimed at it reveals its inanimateness, because such initiatives are not followed by a circular action-reaction response and thus do not lead to any exchanges. Thus, engaging in dialogue becomes the child's criterion in distinguishing the animate from the inanimate.[7]

This being the case, we may legitimately use the construction of the converse of Spitz's proposition in order to frame our theses more clearly. Thus we may concede that the criterion according to which a nascent person judges himself animate or inanimate, that is to say 'spiritually alive' or 'spiritually dead', is whether or not he is singled out as a subject with whom to interact dialogically. By the same token, when the dialogic dimension fails to unfold, an infant cannot be said to possess a criterion whereby he may at least perceive himself as animate. Without dialogue, in fact, an inchoate person is already inwardly dead, for the specific reason that his mind is not allowed *to be born* – in the rigorous and literal sense of the verb.

The actions which a developing self directs towards the inanimate world may be inessential for maturational purposes, in the sense that they are linked at the most primal relational level, since inanimate objects do not respond to his initiatives. Thus the interactive potential diminishes (or, in extreme cases, may vanish) when it cannot be integrated into a more complex interactive structure. When parental presence comes across in its more inanimate form – that is when the mechanical, animal-husbandry aspects of the 'relationship' predominate (the inadequate 'feeding satisfaction' spoken of by Winnicott) – an infant is truly 'genetically' damaged in his potential for becoming a thinking individual. In fact, if we for instance regard genital organs as a biological symbol of the capacity to generate, we may be able to see in the drama of Oedipus a mythical quandary spun from 'mental' experiences of a drastic and dramatic nature. The stifling of the symbolic function is perpetrated not by inflicting damage to something existent, but rather by the obtuse ferocity of a non-listening attitude which may be at work under the guise of the most impeccable 'rearing', and which may ultimately impede the birth of thought. The point at issue is not the damage to something functioning but the failure to allow something to exist and function.

The dialogic attitude, then, joins forces with biological life at moments of frustration, when the infant is exasperated by the opposed polarities of instinctual expectation and its negative realization; the dialogic dimension links with biological life through affective participation – a sympathetic sharing of world views and epistemic frames of reference. 'Language is a social *art*,' remarks Quine.[8] Thus the dialogic approach represents the personalized, authentic articulation of what the other, the infant, is as yet incapable of expressing fully. And this is why a nurturing presence acts as an anticipated potential for assuming the task of symbol-formation and provides the listening responsiveness which nourishes the infant's mental growth. It is an endeavour to attract the infant towards dialogic life. Such a presence stands in opposition to any sophisticated form of animal husbandry even where it takes perfect care of biological needs. To the extent that a parental figure uses any expression of physiological imbalance as an opportunity to communicate, he contributes to the production of the symbolic instruments destined to lead to the conjunction of the opposites in question (desiring and waiting, imagination and objects). Conversely, we may posit that a root cause of pathology lies in an inability to cope with affective and cognitive opposites which cannot be contained within the mind when there are no symbols which may function as vehicles or bearers. The more or less disastrous unfolding of such vicissitudes is manifested in the distortions of object-relations, invariably marked by an obstinate infantility.

By gratifying an oral drive in the absence of a dialogic relation (still, possibly, at a pre-verbal level), one may be performing one of those innumerable microscopic interactions in which one caters to a physiological need while remaining deaf to the needs of the person's epistemophily. It is as if the adult were incapable of imagining the desire to be born psychically, for the mind to spring to life. Further-more, in each of the countless relational sequences wherein biologi-cal needs are satisfied while the dialogic propensity for enhancing thought is ignored, the latter faces the danger of extinction. This is the worst form of damage, for it nips in the bud those emergent primal significants by means of which the inchoate person can try to achieve a link with reality.

Meaning may derive from interpersonal negotiations regarding something on which there is agreement because it is shared. Meanings which have been reciprocally agreed upon are of course such that they grow, change and are an object of dispute in the relation. In this sense meanings are a form of shared possession. In the absence of reciprocity in the development of meanings, 'good' may even mean non-existent or inanimate, and 'bad' may even mean resilient and surviving. And of course the relevance of the nego-tiation of meanings extends from the relatively easy description of quantifiable external situations to the attempts to describe dynamic inner states. Hill suggests:

> The very special interest that attaches to meanings in the intentional way is rooted in the fact that when someone says something, or in some other manner undertakes to convey a meaning, what people most commonly want to know is not what the expression that he uses could be used to lead a respondent to apprehend ... but what the agent in fact intends to lead a respondent to apprehend.[9]

What the utterer intends his hearer to understand is not only his meaning but the fact that this meaning is intended.[10]

In this connection I am trying to suggest that the celebrated oedi-pal anxieties of quandary are but a tangible, conglomerate version of the countless, imperceptible repressive experiences accumulated in an environment which only in appearance has a formative value. In a developmental perspective, therefore, it is amply justifiable to adhere to Winnicott's daring statement: 'It is indeed possible to gratify an oral drive and by so doing to violate the infant's ego-function, or that which will later on be jealously guarded as the self, the core of the personality.'[11]

Unless the satisfaction of needs is carried out in joint synergy with the infant's epistemophily and kept in harmony with it, a situation conducive to pseudo-relationships may arise, since the inchoate person will only imitate the adult's (unintelligible) 'language'. What transpires is not a symbolic life originating within the infant, but passive mimicry, both pseudo-adaptive and acritical. It will remain invisible and beyond reach, precisely because it is a survival technique designed for passively mirroring the adult. This state of affairs certainly amounts to a violation; it is a threat to the very genesis of mentation.[12]

Success in educating a person (as in conducting an analysis) that is measured in terms of a 'good rapport' may all too easily conceal the adult's overwhelming logico-linguistic power. Whenever listening is not sufficiently cultivated, any measure of logocratic power will detrimentally prevail in any dialogic interaction. Innumerable microscopic acts of curtailment perpetrated to the detriment of the evolving symbolic life are glossed over by such overwhelming power – an expressive power which can speak but cannot listen. If symbols are the tools which humans use for shaping and using possible worlds, and if the progressive ordering of such tools is hindered, the basic manner in which the subject relates to the world in general will be impaired. Thus oedipal vicissitudes revolving around the desire to attain a mother-figure and the concomitant anxieties of retaliation are to be viewed as an account in fable form – a story that we can visualize – of the more crucial (impossible to grasp) experiences affecting the development and inhibition of our symbolic capacity and influencing the genetic core of mental life.

By offering themselves as interpreters of the infant's anguishing experiences, sufficiently good parents contribute to the transformation of a biological event into a dialogic one. By 'explaining' to the infant that they are trying to understand what he is living through, parents are really nourishing him not only with their 'explanation', but also with their readiness to comprehend, to contain with their own adult ego his tumultuous fantasy experiences. Adults generate humans to the extent that they can enhance biological *and* epistemic growth in conjunction. A disjunction, on the other hand, produces biological growth but mental impairment – a practice which is liable to obscurity because it is apparently unobjectionable. The process of psychoanalytic interpretation might possibly be conceptualized as the task of making good such early interpretative shortcomings.

If we suggest that the dialogic use of instinctual events allows something syntropic to be obtained from aspects of entropic phenomena, we are positing a loose analogy between the concept of entropy and certain conditions of mental confusion out of which the infant strives to surface. Winnicott reminds us that 'At the stage which is being discussed it is necessary not to think of the baby as a person who gets hungry, and whose instinctual drives may be met or frustrated, but to think of the baby as an immature being who is all the time *on the brink of unthinkable anxiety*.[13]

When Winnicott insists that it is possible to gratify an oral drive and in so doing violate an ego-function, we wonder to which ego-function he may be referring. For at the onset we cannot, in fact, identify any observable behaviour which would allow us to ascertain the existence of an actual reasoning life. It seems that the profound significance of Winnicott's thinking lies precisely in its aim of highlighting a basic aspect of parental presence, namely the ability to adopt a dialogic role *vis-à-vis* the infant and extend him the credit in advance by attributing to him a thinking life which may not, as yet, be said to exist. However, if such dialogic credit is not forthcoming and more satisfactions are offered instead, then the development of those peculiarly human functions which were not credited with being able to spring to life and evolve will surely be impeded.

The symbolic dimension made available by the adult's listening presence functions as an anticipated potential within the process of structuring the infant's relational space-time. By assuming that the infant can, or could, understand, and consequently offering themselves for dialogue, it may be possible for adults to 'invert time' so to speak: something which does not yet exist is anticipated, while at the same time adults become attuned once more to aspects of their own earlier growth. It is a simple and vital form of dialogic philosophy: we do not teach the vocabulary of merely one specific epistemology but rather try to step out of our own world view and show a propensity for exchanging vocabularies in order to create greater complexity and richness.

On the other hand, when there is a failure to bring opposites together through a process of symbolization, the knowing subject in the making will take its bearings from a relational pattern based on splitting and negation, thus leading to the 'ossification' of narcissistic, schizoid defences and to the disjunction (disconnection, dissociation, separation) between physiological growth and epistemophily.

And so we have possibly reached the conclusion of our attempt to answer the provocative riddle posed by Winnicott's statement implying that a satisfying feed may prove harmful to the mental life of the human infant. As we said earlier, the true nourishment for growth is the ability to employ expectations, frustrations and instinctual satisfactions in order to lay the basis of an interaction conducive to the birth of an authentic (and not simply imitative) phatic function. True parental nourishment consists in a dialogic presence eager to proffer itself as an anticipated potential which *attracts* linguistic growth. Although the infant does not speak, the sufficiently good parent addresses him as if he were truly capable of understanding and expression.

On Interactive Interpretations

As pointed out above, a salient feature of psychoanalytic therapy consists in the effort to re-create a process of psychic conception, birth and growth whereby the subject's inhibitory vicissitudes may be worked through again so as to regain a direction towards development. During the analytic experience one inevitably retreats from the level of neutral, abstract descriptions and becomes involved in the inner life of the person, reverberating with the ancient, formidable opposites of good and evil, life and death, integration and fragmentation. It is the perspective of a dialogue stemming from the relationship itself which, in my opinion, permits freer transitions from the abstract to the concrete, from the universal to the existential, and vice versa.

Inasmuch as the efficacy of interpretations is thought to be rooted in the coincidence of certain analytic experiences with the sequence of ontogenetic events, one may justifiably consider the analytic journey as a laborious process of reorganization. We shall now try to focus on a possible convergence between the interpretative side of analysis and the processes whereby early narcissism is surpassed and the formation of fuller relations is inaugurated. In regard to a subject's history of self-creation, the development of the ability to use symbols emerges as one of the most significant results achieved in working through the 'depressive position', this task being viewed as overcoming the experience of loss through symbol-formation. The nascent capacity to live out mourning – to deal with a loss – appears as a necessary condition for the unfolding of the ability to initiate any form of symbolic thinking. It is through the labour of mourning that it can begin to dawn on the infant that his desire and the lost object are not one and the same thing. If, however, the infant were totally incapable of using 'something' mental, or internal, in order to refer to 'something' external which has been lost, then he would be unable to cope with mourning at all. Each of these activities – symbol-creation and work of mourning – implies and sustains the other in the primal vicissitudes of mentation. In the early phases of development, symbols act as the essential metabolites by means of which the energy involved in combining an instinctual expectation with the cognitive realization of its negation comes to be channelled into some understandable feature of reality.[14] When the infant's overall condition enables him to tolerate the denial of his expectations, the absent external object can then be internalized, transforming a mental trace into a symbol, and this in turn renders the feeling of the endured frustration more bearable and even meaningful.

In regard to the psychoanalytic interaction, we may note first of all that its remarkable feature is the absence of gratification, by which is meant the systematic non-fulfilment of affective expectations, however expressed. As a consequence the subject may come to relive the self-same experiences of early object-formation within the analytic journey. He finds himself once again confronting those critical situations in which there is an expectation, namely an emotional investment in the other partner, and the negative fulfilment (the non-satisfaction of the demand). In fact the commitment and probity of the analyst will neither further nor provide gratification within the analytic setting, for such gratification in itself would be devoid of any maturational value and, hence, would not have the least bearing on the individual's development. In the analytic setting, therefore, the subject is once again faced with an affectual expectation and its negative realization.

When a person expresses a sudden surge of emotion to the analyst, what he receives is a symbolic reply offered as a substitute for the satisfaction of the expectation. Frustration is mediated by a verbal message which uses the impeded emotional investment as a means for conveying the frustration into a symbolic circuit catalysed by the analyst. As Manfredi Turillazzi points out, when the interpretation is articulated with sufficient precision it is possible to restore contact between the isolated parts of the mind as well as between self and world.[15]

In this manner some measure of inner order may be established which is conducive to the process of integrating reality, with the consequence that the subject may begin to pursue these goals for and by himself. Interpretation is seen, thus, as setting in motion the dynamics through which it is possible to effect inner reconstructions.

Interpretation is a symbolic message which is offered as a meaningful alternative in response to an emotional demand which is not met. It is to be noted, incidentally, that were the expectation to be accompanied by gratification the interpretative work of restructuring would be neutralized and debased to pseudosymbolic utterances.

When interpretation is not referred to something throbbing with life, or when interpretation is lacking, a subject tends to languish in a condition of isolation and splittings, a condition that is contrary to integration and, hence, to life itself: whenever we internalize something which cannot be properly integrated, we receive a sterile and costly acquisition dominated by the principle of extinction.

Whenever interpretation takes the form of a symbolic message offered in response to a specific emotional investment, it inevitably involves risk and commitment (the purpose of which is to conduct an analysis which offers the opportunity for authentic reorganization). The task of mediating relations between mutually antithetical parts of the self involves an effort progressively to bring forth meaningful inner life, an effort which entails both opposing and coping with the mechanisms of splitting, separation and fragmentation which tend, inevitably, towards a state of inanimate stillness.

Strachey lays emphasis on the recognition that analysis works with live impulses, that is by exploiting existing interactive situations:

> Instead of having to deal as best we may with conflicts of the remote past, which are concerned with dead circumstances and mummified personalities, and whose outcome is already determined, we find ourselves involved in an actual and immediate situation, in which we and the patient are the principal characters and the development of which is to some extent at least under our control.[16]

In effect, it is a lively relationship alone which can provide the basis for a mutative impact. Reciprocal verbal exchanges of lifeless, peripheral messages concerning issues far removed from the complex interaction would be an activity free of risk and personal commitment; the 'rapport' would be relaxing for the parties involved, but it would yield little of benefit, apart from some momentary, cathartic relief. The points stressed by Strachey develop along lines clearly convergent with a position which views symbol-formation as that element of awareness which is the mediator and irreplaceable container of affects.

The purpose of a variety of works covering the problem of interpretation is relevant not only for a more accurate appreciation of any therapeutic dialogue; it also aims at fitting such accounts into the framework of the theory of the formation of human thinking, of the way in which a subject evolves – for which the term *Bildung* is frequently invoked. Strachey's vast contribution focuses, essentially, on the search for what is full of life, for this – and this alone – can be used by encoding it in a new symbology which moves away from cognitive and affective degradation. Outside such a dialogic framework, we might very well be reduced to dealing 'with conflicts of the remote past, which are concerned with the dead circumstances ... whose outcome is already determined'.[17]

Where symbolic instruments are lacking, a gratifying object which is lost (or absent) turns into a persecutory entity; when a symbol is available, however, it becomes merely a not-too-good object, because it is temporarily absent, or out of proportion to the expectation, or simply other than the self. Interpretation, therefore, connects and re-joins a primal fantasy object with a real one.

Interpretative work may either induce transformation or end in verbal futility. The crucial role of interpretation, therefore, compels us, as it were, to address ourselves more painstakingly to the complexity of the symbolic function. The development of that capacity, in fact, determines the mode of transition from being ruled by unconscious fantasies to the organization of awareness expressed in the almost unimaginable richness of relational life.

Let us now try to attain a better grasp of the meaning of Strachey's suggestion that a transference conflict should be approached in such a way that 'the patient chooses a new solution instead of the old one, a solution in which the primitive and un-adaptable method of repression is replaced by behaviour more in contact with reality.'[18] It is clear that, according to Strachey, analysis ought to set about restructuring those basic areas that constitute the inner code governing relational experience in general. If the code is static, all experiences are channelled invariably into the same circuits: any mutative interaction with reality is avoided and new information is invariably fed into the *same* cognitive paradigm. Strachey's solution would involve, essentially, putting a stop to repression: as the derivative of splitting, repression remains active indefinitely, precisely in those areas where symbolic tools which could hold together contrasting elements or give voice to a conflict are absent. And those defensive processes of splitting which propagate indefinitely come down to the negation of any interactive potential, or mental degradation, at the service of extinction.

This new solution, which Strachey terms 'behaviour more in contact with reality', cannot but rely on symbolic coding which links – not in a jumbled way but in a pattern – the primal opposites of 'good' and 'bad' which dominate our inchoate condition. If adequate means of connection or channelling (as provided by interpretation) are unavailable, the infant-in-the-adult may not know how to surface out of chaotic conditions which threaten him and will continue, instead, to rely upon the usual mechanisms of splitting, separation and negation as the only means for confronting the threat of detrimental confusion. These mechanisms will be ever more ornate, romantic and extensive to the extent that they interlock with the expression of the cultural trends in vogue. Blocking maturation involves the enormous cost of maintaining a psychic structure based on splitting, and it is on this waste of life that analytic work focuses, for what has been repressed, while certainly unconscious, is above all isolated. What Strachey is recommending, in essence, is an effort to create in the patient an ego-structure with a creative propensity. In this sense it is just not a particular technical device. He expresses the hope, in fact, that 'The solution of the transference conflict implies the simultaneous solution of the infantile conflict of which it is a new edition.'[19]

What is being suggested here harks back to the clinical concept whereby splitting is the precursor of repression and the fact of being unconscious is, ultimately, less important than being isolated, detached, out of touch and thus prone to disintegration and degradation. And of course the separation or splitting of thoughts and affects is one of the most damaging threats to the life of the mind – however liable to obscurity this process may be.

Strachey says that 'A mutative interpretation can only be applied to an id-impulse which is actually in a state of cathexis.... The function of the analyst is merely to ensure that the energy shall flow along one channel rather than along another.'[20]

But how are the analyst's words to ensure that the energy flows along one channel rather than another? Once again we are confronted with an early situation in which there is an intense emotional expectation and the frustration of that affectual investment; for by no means are instinctual demands to be satisfied within the analytic setting. What the analyst strives to do is to offer a symbolic mediation which establishes a meaningful link with the emotional investment. In this way the impulse will be conveyed into a structuring activity and not flow back into the depths of the self as yet another negative element to be detached and expelled, thereby perpetuating the old impoverishing circuit. 'At any given moment some particular id-impulse will be in activity, *this* is the impulse that is susceptible of mutative interpretation at that time, and no other one,' writes Strachey.[21] And once more we come to the realization that therapeutic work can be performed with live thoughts alone. There is general agreement that the most extensive intellectual knowledge of psychoanalytic culture does not in itself enhance developmental transformation in the slightest.

Basically an analyst is credited with performing a twofold function: (1) using himself and the setting, he contains the patient so as to provide him with a well-defined space in which he may try out new relational styles in an attempt to break free from the repetitiveness of his constraints, while safe from the risks of an inability to cope; (2) in addition to 'holding' the patient's inner movements, the analyst also intervenes with interpretations. He thus provides the means whereby the analysand may connect any two elements of his inner life exactly when the creative energy of his messages may make the most of the metabolic, interpretative vehicle.

A truly mutative interpretation, as Manfredi Turillazzi suggests, is carried to completion not by backing out of transference but by passing through it in the direction of the subject's innermost structure. For instance, hostility towards the analyst may indicate an attack on an aspect of one's own self; an enlivening interpretation should therefore adequately articulate into consciousness not only that aspect of the mind which is making the attacks but also the part which is being attacked.[22] An interpretation is to be experienced as an event apt to contain conflict, to mediate between any two parts which cannot coexist functionally and which thus quench the subject. Interpretation is precisely a live symbolic response which restores, or creates a path along which to proceed, thereby conveying 'energies' (emotions, feelings, ideas, urges) which might otherwise flare up or neutralize themselves in a paralysing friction.

Strachey observes:

Extra-transference interpretations are far less likely to be given at the point of urgency. This must necessarily be so, since in the case of extra-transference interpretation the object of the id-impulse which is brought into consciousness is not the analyst and is not immediately present.... It follows that extra-transference interpretations tend to be concerned with impulses which are distant both in time and space and are thus likely to be devoid of immediate energy.[23]

In a devitalized context one runs the risk of reinstating a condition of passivity in the patient, who thus will manage, at best, to introject some verbal articulations; such messages will determine pseudo-structures which are of no use for attaining maturity. At most, one may induce introjections of a prevalently imitative nature which in the long run will reinforce a false self; although it may be a socially functioning one, it is of little avail for purposes of overall integrated evolution.

Strachey further stresses the relevance of affects as indispensable factors in any constructive interpretation when he reminds us that the term 'interpretation' is often used in more than one sense; hence, it is perhaps only a way of reasserting the proposition 'Make conscious what is unconscious', so that it ultimately shares the vast ambiguity of that statement. 'For in one sense, if you give a German/English dictionary to someone who knows no German, you will be giving him a collection of interpretations.... Such descriptive interpretations have evidently no relevance to our topic.'[24] Once again, we seem to be dealing with a simple (and not necessarily harmless) pastime revolving around a pseudo-communicative exchange of dead thoughts, in which the words do duty as decoys to divert attention from an unwitting, mutual collusion against authentic listening.

The Interpretative Effort

We may draw inspiration for a progressive clarification of the risk-fraught dynamics implied in the psychoanalytic relationship from the following 'meeting of the minds' between Klein and Strachey:

> Mrs Klein has suggested to me that there must be some quite special internal difficulty to be overcome by the analyst in giving interpretations. And this, I am sure, applies particularly to the giving of mutative interpretations.... All this strongly suggests that the giving of a mutative interpretation is a crucial act for the analyst as well as

for the patient, and that he is exposing himself to some great danger in doing so. And this in turn will become intelligible when we reflect that at the moment of interpretation the analyst is in fact deliberately evoking a quantity of the patient's id-energy while it is alive and actual and unambiguous and aimed directly at himself. Such a moment must above all others put to the test his relations with his own unconscious impulses.[25]

In a conventional, risk-free hermeneutics, pathology may well remain mute and obscure. Psychoanalytic hermeneutics, though, is marked by personal involvement, in the sense that it particularly seeks confrontation with whatever is most opaque and illusive, even threatening. A mechanical, theory-dependent translation can be a mimicry or authentic interpretation, that is the effort to learn someone's language for the purpose of letting it grow together with the person hitherto trapped in his own inadequate vocabulary. And there seems to be no backing away from this prospect as psychoanalysis slowly brings to light the rich nature of interpretation within the relationship; it is the critical moment when the patient's affects are directed towards the analyst who exposes himself to, or even invites, the onslaught of emotions.

Should one manage only later to identify the emotional urgency in a message – for instance while mulling over a segment of analysis or reading over one's notes – it may be argued that the affects directed at the therapist went unidentified for some good enough reason. Possibly a 'short circuit' (in its full metaphoric sense) had to be averted in the analyst's pattern of awareness if the dynamics directed towards him could not be met by an inner organization capable of bearing such loads.

It is often said of the 'neurotic' subject that he does not see certain aspects of reality because of an inability to construct a sufficiently complete array of relations with himself and with others. If the 'neurotic' does not accept certain facts, it is because he cannot face them – affectively and linguistically they are just too burdensome. Whatever may be assumed as regards the afflicted person is equally applicable to the person of the analyst in the sense that his limited ability to pick up a subject's emotional vicissitudes reveals his own shortcomings and fragility. The latter, however, may actually use such failures in order to focus gradually on features of his own inner reality. An analyst may develop his therapeutic potential, not so much by deepening his erudition but rather by striving to organize a more resilient structure of awareness capable of receiving the emotional impact of the patient within the here-and-now of the relationship.

I believe that the transition from 'judging' to listening indicates a shift from a general outlook emanating from a self-sufficient epistemic frame, to a cognitive stance rooted in the effort to negotiate between rival epistemologies, and even migrate from one to another. Unless we have previously engaged in the effort to abandon acquisitive and imitative habits of *having* in favour of the challenging practice of *being*, our proclaimed preference for understanding – with respect to judging – may amount to nothing more than a romanticized version of our favoured epistemology; having and being may, in fact, be connected through vocabularies and theories. The point at issue is the need for a capacity to cross the boundary between 'knowing' (a psychoanalytic language, for instance) and knowing our way around inner suffering.

The ultimate issue to be confronted is the analyst's need to overcome the condition of *having* the notions of holding, neutrality and interpretation, by means of a transformation which allows him to *be* an instrument of containment, acceptance and mediation.

Let us ask what is required of an analyst in order that he can incline towards achieving structural transformations rather than superficial verbal transactions. Which indispensable factors enable an analyst to receive the affects directed towards him and to use them to make an interpretation which leads to a liveable reconnection of isolated meanings? We may also enquire which conditions must obtain if the therapist is no longer to limit himself to grasping emotional intensity and immediacy only *after* an intense surge of emotions is spent. Ultimately, one is perhaps asking the analyst to opt for participation rather than mere 'knowledge of something'. The main component of therapeutic strength may well be the willingness to risk facing the facts of living thought (so as to give live interpretations) and not confine oneself to rehashing extinct, fictitious messages.

Unless genuine participation, which positively welcomes affects expressed under the most varied guises, is supported by structures capable of conducting these affective charges, the relationship's emotional overload may be turned aside by means of certain defensive manoeuvres which are worthless from a mutative point of view. Hence, one of the greatest temptations for the pseudo-psychoanalyst (or for the fictitious part of any analyst) is that of satisfying, in the short term, the patient's entreaties in order to avoid having to deal with them at psychic, analytical level by means of interpretative responses. Any compensatory giving in (ultimately curtailing and inhibitory) actually prevents the establishment of new, symbolic circuitry: it denies and ignores the patient's self-healing impulse, placing him under a primal obligation to acknowledge the analyst's 'superior goodness' – which he finds unacceptable and useless. And so the archaic, most destructive experiences, the very causes of his inadequate relational development, are sadly reconfirmed. Unable to help the patient to transform a frustration of his affective request into an inner structure capable of better organizing his own mind-relations, one may be tempted to give in to his plea, and thus postpone indefinitely his steps towards developmental transformation.

The inadequacy of inner conducting structures ('having' a vocabulary without 'generating' it) could cause the analyst to ignore, shun and therefore fail to take advantage of the living messages directed towards him. Should a therapist not manage to gain awareness of his interpretative shortcomings, there may be a risk of keeping the analysis 'alive' in hibernation, as it were, so that it proceeds as smoothly as when 'good children' are raised in a psychic climate which abhors structural changes and the urge to self-creation.

Unfortunately one may avoid the effort needed in order to respond with adequate interpretation to an affective request simply by admitting verbal exchanges concerning any topic at all, provided the topic is set in such a way as to form a triangular pattern, as it were, which conducts the deeper and more meaningful issues out of the bi-personal field. Within such a defensive triangle one may expatiate on any 'interesting' topic without either risking personal commitment or giving rise to a confrontation. Such peripheral messages may not be regarded as properly symbolic, for they will never be metabolic in the sense of being able to initiate and sustain a growth process. If analyst and patient tend to focus on issues alien to their own dialogue, they are in fact colluding in the avoidance of an understanding of what goes on in their relationship.

The effort required to maintain an adequate level of inner communication proves indispensable to any interpretative work which neither degrades into retaliation or collusion, nor confines itself to returning projections mechanically without letting them resonate in, or flow through, the inner depths of the therapist. Sensing the danger of a too costly inner resonance, one may be tempted simply to hand back projections together with some intellectual comment. The gap between the patient's live messages (even when couched in most defensive terms) and an inanimate pseudo-interpretation might be the unhappy re-edition of the self-same early experiences which failed to allow the emergence of those maturational dynamics to which the patient fervently aspires; for he is not only a person who is suffering, but also and foremost – because he is involved in dialogue – a person who wants to evolve.

Reciprocity in Early Dialogue

The early vicissitudes in one's self-creation, that is the experiences whereby we may become fully human, evince clearly the indelibly relational nature of the human condition. Within the original parent–infant relationship, the critical threshold where one 'changes' from simply being there to existing is closely associated with the events of inchoate self-awareness. Such incipient consciousness could be outlined as follows: self-awareness may only be achieved if somebody else is sufficiently cognizant of our potential for self-awareness. And since it constitutes personal individuality, self-awareness appears to be closely dependent on interpersonal conditions in which we come to recognize ourselves as not only endowed with symbolic capacities for expression (of needs) and for description (of the external reality), but also gifted with metasymbolic faculties capable of awareness of one's inner life and of one's relations with others. Paradoxically, the more such potentials can be described as 'intimate', 'profound', 'subjective', the more their development is dependent upon the quality of the interpersonal relationship in which the change from simply being to existing is either aided or hindered. In fact, it is only if the nascent self is able to perceive himself as a party to a relationship of mutual recognition that he can face the challenge of self-awareness.

Experiences within a relationship alternate between two virtual extremes: each one may perform the role of being recognized while the other acts exclusively as the one recognizing. However, a primal dialogic condition may exhibit an asymmetric disparity between the two persons concerned. In fact, a style may prevail such that the parent, for example, relies upon the recognition offered by the infant who, in his extreme dependence, cannot but turn to the principal source of gratification (howsoever or whatsoever this may be). Conversely, the infant's nascent psychic life may depend mainly upon being recognized by the parent as guarantor of both his existence and his growth. As can be seen in the fluctuation between such extremes, neither of the two exhibits full self-awareness, for each draws on the other's recognition: that is to say, each strives to sustain his personal identity by seeking to perpetuate the condition of being recognized by the other. While in this way one consolidates a 'supremacy' based upon the acknowledgement drawn from the other, there is a growing dependence on this recognition which may culminate in being totally subjected to the other in so far as one is totally dependent on the other's recognition. Social and existential cases wherein survival is possible solely when locked into parental or infantile roles are in fact numerous, disparate and certainly worthy of careful scrutiny. For some humans it seems almost impossible to survive outside a cognitive framework in which they feel contained and sustained by the 'gaze' of some well-established 'ratiocination' functioning as a parental frame which alone grants recognition and the right to function. They seem almost unable to risk being lost sight of by whoever it is that epitomizes the parental role in any cultural context.

Conversely, others may develop a fixation for seeking parental roles. As long as they can stage cultural interactions in which dependent figures look up at them as parental referents, or irreplaceable sources of cognitive life, they may well abandon their own maturational journey; the sufficient condition for their identity may amount to no more than exhibiting features of parental 'authority' however circumscribed.

Inasmuch as it applies to the recognition of only one of the individuals involved, primal asymmetry turns out to be a fictitious situation in early dialogue. Were it a possible condition, the partner used as a source of recognition would be unable to perform the role forced upon him, since his affective and cognitive functioning could not possibly endure without some response from the other; and who would want to be recognized by a 'mentally worthless' being?

If, for example, we force the primal situation to a 'pathological' extreme in which there is no personal requital of the infant's efforts (to be complaisant, admiring and ingratiating) because the parental figure regards him as being solely governed by biological factors, we are drawn to an enigmatic conclusion: paradoxically, the infant, being perceived as a mere biological and not dialogic entity, might well go on existing as such and thereby prove to some degree even independent, while the parental figure would ultimately be incapable of using the infant for the purposes of his own personal recognition. In fact, if the infant is relegated to a biological level, he will never be able effectively to perform the role of the defenceless child 'lovingly' turning to the omnipotent parent (recognizing him), and thus he may not function as a source of recognition for the parent.

The relationship is of no use unless the infant can also seek for himself those same responses that parents may want to elicit from their offspring. Conversely, the extreme hypothetical condition of a child opting for the role of the suckling who only wants to take and who only makes demands of recognition from figures that he tries to force into the fixed roles of providing parents would ultimately turn out to be self-defeating. In fact it would be an outright rejection of his demand that they comply with his primal choice; for it is not known how they could be 'mighty' parents if immobilized in the role that he tries to force upon them. And of course 'parents' and 'children' could be construed as indicating emblematic attitudes which characterize a wide range of cultural practices.

Hence, the onset of a dialogue may not be placed outside a joint interaction of awareness. A facilitating dialogic condition seems to require that each sees that the other is doing just as he himself is doing; within the formative process, the inchoate person (and likewise the parent) strives to behave as he demands of the other to behave, and moreover manages to act as he does only in a setting which is sufficiently symbolic to enable him to *know* that the other is attempting to pursue just the same goal. A unilateral approach seems scarcely effective for maturational purposes, since the transformation of the biological condition into a dialogic function can be achieved primarily through the joint efforts of the partners involved.

Where the symbolic horizon virtually approaches the level of zero, the two 'leading characters' appear as strangers who just happen to be juxtaposed; they neither confront each other in a clash nor extend mutual recognition. Each seems to accord the other a status of indifference, as if he were a thing.

Forming oneself into a person, however, constitutes a step beyond dialogue, inasmuch as it implies advancing, or letting oneself travel, even beyond the symbolic grid which underlies the interactions of a phatic community; for it means subsisting, at least potentially, free of the dynamics of recognition. Clearly the potential for individuation resides in the ability to forgo those linguistic customs as well as those reassuring paradigms which are a guarantee of reciprocity. In dialogue among humans, there seems to be an intrinsic need for each of those involved to prove to the others that he exists as an individual (as a subject and not as an object), that is a person and not a thing. And this may come about through a tension which links the affective and cognitive levels so that the more a subject in the making accepts manageable encounters with the experience of epistemic isolation the more he consolidates his ability to test his creative potential. As coming to face enigmatic situations or radically different symbolizations are occasions involving laborious integration, one is offered the opportunity of organizing an autonomous symbol-generating capacity.

The Dynamics of Challenge

Self-awareness could not be construed as solely dependent upon the recognition of others, however extended it may be. It also rests upon the symbolic language whereby the subject perceives himself; and that vocabulary of self-perception is a truly autonomous and innovative construct, capable of providing an awareness of one's own incipient independence and identity. The most varied and frequent attempts at challenging parental figures, or functions, are dramatically evident during early infancy in the extremely tenacious efforts to define one's own identity and uniqueness. In early experiences a challenge is to be understood as a radical challenge for life. Or, from another point of view, the subject in the making seems engaged in risking the sort of life that he 'despises' as an excessively natural form of being (and hence insufficiently individual). His defiance of danger is therefore a means of defining a break with an excessively natural life (a mere biologic survival) which seems to hinder the development of identity.

In its radical sense, a challenge is ultimately a defiance of death and a confrontation with it. But this by no means implies an inclination for self-destruction. The goal is not extinction but the challenge itself or, more precisely, the radical quality of that challenge. As a biological fact, death is nothing but the negative side of life, and may thus be an overturning of that self-same 'excessively natural' life which is no longer acceptable.

The developmental function of challenge is, however, susceptible to pathological degradation. That susceptibility is closely dependent upon the degree of symbolic awareness and of the pseudosymbolic falsifications which may infiltrate one's standard vocabulary. In fact, the dynamics of challenge may become perverted, in the sense that the effort to achieve a way of life marked by independence and self-awareness may deteriorate into self-destructiveness. Maturational goals are reached by means of the 'thrill' of the challenge and not the 'thud' of destruction; that is to say, they unfold through risk and not through ruination. But what, then, is the essential circumstance which may be eluded and falsified to such an extent as to lead to self-destructiveness instead of inducing the exercise of negation, challenge and risk? What makes possible a maturational outcome from the defiance of danger is probably the tendency of our symbolic function to seek after an inner truth – in the form of an openness towards oneself and towards reality in the making.

Another form of anti-evolutional deterioration in the need for defiance may be seen in the diverse subtle methods of neutralizing any challenge and making it banal, in short a non-challenge. Under such circumstances, one may continually launch and accept challenges while following the most stereotyped and impersonal of vocabularies, precisely those which rule out awareness and creativity. The individual deflates his challenges to the level of conventional games carried on in the context of an anti-evolutional collusion. As a fictitious challenge is a habit which impedes maturation and is therefore falsely symbolized, it seems that it could ultimately be used to ward off the risk of any authentic confrontation.

12

The Maturation of Knowledge

Interactive Dialogue and Awareness

Attitudes of unassailable narcissism – and hence pseudo-interactive outlooks – may be at work in any of the cultural emanations of our thinking. In an attempt to explore the elusive and pervasive features of such an approach we could, for instance, invoke some working model of psychoanalytic dialogue: this we might regard as a possible paradigm-setting wherein the aim is to bring to light and resolve the defensive structures which hinder dialogic contacts with world and persons. Tentatively resorting to such a frame of reference, we may view the figure of the analyst as an interlocutor responsibly engaged in maieutic dialogue – in fostering the birth of thinking.[1]

Narcissistic forms of life may come back into play during psycho-analytic work in conjunction with the need to deny any resurgence of envy *vis-à-vis* the person administering therapy, effort or attention. Envious resentment may at times show through (and hence become utilizable) when there are complaints about the (miserly) attitude of the therapist, when, for example, the subject protests that the analyst, who is 'an expert in the science of the mind', refuses to answer his anguished queries in such a way as to provide a complete solution: although the analyst 'has' such an answer to give, all his responses are contingent and incomplete. The analysand thus wonders why he should put his efforts into analysis and really listen, when anything he ever receives in return is partial and insufficient. As we see it, the main point is to appreciate that such a protest is an indication that the subject's narcissistic enclosure is giving way, while not using it as an opportunity to defend the worth of whatever is being offered. In fact, it is not just a question of being able to recognize the desire for complete possession of the analyst's mind, but also, and in particular, a question of the subject's ability to let his most intense desires show through in understandable form, so that a therapeutic interlocutor may grasp and clarify them. In such a way the subject's healthy core can recognize, with relief, that the overall relational pattern is being understood and that it is even possible to work within the relationship. It is when a narcissistic subject manages neither to engulf nor magically ignore the partner that he may come to perceive that it is possible to strive to make himself understood and even actually *be* understood. Obviously, this is not the end pursued by the omnipotent, narcissistic aspect of human beings. And yet it is not easy to turn a blind eye to the inputs received, nor can these be totally ignored, inasmuch as they have such a close, specific connection with what was desired and not received. Such a subtle, yet crucial, type of clarification is made possible by means of a dialogic alliance with the vital, healthy part of the self. That alliance draws its strength from a well-grounded expectation that the strenuous labour needed in order to penetrate narcissistic defences is also, or primarily, intended to enhance the development of the healthier and more vital aspects of one's inner organization.

In accordance with Rosenfeld's observations,[2] we could note that it is only gradually that a subject allows himself to admit that a refusal to change his outlook may derive from the 'need' to hold on to the idealization of his defensive inner frame, to protect it against any likelihood of 'cracking'. Any admission to this effect may involve suffering or distress which can be eliminated by withdrawing the admission itself, even though there is no denying that the interaction in question, inasmuch as it has induced such awareness, is proof that there is a dialogic relationship of real value.

The disconcerting point is that both suffering and awareness can be eliminated with a single turn to selective blindness which may then perpetuate itself. On any occasion when a subject might opt for an opportunity for self-understanding, and whenever he might forgo triggering projections, he may confront serious danger inasmuch as he has to come to grips with his own feelings of anguish and depression. 'But why should I be the one that disintegrates and sinks?' a person seems to be asking while making his most demanding steps towards maturity. It is at such stringent junctures that a listening presence – that of the analyst, for example – is both essential and decisive; for the deeper meaning of a therapeutic alliance is, in fact, the promise that giving up projective inclinations will be something gradual, contingent, expressible and recognizable. The analyst's word of interpretation is the tie, the safety line which allows the developing self gradually to make efforts to break the spell of envious or idealizing negations. A suffering individual often puts forward all-compassing, overwhelming requests to which the analyst responds with words of interpretation which, on the contrary, almost 'force' the individual into minimal, piecemeal, circumscribed transformations, obviously apt to be condemned and disparaged as being fragmentary, incomplete and insufficient.

With reference to narcissistic conditions, Rosenfeld remarks that 'We discovered that whenever the patient acknowledged any real understanding about himself and tried not to project his feelings, he became anxious and depressed.... I then showed him that what was endangered in such a situation was not his sane or good self but his omnipotent mad self.'[3] Let us ask whether this is enough to show that what is 'endangered' is not a subject's true, live self, but a narcissistic encrustation, or whether, in fact, it will be necessary to provide further 'demonstration'. How can one show or demonstrate all this? And how can we reasonably believe that our demonstration will be accepted or will create any impact at all?

We might attempt some conceptualization of what one is trying to accomplish within any authentic dialogic relationship, or within a specifically therapeutic relation, along the following lines. Permission to commence the laborious work of dismantling is granted by that live, healthy part of the subject which has never been able to make itself heard, and which makes its first appearance by allowing such interaction to spring to life. Were it not for the existence of that part of the self, it would have been impossible even to begin the task of coping with narcissistic propensities inasmuch as the whole enterprise is a response to the first, daring message sent out by the healthier aspect of our inner world. The decisive factor determining the success of the interpretative effort is in fact the creation of contacts with the healthy parts of the self. The person ought to become aware that it is he (by means of the more cognitively sound aspects of the self) who has in some way originated, or allowed, the task of eroding the narcissistic defences. What a therapeutic listener is trying to piece together is a dialogic reply to that 'secret' inter-locutor who is alive and well, but who has never been in a position to speak out or has never succeeded in making himself understood and who, moreover, would be subjected to still further outrage if he were not understood. At the relational juncture brought about within the analytic process through the action of a healthy core, a signal may be given out indicating the time to intervene, almost inviting a dialogic 'loosening', or *dissolution* (according to the etymology of the terms 'analysis' and 'dialysis'), of narcissistic, pseudo-cognitive incrusta-tions. This is a response to a suffering subject who is no longer considered in unrelated abstraction but as one of two partners on a long journey. A patient (*patiens*) in analysis is not just a person who is suffering but, inasmuch as he attempts analysis, primarily a person who wants to know, to become aware – to evolve.

In other words, the gradual dismantling of solipsistic barriers must be lived out knowingly as a vital reply directed to that sounder core of the self which wants to express itself, to get its inner world across to others and get to know the experiential situation as a whole. When all the multifarious elements at hand are being utilized in the thick of the process in order to assemble an interpretative inter-vention capable of striking home, it is often essential to make clear that we are only saying what the analysand is 'forcing' us to say; he is letting us know that all we are doing is providing a response, that in fact it is he who never misses the mark and who offers a perfect pres-entation of his life's experiences for which he demands a mutative answer. He tells himself that the analyst could not answer him with any other interpretation, though the analyst's words might even appear to be 'depressing'. An interpretation is offered inasmuch as the patient's skill at sending messages has put the analyst in a position to understand something of vital importance. In fact the therapist *could not* avoid responding, since it is the subject himself who has skilfully managed to make himself understood. Whatever words may then painfully tear away narcissistic incrustations are only a reply that the analysand himself, priceless ally to the analyst, has been laboriously preparing in advance.

The Development of Otherness

As the 'interest' of the healthy core for the 'ill' part of the mind is being brought to light and as analysis makes use of such cognizance, a patient's awareness of his own dynamics may become more bear-able and viable, inasmuch as a 'bridge' has been built on which such awareness may rest, or over which it may be conducted. Should a dawning awareness prove too painful, it would not be possible to engage in analytic work and the narcissistic pattern could only be made more rigid, almost as if the individual were asserting his own survival above all else and preferred 'illness' to disintegration.

The question that stands out when one is confronting narcissistic attitudes concerns the reasons which make it so unbearable to recognize otherness and dependency, not to mention relational asymmetry, and, consequently, conditions of needing and receiving. One might possibly venture a tentative reply by positing that no sufficient structures have formed within the individual such as are capable of allowing the symbolization and the cognitive realization of interpersonal dimensions; in fact, it is often 'evident' how necessary it is to deny the existence of such dimensions through inexhaustible sequences of narcissistic ploys, from the most tangible to the most abstract.

Dependency and otherness must be denied (or circumvented) for the very good 'reason' that the inner dynamics involved in admitting need cannot be accepted or conceptualized in any way. Even the most impervious, narcissistic pattern thus reveals itself as a survival system used in order to avoid bursting or melting down one's frail internal connections with affectual short circuits. There is nothing to be gained, then, from launching massive verbal messages in an attempt to breach a subject's narcissistic defences. What is called for is action at the microscopic level, offering the symbolic elements that each interaction requires in order to resolve (cope with) the instances of denial and deafness which interpretation is gradually bringing to light.

One of the ploys used for sustaining one's denial of otherness consists in an attempt to merge oneself magically into the other, the analyst – or whoever it may be. A 'narcissist' may cleverly draw upon his intellectual resources in order to frame highly sophisticated, meta-psychological syntheses of the analytic process and thus give the impression of an idyllic agreement or a meeting of minds with the therapist. Under such circumstances one is pitted against a set of genuine intellectual abilities, which are, however, shackled to the magical, reabsorption-seeking aims of dominant narcissism, with the result that any likelihood of a healing or evolutionary relationship is placed in jeopardy. And yet such attempts at intellectual seduction, which tend essentially to slow down any maturational process, reveal their equivocal nature, if we can view them from the standpoint of the symbolic function, specifically with regard to the value of interpretations as symbolic responses to the expression of desires. If the patient has gone into a narcissistic loop which precludes recognizing otherness, his aim is to show that his views substantially match those of the analyst. It is for this purpose that he (astutely, subtly) reiterates the main psychological assumptions deriving from the analyst's interpretations, although of course at a point of discourse removed from the context in which the parties are meeting and clashing. At that point the discourse has relinquished its true symbolic potential, namely that of creating internal bearers of affective and cognitive life. The flow of intellectualizing words used out of context are only pseudosymbols, dead utterances, noise. One almost risks falling victim to the secret weapon of narcissism, while at the same time dimly perceiving a seductive threat: 'See, we agree completely; there are no differences of opinion between you and me and I have understood everything perfectly.' But what we are really facing is an attempt to devitalize the relationship and turn it into waste matter while reducing symbols to a confusing noise. Prudence is truly called for when facing apparently friendly approaches such as these (however subtle and elegant), where one is constantly dealing with the destructive aspect of the subject, its existence being indicated by his profound and irrelated suffering. The efforts put into devitalizing dialogue could thus be construed as a relief from the perils of a relation potentially involving gratitude, dependency, individuation, exchange, negotiation.

In the analysis of persons exhibiting a narcissistic organization of character it often transpires that they picture the relationship as a perfect co-operation, totally satisfying for analyst and patient alike. The bipersonal field could be thus illusively described: 'I co-operate with a fantastic person and I am his ideal patient.' Such a way of construing the 'relationship' is induced by a propensity to run together the separate identities of patient and analyst, a fusion that is, moreover, defensively idealized by proclaiming the relation 'perfect'. This condition may be even more enlightening if viewed in connection with the primal stages of development – when a distinction between any two identities may have been hardly possible. Differentiation entails a capacity to recognize and connect different elements, distinguished by their displacement from one another in time or space. Whenever it is not possible to create the symbolic connection which governs the recognition of otherness and separateness (and a distinction between symmetry and asymmetry), a subject is forced to devise ever new manoeuvres for maintaining a symbiosis marked by an illusory merging of identities and aspirations, which constantly threatens to interfere with development. A subject may tirelessly adjust his own perceptions in such a way as to be able to claim that things could not go better. His aim is in fact to mount a stubborn defence against any gap or discrepancy which might rekindle the primal drama of separation which would necessarily involve the need to create the inner symbolic connections by means of which he may cope with separation itself. Such junctures call for an obstinate patience in seeking out and using even the slightest hint available in order to clarify the obscure interactive and differentiating predicament which none the less continues to unfold between the two. The analyst must be patient. Rosenfeld observes:

> To bring about an improvement, the omnipotent narcissism of the patient and all the aspects related to it have to be laid bare in detail during the analytic process and to be integrated with the more normally concerned part of the patient. It is this part of analysis which seems to be so unbearable. Splitting results again and again when either the normal or the omnipotent parts of the self are denied. Often the attempt at integration fails because mechanisms related to the omnipotent narcissistic self suddenly take over control of the normal self in an attempt to divert or expel the painful recognition.[4]

According to Rosenfeld, therefore, the factor that makes the difference and decides the outcome of any interpretative effort may be traced to the degree of ability or inability to endure 'the painful recognition' that the realistic as well as omnipotent aspects of one's experiential organization actually 'coexist' without being sufficiently integrated.

It is when the development of the symbolic function is enhanced, as by undergoing anew a process of birth and regeneration of consciousness, that supporting structures may be achieved (established) which are capable of bearing the burden of connecting diverse parts of the self. As a symbolic form is precisely that which links and joins together different elements, the relative ability, or inability, to endure the effort (and even the pain) of the analytic process may be seen as depending upon the degree to which the symbolic function has developed. There is no apparent reason, moreover, why an individual ought to make the effort to accept an interpretation if it were only conducive to a harmful affectual short circuit.

Where relations of the narcissistic type tend to prevail, defences are being continuously raised against any recognition of separateness between the self and the object, since the awareness of such separation could induce feelings of dependence – ultimately too difficult to tolerate. Indeed, dependence upon an object, when combined with a nascent awareness of it, does involve a variety of attitudes which may prove too risky and demanding for one's inner mental organization. Feelings of dependency may in fact imply the need to 'love' as well as to recognize the value of the 'other' so that one constantly faces both one's own fear of losing the object together with one's potential 'rage' towards anyone or anything for never allowing itself to be possessed completely – for its being something hopelessly *other* than oneself. But mental events are profoundly and dangerously interwoven with the dynamics of primal envy which flares up anew at the prospect of recognizing the worth of anyone or anything. If we adopt such a hypothesis concerning the primal vicissitudes of our mentation, we may well suppose that a subject may have patterned himself in an unrelated, narcissistic manner for the purpose of eliminating, in illusory fashion, both the intrusion of aggressiveness towards an object which proves obstinately other than the self and the emergence of envy for an object which is none the less needed and longed for.

Let us now turn to the basic issue which also constitutes our central concern thoughout the work, and ask how the formation of symbols interacts with such vicissitudes and why the impending awareness of separation and envy may turn out to be so unbearable. Invoking these two questions, which to some extent imply one another, we shall be in a better position to identify the specific function of symbols in relation to the primal issue of separation and envy. A recognition of separateness is unacceptable to the extent that such a prospect is unbearable; in order to be capable of enduring a loss, an inchoate self must be prepared to forge the tools with which to 'feel regret' for what may be lost and to establish some sort of inner reference to something which has previously been present and has subsequently vanished. It is specifically when one is capable of experiencing some conscious attachment to an object that this becomes in some sense 'recoverable', somehow meaningfully substituted or symbolized. Symbols constitute the cognitive tools with which one compensates for loss and thereby achieves a better position for bearing the separation-loss of the object. As the ability to endure detachment develops, the conditions arise that enable one to enjoy a relationship, namely a connection with something unexpectedly *other* than oneself, something which gradually grows into a concreteness of its own – an entity in its own right.

As has been suggested, primal envy exhibits such narcissistic features that any feeling of envy which invades the inchoate mind spreads indefinitely throughout it, inducing an undifferentiated space-time dimension; such envy is unconditional and absolute. Conceived of as a bridge connecting any two different elements, a symbol can thus join up two well-defined, exact 'points', which, when connected, form a link that spans across any overwhelming stream of envious emotions. The symbolic process thus springs to life as a function of mentation capable of eroding and neutralizing conditions of invasive primal envy.

From the Flow of 'Emotion' to the Exchange of Communications

A subject involved in analysis, or even in a variety of other relations, may come to 'feel better' thanks to the opportunity of being understood, a condition in which his 'thoughts' course smoothly through his partner, who functions as a container capable of absorbing the stream of emotions emanating from deep affects. It is thus as if there were nothing interpersonal in the bipersonal field and as if the other person were a 'physiological' extension of the self, or even its mirror image. In the myth, Narcissus mirrors himself in the pool, delighting in his own idealized image until he actually drowns in it, with the result that his idealized reflection ultimately turns into a fatal narcosis. The fact that the term 'narcissism' may be traced etymologically to the root *narche*,[5] from which 'narcosis' also derives, may help us towards a better insight into the significance of such tragic cognitive torpor which threatens humans at large and which may even bind our linguistic forms of life into ways of extinction.

The danger implied in any such pseudo-relational situation is that a subject may be unaware of the dynamics at work, in the sense that the situation could appear to be no more than a smoother flow of emotional traffic, inasmuch as the psychic means for containment are being supplemented by the availability and participation of the analyst, or of any other partner. A subject may fail to realize the situation and thus confine himself to the experience of a transient relief which is not in itself sufficient to determine an authentic advancement in inner growth. A therapeutic presence may be decisive inasmuch as it induces in the patient some measure of awareness of the ongoing situation. A person may thus attempt to respond to the understanding shown him by the other and he will do so to the extent that he becomes aware of receiving something, and of benefiting from the understanding of someone who is laboriously revealed as something *other* than the patient himself. It is only by responding in some way to the event of his being understood that a subject may begin to function independently and moreover realize that he does have a mind which can work in such a way as to grasp both personal and interpersonal occurrences. During analytic dialogue a subject might exclaim that 'of course he certainly understands' or that 'the interpretation is abundantly clear', and immediately switch to some other absorbing topic in order to avoid processing inwardly (actually assimilating) the awareness of having received something – an interpretation, for instance. It is almost as if he were asserting that he has understood the situation perfectly well so as not to have to go any further, recognize anything more, and thus postpone the labour of developing his own symbolic structure, which is the main support in the advancement towards a realization of otherness.

'Narcissists' may experience considerable irritation when they perceive that they are being drawn towards a realization of the awareness that there is a dual condition wherein somebody-other-than-oneself is participating intelligently in his own inner life. It is when an individual is brought to understand something (that he was previously unable to grasp) through the wise utilization of his own inputs that his emotional suffering may paradoxically grow intense. A subject's rage may be overwhelming and subtle at the juncture where he is preparing to make his way from the unwitting use of persons (which might be conceived of as the condition of a suckling infant) to an inner cognition (a visualization, almost) of the variety of relational modes between the self and others.

If in the course of analysis a subject offers a profusion of dreams or detailed narrations of events, this does not necessarily imply the development of a mutative evolutional relationship; it is possible that the subject's latent confusion is just overbrimming his mental margins, while he has the illusory belief that he is even 'feeding' and enriching his listener. The risk is that the overflowing person may perpetuate a confused condition wherein he is unable to distinguish his own workings from the way in which others function, under the infantile illusion that he is offering precious gifts, whereas he is unwittingly using his neighbour as a conduit for what is going on inside himself, his own inner structures not being up to the task. A psychic extension of his mind is magically constituted.

It does not serve the purposes of maturation to repeat such symbiotic conditions unless there is the added ingredient of a growing insight into the different roles played by the persons involved: an increased understanding that it is an asymmetrical relation wherein, for example, one of the two provides a suitable container into which the other brims over. When consciousness requires an effort such as this, there is an escalation in the number of attacks intended to confound the bipersonal field, to be reabsorbed in regressive fusion and to keep things at the level of mere utilization. By so doing one avoids the labours of forming 'organs of awareness' through which alone one may perceive the asymmetrical relationship between oneself and others, recognize one's need for others and become responsible for the quality of events. And one way of becoming responsible is to assimilate and metabolize the interpretations offered.

The cost of accepting one's dependence is quite high, because it involves an inner restructuring that can bring out an awareness of the dependency context itself. At this point, in fact, we might conjecture (suspect) the influence of regressive factors capable of luring the mind into the most grandiose and unreal of imitative fictions and of inducing illusions that allow any danger of developmental learning to be warded off. We are sometimes faced with an output of imitative pseudosymbolizations which are absolutely devoid of any constructive value. It is almost as if the symbolic dimension acquired by humans were used by a destructive form of narcissism as a clandestine mint for coining an immense, counterfeit wealth. What is involved is an inexhaustible supply of fake symbols, or diabols: through their grandiosity and their overwhelming numbers, they are capable of wiping out relational, symbolic ties. In any case, they ultimately impoverish the subject, reducing him to a fiction drained of any life. Deceived by his own pseudosymbolic fictions, a subject can do no more than to replace one falsehood with another and go on to stage further (linguistic) fakes.

Let us ask how we could illustrate the characteristics of such a crucial dialogic confrontation, which is to be faced by the person in whom therapeutic trust has been placed. In the more serious cases of narcissistic trends, fictional grandiosity is not to be regarded in isolation, as if it were something uprooted from the interaction; were this to be done, there would be a risk of calmly discounting the utterances of the suffering person inasmuch as they may come across as something unusable: while their content is possibly valueless in itself, it is quite precious as an element suited to bringing out the paradigm of the relationship. Under different circumstances an interlocutor might submit to such manifestations passively and (or) with hostility; relations along such lines can achieve little more than to bring a transient relief to one's emotional turmoil – a lull which occurs as a result of the mere process of the ebb and flow of affects. A person will keep exercising his unique maieutic role as long as he is able to pick up the meta-communications within communication, in other words, as long as he is capable of grasping the personal meaning of the messages borne out by those apparently 'mad' expressions. The analyst takes up the challenge offered by the vital core within the patient, that is to say by the very ally which allows what is false to be traced and removed from the pseudosymbolic wrapping in which it is swathed. The challenge is a serious one and not just verbal fencing, for whenever one points to the 'falsity' of a subject's narcissistic defences one risks having to cope with the anger triggered by the interpretative work, which nevertheless continues to be the foundation upon which the survival of the relationship rests. When something happens to disturb the subject's solipsistic gazing at himself in the interlocutor-mirror, his narcissistic parts may actually become irate, so to speak; such mirroring is in fact uncognitive and ultimately benumbs the self. Authentic listening threatens to disturb such a condition. If the analyst fails to recognize the false omnipotence in a subject's narcissistic organization, if he does not take up the challenging invitation to recognize its falsity, then he will truly be abandoning the subject by letting him mentally drown. The subtle 'voice' of a live co-operative self confers upon the analyst the task of understanding that, whenever anger and discomfort are expressed, it is not just a question of personal emanations but of a 'secret message'; it is up to the analyst to seize upon it as possible evidence of the subject's suffering. And yet, when a patient comes to accept that the other is perceiving, sorting and making connections at a symbolic level, he may eventually begin to make creative use of this understanding on his own behalf.

The heavier attacks intended to knock the analyst off balance are encountered particularly in cases where there is an attempt to recognize one's dependence upon analytic work. And if the therapist's patient work of interpretation comes to be dimly perceived as the main thing behind the subject's efforts to make inner transformations, the attacks may become especially astute and insidious, intended as they are to throw the listener's ability into disarray. But if the offensive is interpreted as a message emanating from a bipersonal field created by such an 'impossible' but authentic dialogue, then the task of transforming a flow of emotion into a flow of information (of progressing from a biological level to a dialogic dimension) will be performed; this is beneficial to the development of the self, given that an emotional experience may be transformed, as result, into an inner structure of cognitive connections. The latter opportunity may well heighten a subject's rage, as he may realize that the interlocutor is not doing what he is trying to force him into doing, namely to 'retaliate' with a mirror-image escalation of provocations – or collusions – which would pervert and annihilate the progress of symbol-formation. There is no place, therefore, for a sterile, irrelated disposition in interpretative work, since interpretation is performed solely by dint of intense, personal effort.

Mechanisms of Splitting and Deterioration of Cognitive Life

According to Strachey, it is evident that there is a 'lesser' sense in which a patient can become conscious of an unconscious trend; he can be made aware of it by the analyst in some intellectual manner, without becoming 'really' aware of it, and it is at this point that the practical lesson emerges: the main task of the analyst is not so much to investigate the unacceptable unconscious trend as to get rid of the patient's resistance to it.[6] Such resistance may possibly be conceived of as a state permeated by a constant dissipative tendency which hinders integration of the self.

Once again invoking Strachey's thesis as regards interpretation, notably where he would have it that during transference vicissitudes a patient chooses a new solution whereby his earlier strategies of suppression are replaced by more integrated behaviour, we should recall these incisive remarks:

> But if we bring it about that in this revivified transference conflict the patient chooses a new solution instead of the old one, a solution in which the primitive and unadaptable method of repression is replaced by behaviour more in contact with reality, then, even after his detachment from analysis, he will never be able to fall back into his former neurosis. The solution of the transference conflict implies the simultaneous solution of the infantile conflict of which it is a new edition.[7]

Expressions indicating the prospect of 'never' falling back into former difficulties and of 'simultaneous' solution of conflicts manifestly bear witness to Strachey's clinical convictions. And yet in a secondary fashion, however, they also point to a more general necessity of a joint approach to cognition and affects. The issue is whether we can derive knowledge from emotions and recognize affectual components in our reasoning. And the question, moreover, is how to bring about a transition from dynamics which are apparently disruptive (those, for instance, which detach experience and feeling) to ways of functioning which are prevalently aimed at integration and to ever new symbolic linkages.

When primal splitting during the subject's ontogenetic history has prevailed outright, and no mitigating symbolic instruments have been established, subsequent dynamics of suppression will be likely to prove both extensive and pathogenous, because processes of fragmentation and segregation will come to prevail in our mentation and the ego itself will be subtly bound by anti-vital deadening inclinations. While we recognize that splitting and suppression are none the less essential features of development, we may construe that, when symbolization renders splitting less rigid, the ensuing suppression will not prove excessively damaging to the mind's equilibrium. As a result the unconscious and instinctual sources of 'energy' will be better able to communicate with the conscious mind, thus providing opportunities for the latter's enrichment; the origin of such enrichment being, above all, a laborious recovery of the deep-seated layers of mentation. Indeed, as Rosenfeld suggests in regard to the destructive aspects of narcissism, when a subject gradually acquires the ability to use the healthy part of himself in order to establish a dialogic relation, he will also be in a position to attempt to become aware of (and thus monitor) the more omnipotent and destructive aspects of his own personality. Such aspects may in hidden ways dominate a subject's whole mental life, and the extent of their power is possibly directly proportionate to the degree to which destructive aspects are covert and isolated. The clandestine, secret nature of a subject's destructive trends is antithetic to the symbolic function, which is the basic means for establishing inner connections; we may therefore claim that the destructive aspects of narcissism are ways of functioning which oppose the symbolic function. As analysis creatively and constructively uncovers those parts of a subject which are split and deadening, a patient becomes gradually cognizant of being ruled by an infantile and omnipotent part of his own self which not only pulls in destructive directions but also incessantly infantilizes and impedes growth.[8]

We believe that it is due to the action of such archaic narcissistic factors that violent, repeated attacks are aimed against every form of linkage between life and daily experience, digital performance and analogic functions, between 'past' and 'present', events and achievements, destiny and responsibility. Such disconnections, moreover, are permanently vulnerable to obscurity.

Besides being ruthless in their degradation of the mind's life, destructive drives which in covert fashion may gain control of thought are downright mesmerizing inasmuch as they tighten their hold by promising perfection, grandeur, ultimate solutions aimed at overshadowing the modest course open before those patiently seeking provisional and contingent truths. If we could illustrate our point through analogy, what readily comes to mind are criminal organizations which lure their recruits by dangling glittering prospects of gains before them: members are induced into an infantile dependency which is almost invariably as detrimental as the false promise is high; and the promises may range from very practical to highly 'philosophical' types of gains.

Whatever their nature, such organizations can only operate in absolute secrecy or by completely and drastically concealing their ultimate senseless aims. In fact, the most sadistic reprisals are directed against those who attempt any dialogic venture or those who try to see things in their full perspective. The basic rule in a 'criminal' code of conduct is in fact not to breathe a word, not to ask for explanations, to return gradually into a 'morbid' infancy in the strict etymological sense of *infans*, he who does not speak – a return, as it were, to being someone who keeps silent or forsakes the chance of authentic linguisticity.

Chronic resistances that deride or underrate the travails of dialogue could thus be seen as offensive manoeuvres developed by destructive aspects of narcissism. This pervasive hostility is manifested through condescension towards interlocutors, its purpose being to attack symbolic connections, to annul the worth of dialogue, to cut through it inasmuch as it is a symbolization which links diverse elements. It would be difficult, otherwise, to understand how a good interpretation of the relationship, really just a few unassuming words, could release such a massive aggressive response intended to wrench the self away from every inchoate attachment to persons and thoughts and to absorb everything into the reflection of Narcissus' lethal mirror.

An analyst, therefore, will often find himself 'seduced' into doing almost anything at all, as long as he can avoid practising psychoanalysis: doing anything at all as long as the subject can remain infantile and mute, accepting any idealized distortion of the relationship as long as the real interactions at work are not symbolized. Every kind of concrete assistance will be requested, provided that symbols, as tools for communicating both inwardly and with persons, do not spring to life in order to attempt a change of course. Within a therapeutic relationship, some menacing, seductive kernel goes as far as to say: 'If you don't provide me with the compensations I want, I'll break off dialogue, because it means you couldn't care less.' The stakes are high: it is a question of leaving behind disruptive degradation in favour of more vital ways of symbolization.

Towards a Notion of Symbolic Integration

The celebrated remark of Freud, 'Where id was, there ego shall be,'[9] is not to be construed as referring 'quantitatively' to a territorial ego extension, as if rational faculties were progressively gaining ground at the expense of the instinctual, unconscious side. What it refers to is rather the ultimate aim of analytic work, namely the effort to create developmental propensities such that integration may prevail over pathogenous mechanisms of splitting. The 'antithesis' is not between the conscious and the unconscious, I believe, but between a potentially coherent self and mechanisms of splitting. The essential point is that the nature of that which is suppressed is characterized not by its condition of unconsciousness (although in fact it *is* unconscious) but, much more importantly, by the fact that it is detached as well as unwittingly segregated from the integrated mind.

Processes of internalization are directed towards progressive overall integration, whereas suppression, denial, repression – generally speaking – fight against any such coherent mental organization, by keeping a share of the mind's life at primitive, less organized levels of functioning.

Invoking the analogy of metabolic processes, such integration involves a destruction of primitive affective and cognitive approaches into their elements and an inner reorganization of these parts with a different setting implemented by symbolic links, so that novel but in some way related structures may evolve. Thus language, according to Cassirer, 'becomes one of the human spirit's basic implements, by which we progress from the world of mere sensation to the world of intuition and ideas. It contains in germ that intellectual effort which is afterwards manifested in the formation of scientific concepts.... Here lies the beginning of a universal function of separation and association.[10]

As Loewald points out, the maturing ego, rather than defending itself against threatening contents by means of suppression, will at times summon its resources in order to accept, resymbolize and internalize vicissitudes into its own cognitive pattern. How does defence by suppression come to be replaced by acceptance? What really 'happens' is that our whole outlook shifts as soon as we adopt the perspective of our *potential* for cognitive and affective development. Inasmuch as we speak of cognition as the function which might tend to include rather than to exclude, to represent rather than to distort, our perspective will necessarily be referred to the mind's urge for assimilative integration – our 'natural' epistemophily.

Seen in this perspective, we might suggest that any form of linguisticity which maintains mental processes at lower integrative levels – where no interepistemic questions are to be asked – is under the sway of destructive forces (however these may be conceptualized or imagined in human cultures), while symbolic internalization, in so far as it enhances an enriched mentation, is motivated by life forces, however these may be articulated. And such a view, of course, allows for a share of the other polar trend in both propensities.

The infusion of affect into thinking and the extraction of thoughts out of emotions entail that the exploration of our deep inner life through 'rational' means provides our ratiocination with an inexhaustible source of knowledge. Our deep mental life is possibly unfathomable and the venture of symbolizing it in such a way that some of its primal force is transferable into cognition is truly an immense prospect.

Symbol-formation could be construed as a continuous extraction (by whatever mental structures we have achieved) of ever new possibilities deriving from unconscious domains of mental life. Conversely, we could suggest that our profound 'being' pours into our cognitive life to the extent that symbolic channels are created for this vital process.

Notes

Chapter 1   Language and Symbolization

1   P. Filiasi Carcano, *Introduzione alla lettura del 'Tractatus' di Wittgenstein* (Rome: Editrice De Santis, 1966), p. 26.

2   D. Davidson, *Inquiries into Truth and Interpretation* (Oxford: Clarendon Press, 1985), p. 280.

3   L. Wittgenstein, *Remarks on the Philosophy of Psychology*, vol. 1 (Oxford: Basil Blackwell, 1980), p. 157e, para. 891.

4   'Ontology recapitulates philology' (J. G. Miller) is quoted as an introductory remark in W. V. O. Quine, *Word and Object* (Cambridge, Mass.: MIT Press, 1981).

5   B. L. Whorf, *Language, Thought and Reality: selected writings of Benjamin Lee Whorf*, ed. J. B. Carroll (Cambridge, Mass: MIT Press, 1973), p. 156.

6   E. Cassirer, *The Philosophy of Symbolic Forms*, vol. 1: *Language* (New Haven, Conn., and London: Yale University Press, 1953–5).

7   P. Ricoeur, *Freud and Philosophy: an essay on interpretation* (New Haven, Conn.: Yale University Press, 1972), p. 10.

8   Ibid., p. 10.

9   W. V. O. Quine, *Ontological Relativity and Other Essays* (New York: Columbia University Press, 1969), p. 1. Quoted with reference to the chapter entitled 'Speaking of objects' in Davidson, *Inquiries into Truth and Interpretation*, p. 191.

10   *National Geographic*, official journal of the National Geographic Society (Washington, DC), 174, 6 (December 1988).

11   *Dialogue*, a quarterly journal of significant thought and opinion on social, political, economic and cultural issues in the United States (US Information Agency, Washington, DC), 3 (1989).

12   Quine, *Ontological Relativity*, p. 1.

13   Ibid., p. 1.

14   G. Ryle, *Dilemmas: the Tarner Lectures 1953* (Cambridge: Cambridge University Press, 1966), p. 11. In a preceding passage Ryle says: 'Sometimes thinkers are at loggerheads with one another, not because their propositions do conflict, but because their authors fancy that they conflict. They suppose themselves to be giving, at least by indirect

implication, answers to the same questions, when this is not really the case. They are then talking at cross-purposes with one another.'

15   L. Wittgenstein, *Philosophical Investigations* (Oxford: Basil Blackwell, 1988), p. 122e, para. 402. Possibly arguing to a similar effect, Quine remarks that 'issues are connected with surface irritations in such multifarious ways, through ... a maze of intervening theory'. Quine, *Word and Object* (Cambridge, Mass.: MIT Press, 1981), p. 276.

16   On this issue, see R. Rorty, *Philosophy and the Mirror of Nature* (Oxford: Basil Blackwell, 1980), Introduction, esp. p. 6.

17   'And is it complicated? Well it is complicated a bit; but life and truth and things do tend to be complicated. It is not things, it's philosophers that are simple.' J. L. Austin, *Philosophical Papers* (Oxford: Clarendon Press, 1961), p. 239.

18   Cassirer, *The Philosophy of Symbolic Forms*, vol. 1: *Language*, pp. 85–6.

19   L. Lugarini, 'Cassirer e il compito di fondazione delle scienze umane', *Il Pensiero*, 2 (1967), pp. 142–61.

20   P. A. Schilpp (ed.), *The Philosophy of G. E. Moore*, The Library of Living Philosophers, vol. 4 (La Salle, Ill.: Northwestern University and Southern Illinois University, 1968), p. 14.

21   Cassirer, *The Philosophy of Symbolic Forms*, vol. 1: *Language*, p. 77.

22   See chapter 7, 'Pseudosymbolic Language', pp. 80–108.

23   Cassirer, *The Philosophy of Symbolic Forms*, vol. 1: *Language*, p. 76.

24   As is known, the central notion of Goodman's theory of symbols is that of 'reference'; he regards reference as a 'primitive term covering all sorts of symbolization, all cases of standing-for'. N. Goodman, *Languages of Art: an approach to a theory of symbols* (Indianapolis and Cambridge: Hackett, 1976), p. 55. See also *Ways of World Making* (Indianapolis: Hackett, 1978) and *Of Mind and Other Matters* (Cambridge, Mass.: Harvard University Press, 1984).

25   'Talk of ordinary physical things he [our philosopher] would then see as, in principle, a device for simplifying that disorderly account of the passing show. But this is a misleading way of depicting matters, even when the idea of a sense-datum "language" is counted frankly as metaphor. Quine, *Word and Object*, p. 2.

26   'The ostensive teaching of words can be said to establish an association between the word and the thing.' Wittgenstein, *Philosophical Investigations*, p. 4e, para. 6.

27   The word *symbol* derives from *syn* ('together', 'with', 'according to') and *bolon* ('that which has been thrown'; from *ballo*: 'I throw'). During the classical Greek period *syn* was mainly used by poets, while in ordinary language the word *meta* was also employed to mean 'with' or 'together'. *Meta* was also used in combination with *ballo*: hence *metabol*. But here the original meaning of 'throwing together' has developed into that of 'turning into', 'changing', 'substitution'. In my opinion, only symbols can be metabols, and only vicissitudes which are sufficiently symbolized can

be metabolized in a process of growth. A pseudosymbolic process which has the appearance of symbolism but is not conducive to construction and fruition is 'diabolic' in the etymological sense of the word: the Greek verb *diaballo* is a compound of the word *dia* ('across') and the above-mentioned verb *ballo*. Hence a 'diabol' is something that flings things across and, as a consequence, jumbles them up. I suggest, therefore – trying to be closer to the vital complexities of the symbolic function – that linguisticity is symbolic when we have activities which lead to a fuller appreciation of reality and that, in so far as this is carried out, the activity is also a truly metabolic one, a vital one. Pseudosymbols are diabolic in the sense that they cannot possibly be metabolic. On this topic, see chapter 10.

28 Whorf, *Language, Thought and Reality*, p. 52.
29 L. Wittgenstein, *Tractatus Logico-Philosophicus* (London: Routledge & Kegan Paul; New York: The Humanities Press, 1961), paras 2.021, 2.03 and 3.32.
30 P. Filiasi Carcano, *Introduzione alla lettura di 'Ricerche filosofiche' di Wittgenstein* (Rome: Bulzoni, 1976), p. 116.
31 On the notion of 'use' and 'consumption' of language, see F. Rossi Laudi, *Il linguaggio come lavoro e come mercato* (Milan: Bompiani, 1968).

Chapter 2   The Concept of Linguistic Community

1 M. Masterman discusses Kuhn's multiple definition of a paradigm and points out that 'it has got to be a concrete picture' used analogically, 'because it has got to be a "way of seeing"'. M. Masterman, 'The nature of a paradigm', in *Criticism and the Growth of Knowledge*, ed. I. Lakatos and A. Musgrave, Proceedings of the International Colloquium in the Philosophy of Science (London, 1965) vol. 4 (Cambridge: Cambridge University Press, 1970), p. 59.

2 'When you are criticizing the philosophy of an epoch do not chiefly direct your attention to those intellectual positions which its exponents feel it is necessary explicitly to defend. There will be some fundamental assumptions which adherents of all the variant systems within the epoch *unconsciously* presuppose. Such assumptions appear so obvious that people do not know what they are assuming because no other way of putting things has ever occurred to them. With these assumptions a certain limited number of types of philosophic systems are possible, and this (group of systems) constitutes the philosophy of the epoch.' A. N. Whitehead, *Science and the Modern World* (New York: Macmillan, 1924), ch. 3, 'The century of genius'; quoted in S. Langer, *Philosophy in a New Key: a study in the symbolism of reason, rite and art* (Cambridge, Mass., and London: Harvard University Press, 1979), pp. 4–5 (italics added).

3 'Scientists work from models acquired through education ... often without quite knowing or needing to know what characteristics have given
these models the status of *community paradigms*. And because they do so,
they need no full set of rules.' T. S. Kuhn, *The Structure of Scientific
Revolutions*, 2nd edn (Chicago and London: University of Chicago Press,
1970), p. 46 (italics added).

4 M. Dummett, *Truth and Other Enigmas* (London: Duckworth, 1978),
p. 452 (italics added).

5 ' "So you are saying that human agreement decides what is true and
what is false?" – It is what human beings *say* that is true and false; and
they agree in the *language* they use. That is not agreement in opinions
but in form of life.' L. Wittgenstein, *Philosophical Investigations* (Oxford:
Basil Blackwell, 1988), p. 88e, para. 241 (italics in the text).

6 'To say of man, in Moore's sense, that he *knows* something; that what
he says is therefore unconditionally the truth, seems wrong to me. –
It is the truth only inasmuch as it is an *unmoving* foundation of his
language-games.' L. Wittgenstein, *On Certainty* (Oxford: Basil Blackwell, 1979), p. 52e, para. 403 (italics added).

7 Dummett, *Truth and Other Enigmas*, p. 452.

8 E. Cassirer, *The Philosophy of Symbolic Forms*, vol. 1: *Language* (New
Haven, Conn., and London: Yale University Press, 1953–5), p. 87.

9 Ibid., p. 89.

10 Kuhn, *The Structure of Scientific Revolutions*, p. 109.

11 Ibid., p. 46.

12 On this problem, see ibid., ch. 3, 'The nature of normal science', pp.
23–34, and ch. 5, 'The priority of paradigms', pp. 43–51.

13 Ibid., p. 42.

14 B. L. Whorf, *Language, Thought and Reality: selected writings of Benjamin
Lee Whorf*, ed. J. B. Carroll (Cambridge, Mass.: MIT Press, 1973),
pp. 152–3.

15 L. Wittgenstein, *Culture and Value* (Oxford: Basil Blackwell, 1980), p. 7e
(1948).

16 See Kuhn, *The Structure of Scientific Revolutions*, ch. 6, 'Anomaly and the
emergence of scientific discoveries', pp. 52–65, and ch. 8, 'The response
to crisis', pp. 77–91.

17 M. Bunge, 'The maturation of science', in *Problems in the Philosophy of
Science*, ed. I. Lakatos and A. Musgrave (Amsterdam: North Holland,
1968), p. 120.

18 Whitehead, *Science and the Modern World*, quoted in Langer, *Philosophy in
a New Key*, pp. 4–5 (italics added).

19 See B. McGuinness, 'Freud and Wittgenstein', in *Wittgenstein and his
Times*, ed. B. McGuinness (Oxford: Basil Blackwell, 1982), pp. 27–43.

20 Wittgenstein, *Culture and Value*, p. 62e (1947).

21 Ibid., p. 62e (1947).

22 On this topic, see G. Corradi Fiumara, *The Other Side of Language: a*

philosophy of listening (London: Routledge, 1990), esp. ch. 4, 'The power of discourse and the strength of listening', ch. 8, 'Dialogic interaction and listening', ch. 10, 'Midwifery and philosophy', and ch. 11, 'Paths of listening'.

23 Wittgenstein, *Culture and Value*, p. 2e (1929) (italics added).

24 Ibid., p. 52e (1946).

25 On this issue, see chapter 11, 'From Biological Life to Dialogic Relations'.

26 Wittgenstein, *Culture and Value*, p. 44e (1944).

27 Ibid., p. 76e (1948).

28 Ibid., p. 80e (1949).

29 Kuhn, *The Structure of Scientific Revolutions*, p. 115.

30 Ibid., p. 115.

31 L. Wittgenstein, *Tractatus Logico-Philosophicus* (London: Routledge & Kegan Paul; New York: The Humanities Press, 1961), p. 188, para. 7.

32 This is a transformation of the celebrated remark: 'What we cannot speak about we must pass over in silence.' Wittgenstein, *Tractatus Logico-Philosophicus*, p. 151, para. 7. We also read in the author's preface: 'What can be said at all can be said clearly, and what we cannot talk about we must pass over in silence.' Ibid., p. 3.

33 C. H. Hamburg, *Symbol and Reality: studies in the philosophy of Ernst Cassirer* (The Hague: Martinus Nijhoff, 1956), pp. 138–9. In this connection he remarks: 'To be sure, one can fail to be logical, and to that extent one will fail to communicate effectively. But interpreted analytically, the maxim merely expresses the conditional that if one cannot use language in conformity to criteria of consistency, then one cannot expect to make logical sense. It does not, however, legislate that we cannot use language in any other way.' Ibid., p. 139.

34 'If "whereof one cannot speak" refers to the semantical impossibility of either having words or of so using them that they clearly designate some state of affairs, then the implication that "one must be silent" is either tautologous or false. It is tautologous, since the lack of direct or indirect linguistic expressions is synonymous with "being silent"; it is false, since the lack of clearly designative expressions has never yet prevented individuals from using language for other than designative purposes. What the proponents of the dictum may want to assert is likely to be something else.' Ibid., p. 139.

35 'We conclude that the prescriptive maxim under consideration is not itself an example of the type of language-use which it prescribes. The self-liquidating consequence can be avoided only if value expressions also are accommodated within the privileged class of those cognitively respectable propositions "whereof one can speak".' Ibid., p. 140.

36 R. Carnap, *Philosophy and Logical Syntax* (London: Kegan Paul, Trench,

Trubner & Co., 1935), p. 28. His well-known remark is worth reporting in full: 'Many linguistic utterances are analogous to laughter in that they have only an expressive function. Examples of this are cries like "Oh, Oh" or, on a higher level, lyrical verses.... Metaphysical propositions are neither true nor false, because they assert nothing.... But they are, like laughing, lyrics and music, expressive. They express not so much temporary feelings as permanent emotional and volitional dispositions.'

37 Langer, *Philosophy in a New Key*, p. 86.
38 Ibid., p. 88. B. L. Whorf, for instance, remarks: 'Science is beginning to find that there is something in the cosmos that is not in accord with the concepts we have formed in mounting the spiral. It is trying to frame a *new language* by which to adjust itself to a wider universe.' *Language, Thought and Reality*, p. 154.
39 Ibid., p. 251.
40 In this connection Whorf argues: 'From the form-plus-substance dichotomy the philosophical views most traditionally characteristic of the "Western world" have derived huge support. Here belong materialism, psychophysical parallelism, physics – at least in its traditional Newtonian form – and dualistic views of the universe in general. Indeed here belongs almost everything that is "hard, practical common sense". Monistic, holistic, and relativistic views of reality appeal to philosophers and some scientists, but they are badly handicapped in appealing to the "common sense" of the Western average man – not because nature herself refutes them (if she did, philosophers could have discovered this much), but because they must be talked about in what amounts to a new language.' Ibid., p. 152.
41 'This language grew as it did because human beings had – and have – the tendency to think in this way. So you can only succeed in extricating people who live in an instinctive rebellion against language; you cannot help those whose entire instinct is to live in the herd which has created this language as its own proper mode of expression.' L. Wittgenstein, Big Typescript MS 213, 423, in G. H. von Wright, 'The Wittgenstein Papers', *Philosophical Review*, 79, (1969), pp. 483–503; quoted in A. Kenny, 'Wittgenstein on the nature of philosophy', in *Wittgenstein and his Times*, ed. B. McGuinness (Oxford: Basil Blackwell, 1982), p. 16.
42 It may be worth recalling that 'The great witch-hunt can in fact be taken as a supreme example of a massive killing of innocent people by a bureaucracy acting in accordance with beliefs which, unknown or rejected in earlier centuries, had come to be taken for granted, as self-evident truth. It illustrates vividly both the power of human imagination to build up a stereotype and its reluctance to question the validity of a stereotype once it is generally accepted.' N. Cohn, *Europe's Inner Demons: an enquiry inspired by the great witch-hunt* (London: Chatto/Heinemann for Sussex University Press, 1975), p. 255.

Chapter 3   On Language and Reality

1   A. Danto, *Analytical Philosophy of Knowledge* (Cambridge and London: Cambridge University Press, 1968), p. 176 ff.

2   E. Cassirer, *The Philosophy of Symbolic Forms*, vol. 1: *Language* (New Haven, Conn., and London: Yale University Press, 1953–5), p. 319.

3   P. Filiasi Carcano, *Introduzione allo studio della filosofia linguistica: guida alla lettura dei 'Principi della filosofia linguistica' di Waismann* (Rome: Bulzoni, 1972), p. 45.

4   J. L. Austin, *Philosophical Papers* (Oxford: Clarendon Press, 1961) p. 89.

5   K. Popper, *Objective Knowledge: an evolutionary approach*, rev. edn (Oxford: Clarendon Press, 1979), p. 119.

6   Cassirer, *The Philosophy of Symbolic Forms*, vol. 1: *Language*, p. 91.

7   Popper, *Objective Knowledge*, pp. 118–19.

8   P. Filiasi Carcano, *Introduzione alla lettura del 'Tractatus' di Wittgenstein* (Rome: Editrice De Santis, 1966), p. 86.

9   Danto, *Analytical Philosophy of Knowledge*, p. x.

10   Ibid.

11   Ibid., p. xii.

12   Popper, *Objective Knowledge*, pp. 120–1.

13   See chapter 2, on 'The growth of expressive modes'.

Chapter 4   The Symbolic Function, Error and Awareness

1   A convergence of affects and paradigms is perhaps suggested by Koffka: 'Where the center of our interest lies, there … a figure is likely to arise.' K. Koffka, *Principles of Gestalt Psychology* (New York: Harcourt Brace, 1935), p. 197.

2   One of Ricœur's remarks is illuminating in this connection: 'I deliberately restrict the notion of symbol to double- or multiple-meaning expressions whose semantic texture is correlative to the work of interpretation that explicates their second or multiple meanings.' P. Ricœur, *Freud and Philosophy: an essay on interpretation* (New Haven, Conn.: Yale University Press, 1972), p. 13.

3   'My point is that symbol formation is not a random but a *directed* process. It results in increased articulation of form and in binding of energy, thereby lending orderliness to the total organism and to its perceived environment. The development of ordered patterns is the prerequisite of organismic existence, be these patterns of visible morphological forms or not directly visible psychological events.' S. K. Deri, *Symbolization and Creativity* (Madison, Conn.: International Universities Press, 1988), p. 62 (italics added).

4   'The principal factors in meaning situations are suggested by the following considerations: every meaning is a meaning of something, is

meant or eventually determined in some way or through some function, and within some setting. Thus every meaning situation may be said to include, in addition to a meaning: a bearer of meaning, a meaning function or way of meaning, and a context. However, in addition to these factors that are plainly common to all meaning situations, *many, and perhaps all, meaning situations also involve other factors* that are often thought of as constituting either crucial aspects or the contexts of meanings or meanings themselves.' T. E. Hill, *The Concept of Meaning* (London: Allen & Unwin; New York: Humanities Press, 1971), p. xii (italics added).

5 'In my conceptualization, "mental schemata" are mental symbols, "tools" with which we perceive and think. If they overrepresent past subjective ingredients at the expense of the realistic features of new stimulation, then they are not true or isomorphic symbols but misinforming cryptosymbols.' Deri, *Symbolization and Creativity*, pp. 74–5.

6 'There are patients whose contact with reality presents most difficulty when that reality is their own mental state.' W. R. Bion, *Attention and Interpretation: a scientific approach to insight in psycho-analysis and groups* (London: Tavistock, 1970), p. 9.

7 S. Freud, *New Introductory Lectures on Psycho-Analysis* (1933 (1932)), Lecture XXXII, 'Anxiety and instinctual life', *The Standard Edition of the Complete Psychological Works of Sigmund Freud*, vol. 22 (London: Hogarth Press and the Institute of Psycho-Analysis, 1964), p. 103.

8 Although operating well 'below' the threshold of language as generally conceptualized by philosophers, infants do communicate meaningfully. Possibly to a parallel effect, T. E. Hill maintains that 'the majority of recent inquiries concerning meaning instead of attempting to take into account the whole range of what is meaningful, have been focused upon language; and even among language oriented studies, the center of attention has often been not meaning as such but linguistic expressions. Most writers who have been directly concerned with meaning of linguistic expressions have been mainly concerned with meanings of particular expressions. Thus despite current appreciation of the importance of meaning, direct and inclusive inquiries concerning meaning remain relatively rare.' Hill, *The Concept of Meaning*, p. vii.

9 A. Danto, *Analytical Philosophy of Knowledge* (Cambridge and London: Cambridge University Press, 1968), p. 155.

10 Ibid., p. 265.

11 F. Nietzsche, 'The genealogy of morals', in *The Birth of Tragedy and the Genealogy of Morals* (Garden City, NY: Doubleday Anchor Books, 1956), p. 217.

12 R. A. Spitz, *No and Yes: on the genesis of human communication* (New York: International Universities Press, 1957), p. 132.

13 Bion, *Attention and Interpretation*, p. 9.

14 In this connection, see G. Corradi Fiumara, *The Other Side of Language: a*

philosophy of listening (London: Routledge, 1990), esp. ch. 9, 'On inner listening', pp. 127–42.

15   K. Popper, *Objective Knowledge: an evolutionary approach*, rev. edn (Oxford: Clarendon Press, 1980), p. 314.

16   R. Rorty, *Philosophy and the Mirror of Nature* (Oxford: Basil Blackwell, 1980).

17   Popper, *Objective Knowledge*, p. 70.

18   E. Fromm, *The Forgotten Language* (London: Gollancz, 1952); Italian translation: *Il linguaggio dimenticato* (Milan: Bompiani, 1962), p. 63.

19   Popper, *Objective Knowledge*, pp. 54–5.

Chapter 5   On the Interaction of Language and Thought

1   'To say of man, in Moore's sense, that he *knows* something; that what he says is therefore unconditionally the truth, seems wrong to me. – It is the truth only inasmuch as it is an unmoving foundation of his language-games.' L. Wittgenstein, *On Certainty* (Oxford: Basil Blackwell, 1979), p. 52e, para. 403.

2   Ibid., p. 24e, para. 166.

3   W. V. O. Quine, *Word and Object* (Cambridge, Mass.: MIT Press, 1981), p. 1.

4   Wittgenstein, *On Certainty*, p. 32e, para. 160.

5   Ibid., p. 23e, para. 154.

6   Ibid., p. 34e, para. 257.

7   Ibid., p. 49e, para. 378.

8   D. Davidson, 'On the very idea of a conceptual scheme', in *Inquiries into Truth and Interpretation* (Oxford: Clarendon Press, 1985), p. 183. The reciprocity of mechanisms influencing popular culture and official knowledge might thus be illustrated: 'For the peasantry, until its outlook was transformed by *new doctrines percolating from above*, witches were above all people who harmed their neighbours by occult means; and they were almost always women. When the authors of the *Malleus Maleficarum* produced quasi-theological reasons to explain why witches were generally female, they were simply trying to rationalize something which peasants already took for granted.' N. Cohn, *Europe's Inner Demons: an enquiry inspired by the great witch-hunt* (London: Chatto/Heinemann for Sussex University Press, 1975), p. 251.

9   B. L. Whorf, *Language, Thought and Reality: selected writings of Benjamin Lee Whorf*, ed. John B. Carroll (Cambridge, Mass.: MIT Press, 1973), p. 247.

10   H. G. Gadamer, *Truth and Method* (London: Sheed & Ward, 1979), pp. 325–30.

11   It may be appropriate to recall that 'The Inquisition took its name from the inquisitional procedure and not, as is sometimes assumed, vice versa: it carried out "inquisitions", or official enquiries, and held

"inquisitorial" trials, along lines which had been worked out much earlier.' Cohn, *Europe's Inner Demons*, p. 24.

12   'The dominance of the public way in which things have been interpreted has already been decisive even for the possibilities of having a mood.... The "they" prescribes one's state-of-mind, and determines what and how one "sees".' M. Heidegger, *Being and Time* (London: SCM Press, 1962), p. 213.

13   S. K. Langer, *Philosophy in a New Key: a study in the symbolism of reason, rite and art* (Cambridge, Mass., and London: Harvard University Press, 1979), p. 4.

14   The issue of recognizable labels could be associated with the remark: 'Knowledge is in the end based on acknowledgement.' Wittgenstein, *On Certainty*, p. 49e, para. 378.

15   With regard to persons who suffer mentally, Wittgenstein asks whether or not it is 'sufficiently observed which language-games these are capable of and which not'. *Remarks on the Philosophy of Psychology*, vol. 1 (Oxford: Basil Blackwell, 1980), p. 37e, para. 179.

16   E. Berne, *Games People Play: the psychology of human relations* (Harmondsworth: Penguin, 1964), p. 162.

17   C. Morris, *Signs, Language and Behavior* (Englewood Cliffs, NJ: Prentice Hall, 1946).

18   'For truly, Custome is a violent and deceiving schoole-mistris. She by little and little, and as it were by stealth, establisheth the foot of her authoritie in us; by which mild and gentle beginning, if once by the aid of time, it have settled and planted the same in us, it will soon discover a furious and tyrannical countenance into us, against which we have no more libertie to lift so much as our eyes.' Michel de Montaigne, *Essais*, vol. 1 (1603), ch. 22; tr. John Florio; quoted as an opening remark in Cohn, *Europe's Inner Demons*, p. 1.

19   The paragraph continues: 'Let us ask ourselves: why do we feel a grammatical joke to be *deep*? (And that is what the depth of philosophy is).' L. Wittgenstein, *Philosophical Investigations* (Oxford: Basil Blackwell, 1988), p. 47e, para. 111 (italics in the text).

20   Berne, *Games People Play*, p. 44.

Chapter 6   The Symbolic Function and the Development of Inner Time

1   H. Segal, 'Notes on symbol formation', *International Journal of Psycho-Analysis*, 38 (1957), pp. 391–7.

2   L. Wittgenstein, *Remarks on the Philosophy of Psychology*, vol. 1 (Oxford: Basil Blackwell, 1980), p. 131e, para. 718.

3   E. Cassirer, *The Philosophy of Symbolic Forms*, volume 1: *Language* (New Haven, Conn., and London: Yale University Press, 1953–5), p. 90.

4　E. Neumann, *The Origins and History of Consciousness* (Princeton, NJ: Princeton University Press, 1954), p. 108 and ff.

5　I. Kant, *Critique of Pure Reason* (London: Macmillan, 1933), 'Transcendental Aesthetic', section II, 'Time', p. 77, para. 6 section C.

6　Cassirer, *The Philosophy of Symbolic Forms*, vol. 1: *Language*, p. 215.

7　K. Popper, *Objective Knowledge: an evolutionary approach*, rev. edn (Oxford: Clarendon Press, 1979), p. 135 ('and' is not in Popper's text).

8　Ibid., p. 135 (italics added).

9　E. Cassirer, *The Philosophy of Symbolic Forms*, vol. 2: *Mythical Thought* (New Haven and London: Yale University Press, 1953–5); *Filosofia delle forme simboliche: Il pensiero mitico*, vol. 2 (Florence: La Nuova Italia, 1976), p. 152.

10　In this connection Jaspers offers a synoptic approach: 'We seek to apprehend the unity of history in images of the whole, which demonstrate the historicity of mankind *per se* in an empirically founded structure – wherein the fundamental fact remains the boundless openness into the future and the short beginning: we are just starting.... History is an open, infinite world of relationships of meaning, which, at any rate from time to time, seem to flow into one growing common meaning.' K. Jaspers, *The Origin and Goal of History* (London: Routledge & Kegan Paul, 1953), p. 263.

11　Cassirer, *The Philosophy of Symbolic Forms*, vol. 1: *Language*, p. 217.

12　Ibid., p. 218.

13　J. P. Vernant, *Myth and Thought among the Greeks* (London: Routledge & Kegan Paul, 1983), pp. 75–6.

14　'Quantification over time is often a useful and classifying device. But it would be absurd as a fundamental explanation of "before" and "after".' G. E. M. Anscombe, *Metaphysics and the Philosophy of Mind: the collected papers of G. E. M. Anscombe*, volume 2 (Oxford: Basil Blackwell, 1981), p. 186.

15　Cassirer, *The Philosophy of Symbolic forms*, vol. 1: *Language*, p. 217.

16　Ibid., p. 222

17　With regard to the escape from distorting and dulling symbolizations of time, Whorf remarks: 'Still another behavioral effect is that the character of monotony and regularity possessed by our image of time as an evenly scaled limitless tape persuades us to behave as if that monotony were more true of events than it really is. That is, it helps to routinize us." B. L. Whorf, *Language, Thought and Reality: selected writings of Benjamin Lee Whorf*, ed. John B. Carroll (Cambridge, Mass.: MIT Press, 1973), p. 154.

18　Popper, *Objective Knowledge*, p. 135.

19　Jaspers, 'The future', in *The Origin and Goal of History*, p. 141.

20　C. G. Jung, *The Structure and Dynamics of the Psyche*, 'The soul and death', *The Collected Works of C. G. Jung*, vol. 8 (London: Routledge & Kegan Paul, 1960), p. 407.

21   Ibid., p. 406.
22   S. de Beauvoir, *Tous les hommes sont mortels* (Paris: Gallimard, 1946).

Chapter 7   Pseudosymbolic Language

1   D. W. Winnicott, *The Maturational Process and the Facilitating Environment: studies in the theory of emotional development* (London: Hogarth Press and the Institute of Psycho-Analysis, 1965), p. 146.

2   S. Freud, *Moses and Monotheism: three essays* (1939 (1934–8)), 'The advance in intellectuality', part II, section C, in *The Standard Edition of the Complete Psychological Works of Sigmund Freud*, vol. 23 (London: Hogarth Press and the Institute of Psycho-Analysis, 1964), p. 113.

3   Winnicott, *The Maturational Process and the Facilitating Environment*, p. 61.

4   W. R. Bion, *Attention and Interpretation: a scientific approach to insight in psycho-analysis and groups* (London: Tavistock, 1970), p. 116.

5   'The poisoning of wells in a country or a city is used as an example of an odious crime – but the sin of using language dishonestly is just as dangerous – alas, the only difference is that one person is not supposed to say much to another about it.' *Sören Kierkegaard's Journals and Papers*, ed. H. V. Hong and E. H. Hong, vol. 3 (Bloomington, Ind., and London: Indiana University Press, 1975), p. 12.

6   S. Freud, *The Ego and the Id and Other Works* (1923–5), 'The loss of reality in neurosis and psychosis', *The Standard Edition of the Complete Psychological Works of Sigmund Freud*, vol. 19 (London: Hogarth Press and the Institute of Psycho-Analysis, 1961) p. 187.

7   M. Heidegger, *Being and Time* (Oxford: Basil Blackwell, 1980), p. 212.

8   Ibid., p. 217.

9   S. Leclaire, *Smascherare il reale: Saggio sull'oggetto in psicoanalisi* (Rome: Astrolabio, 1973), p. 74.

10   Bion, *Attention and Interpretation*, p. 126.

11   L. Wittgenstein, *Philosophical Investigations* (Oxford: Basil Blackwell, 1988), p. 47e, para. 109.

12   Ibid., p. 51e, para. 133.

13   L. Wittgenstein, *Culture and Value* (Oxford: Basil Blackwell, 1980), p. 56e.

14   Wittgenstein, *Philosophical Investigations*, p. 133e, para. 464.

15   M. Khan, *The Privacy of the Self* (New York: International Universities Press, 1974, p. 284).

16   Heidegger, *Being and Time*, para. 37, 'Ambiguity', pp. 217–18.

17   J. Hillman, *Il suicidio e l'anima* (Rome: Astrolabio, 1972), p. 171.

18   Ibid., p. 120.

19   As T. E. Hill suggests, in *The Tyranny of Words* Stuart Chase insists that the roots of many of our current problems lie in our treating signs and symbols as though they had the properties of their referents. His insistence is that only if we are diligent in tracing down the referents of

our terms can we expose the emptiness of our terms lacking referents and grasp the impact of meaningful terms. T. E. Hill, *The Concept of Meaning* (London: Allen & Unwin; New York: The Humanities Press, 1971), p. 147.

20 Heidegger, *Being and Time*, p. 221.

21 Bion, *Attention and Interpretation*, pp. 127–8.

22 Ibid., p. 127.

23 'Every definite view of a perversion is unduly simple, for the perversion of sophistical life is universal. In the very moment when it is being grasped, it has undergone a fresh transformation. The sophist, whose possibility was evolved by the life-order as a nameless warning for the future of man in that order, can only be described as an unceasing perversion. In the very article of formulation he acquires lineaments which are already too definite.' K. Jaspers, *Man in the Modern Age* (London: George Routledge & Sons, 1933), chapter entitled 'What mankind can become', para. entitled 'The sophist', p. 194.

24 Ibid., p. 194.

25 Ibid., p. 194.

26 Ibid., pp. 132–3.

27 Ibid., pp. 197–8.

28 Ibid., pp. 196–7.

29 Heidegger, *Being and Time*, p. 213.

30 Ibid., p. 213.

31 Wittgenstein, *Culture and Value*, p. 37e.

32 Jaspers, *Man in the Modern Age*, p. 194.

33 If we hypothesize a linguistic spectrum ranging from responsibility to renounceability, and if symbolization is constantly linked with expressive modes open to a high degree of recantation, then the adult world may subject the infant world to the systematic, cumulative, undiagnosable expedients of coping with a language primarily generated for lying and inducing confusion. When pseudosymbolization becomes dominant, language loses its metabolic function and is perverted into a dia-bolic use.

34 'The familiar face of a word; the feeling that a word is as it were a picture of its meaning; that it has as it were taken its meaning up into itself – is it possible for there to be a language to which all that is alien? And how are these feelings expressed among us? By the way we *choose* and *value* words.' L. Wittgenstein, *Remarks on the Philosophy of Psychology* (Oxford: Basil Blackwell, 1980), p. 3e, para. 6 (italics added).

35 M. Klein, *Contributions to Psycho-Analysis 1921–1945* (London: Hogarth Press and the Institute of Psycho-Analysis, 1973), pp. 32–3.

36 Ibid., p. 34.

37 Quoted in S. Ferenczi, *First Contributions to Psycho-Analysis* (London: Hogarth Press and the Institute of Psycho-Analysis, 1952), chapter entitled 'The symbolic representation of the pleasure and reality principles in the Oedipus myth', pp. 253–4.

Chapter 8   A Philosophy of Listening

1   P. Ricoeur, *Freud and Philosophy: an essay on interpretation* (New Haven, Conn.: Yale University Press, 1972), p. 13 (italics added).
2   L. Lugarini, *Esperienza e verità* (Urbino: Argalia, 1964), p. 205.
3   Ricoeur, *Freud and Philosophy*, p. 46.
4   M. Heidegger, *Being and Time* (Oxford: Basil Blackwell, 1988), p. 206 (italics added).
5   W. R. Bion, *Transformazioni: Il passaggio dall'apprendimento alla crescita* (Rome: Armando, 1973), p. 182.
6   W. R. Bion, *Attention and Interpretation: a scientific approach to insight in psycho-analysis and groups* (London: Tavistock, 1981), pp. 94–5.
7   E. F. Kittay, *Metaphor: its cognitive force and linguistic structure* (Oxford: Clarendon Press, 1987), p. 313 (italics added).
8   R. M. Rilke, 'Vision intérieure et perspective inversée', tr. L. Brion-Guerry, in *Aesthetik und allgemeine Kunstwissenschaft*, 11, 2; quoted in J. Chevalier, *Dictionnaire des symboles* (Paris: Robert Laffont, 1969), p. xxiii.
9   Heidegger, *Being and Time*, pp. 218–19.
10 Ibid., p. 216.
11 Ricoeur, *Freud and Philosophy*, p. 153.

Chapter 9   Epistemophily and Knowledge

1   S. Freud, 'Negation', *The Ego and the Id and Other Works* (1923–5), in *The Standard Edition of the Complete Psychological Works of Sigmund Freud*, vol. 19 (London: Hogarth Press and the Institute of Psycho-Analysis, 1961), p. 237. The passage continues: 'It only comes into being from the fact that thinking possesses the capacity to bring before the mind once more something that has once been perceived, by reproducing it as a presentation without the external object having still to be there.'
2   H. Segal, *Introduction to the Work of Melanie Klein* (London: Heinemann, 1964).
3   I. Matte Blanco, *The Unconscious as Infinite Sets: an essay in bi-logic* (London: Duckworth, 1965), p. 282.
4   Ibid., p. 145.
5   In a certain way, i.e. in so far as they are infinite sets, all these alternatives are equivalent and, for the deep unconscious, identical. See Matte Blanco, *The Unconscious as Infinite Sets*, p. 293.
6   Ibid., p. 285.
7   P. Martinelli Tomellini, 'Precedenti psicologici della formazione del pensiero razionale', in *Analisi metafilosofica e storia della filosofia*, ed. P. Filiasi Carcano (Rome: Bulzoni, 1974), p. 249.
8   R. Rorty, *Philosophy and the Mirror of Nature* (Oxford: Basil Blackwell, 1980), p. 13.

9   E. Cassirer, *The Philosophy of Symbolic Forms*, vol. 1: *Language* (New Haven, Conn., and London: Yale University Press, 1953–5), p. 148.

10 M. Klein, *Contributions to Psycho-Analysis 1921–1945* (London: Hogarth Press and the Institute of Psycho-Analysis, 1973), p. 237.

11 S. Freud, *An Autobiographical Study; Inhibitions, Symptoms and Anxiety; The Question of Lay Analysis and Other Works* (1926), 'Inhibitions, symptoms and anxiety', Addenda, 'Modifications of earlier views', Repression and Defence, in *The Standard Edition of the Complete Psychological Works of Sigmund Freud*, vol. 20 (London: Hogarth Press and the Institute of Psycho-Analysis, 1959), p. 164.

12 R. E. Money-Kyrle, *Man's Picture of the World: a psycho-analytic study* (London: Duckworth, 1961), pp. 51–2.

13 Klein, *Contributions to Psycho-Analysis*, p. 238.

14 'Symbolic behaviour is directed towards knowledge. This distinguishes man from animal. Man does not simply perceive things, but also perceives the meaning of things. Meaning precedes perception. That which does not mean anything is not, as a rule, perceived." T. Thass-Thienemann, *The Interpretation of Language*, vol. 1: *Understanding the Symbolic Meaning of Language* (New York: Jason Aronson, 1973), p. 3.

15 Under such unfavourable circumstances the person is captured in a specular imitative relation with 'the other' and does not even initiate a process of self-creation. As a cluster of signs exchanged in the verbalizations of the authors (and thus of the authorities) of any micro- or macro-culture, the inchoate person becomes 'the equivalent of a *word* in somebody else's conversation. Survival becomes an impossible question of *either* me or *them*. The child is *spoken* rather than allowed to speak.' A. Wilden, *System and Structure: essays in communication and exchange* (London: Tavistock, 1980), p. 26.

16 Klein, *Contributions to Psycho-Analysis*, p. 238.

17 Indifference may be one of the consequences: 'Our linguistically determined thought world not only collaborates with our cultural idols and ideals, but engages even our unconscious personal reactions in its patterns and gives them certain typical characters. One such character is ... *carelessness.*" B. L. Whorf, *Language, Thought and Reality: selected writings of Benjamin Lee Whorf*, ed. John B. Carroll (Cambridge, Mass.: MIT Press, 1973), p. 154.

18 Klein, *Contributions to Psycho-Analysis*, p. 238.

19 F. Nietzsche, 'On truth and lies in the nonmoral sense', in *Philosophy and Truth: selection from Nietzsche's notebooks of the early 1870s* (Atlantic Hyland, NJ: Humanities Press, 1979), p. 89.

20 M. Milner, 'Aspects of symbolism in comprehension of the not-self', *International Journal of Psycho-Analysis*, 33 (1952), pp. 181–95.

21 D. W. Winnicott, *The Maturational Process and the Facilitating Environment: studies in the theory of emotional development* (London: Hogarth Press and the Institute of Psycho-Analysis, 1965), p. 146.

22 D. W. Winnicott, 'Transitional objects and transitional phenomena', *International Journal of Psycho-Analysis*, 34 (1953), pp. 89–97.
23 D. Davidson, *Inquiries into Truth and Interpretation* (Oxford: Clarendon Press, 1985), p. 184.
24 M. Milner, 'The role of illusion in symbol formation', in *New Directions in Psycho-Analysis: the significance of infant conflict in the pattern of adult behaviour*, ed. M. Klein, P. Heimann and R. E. Money-Kyrle (London: Tavistock, 1955), p. 108.
25 Ibid., pp. 107–8.
26 Ibid., p. 143.
27 Klein, *Contributions to Psycho-Analysis*, p. 34.
28 Ibid., pp. 236–53.
29 Hindrances to symbolic development actually constitute an evolutionary offence: 'Speech is the best show man puts on. It is his own "act" on the stage of evolution, in which he comes before the cosmic backdrop and really "does his stuff".' Whorf, *Language, Thought and Reality*, p. 249.
30 Money-Kyrle, *Man's Picture of the World*, p. 181.
31 W. R. Bion, 'A theory of thinking', *International Journal of Psycho-Analysis*, 43 (1962), pp. 306–10.
32 L. Wittgenstein, *Tractatus Logico-Philosophicus* (London: Routledge & Kegan Paul; New York: Humanities Press, 1961), 'Author's preface', p. 3 (italics added).
33 P. Filiasi Carcano, *Introduzione alla lettura del 'Tractatus' di Wittgenstein* (Rome: Editrice De Santis, 1966), p. 9.
34 Wittgenstein, *Tractatus*, p. 3.

Chapter 10   Genesis of the Symbolic Function

1 E. Cassirer, *The Philosophy of Symbolic Forms*, vol. 1: *Language* (New Haven, Conn., and London: Yale University Press, 1953–5), pp. 89–90.
2 S. Freud, 'The loss of reality in neurosis and psychosis' (1924), in *The Ego and the Id and Other Works* (1923–5), *The Standard Edition of the Complete Psychological Works of Sigmund Freud*, vol. 19 (London: Hogarth Press and the Institute of Psycho-Analysis, 1961), p. 185.
3 Ibid., p. 185.
4 M. Klein, *Contributions to Psycho-Analysis 1921–1945* (London: Hogarth Press and the Institute of Psycho-Analysis, 1973), p. 308. She also suggests that 'the development of the ego and the relation to reality depend on the degree of the ego's capacity at a very early period to tolerate the pressure of the earliest anxiety-situations. And, as usual, it is a question of a certain optimum balance of the factors concerned.' Ibid., p. 238.
5 S. Freud, 'Negation' (1925), in *The Ego and the Id and Other Works*, p. 238.

6 In this connection, see, for instance, 'The Oedipus complex in the light of early anxieties', in Klein, *Contributions to Psycho-Analysis*, pp. 339–90.

7 A. Danto, *Analytical Philosophy of Knowledge* (Cambridge and London: Cambridge University Press, 1968), pp. 159–84.

8 The general notion of a 'quest for certainty' derives from the contribution of John Dewey, *The Quest for Certainty: a study in the relation of thought and action* (New York: Minto Balch, 1929). Human life is not divided between thinking and doing, but between needs, hopes and responses to these in the form of ideas, inquiries, hypotheses and solutions. 'Nothing merely neutral can actually resolve doubt or clarify confusion. At most it can produce only a *feeling* of certainty – something best obtained by withdrawing from the real world and cultivating fantasies.' Ibid., pp. 221–9. On the general idea of certainty, see also L. Wittgenstein, *On Certainty* (Oxford: Basil Blackwell, 1979).

9 Danto, *Analytical Philosophy of Knowledge*, p. 159.

10 On this notion, see M. Heidegger, *Being and Time* (London: SCM Press, 1962); *On the Way to Language* (New York: Harper & Row, 1971); *What is Called Thinking?* (New York: Harper & Row, 1972).

11 L. Wittgenstein, *Remarks on the Philosophy of Psychology*, vol. 1 (Oxford: Basil Blackwell, 1980), p. 110e, para. 591.

12 'It is plain that if a child is to succeed in the conservation task, he must have some internalized verbal formula that shields him from the overpowering appearance of the visual displays.' J. Bruner, 'The course of cognitive growth', *American Psychologist*, 19 (1964), pp. 1–15; quoted in E. J. Peill, *Invention and Discovery of Reality* (New York: John Wiley, 1975), p. 102.

13 J. Lacan, quoted in A. Rifflet-Lemaire, *Introduzione a Jacques Lacan* (Rome: Astrolabio, 1972), p. 114.

14 On this topic, see G. Corradi Fiumara, 'The symbolic function, transference and psychic reality', *The International Review of Psycho-Analysis*, 4 (1977), pp. 171–80.

15 Klein, *Contributions to Psycho-Analysis*, p. 238.

16 Cassirer, *The Philosophy of Symbolic Forms*, vol. 1: *Language*, p. 90.

17 W. R. Bion, 'A theory of thinking', *The International Journal of Psycho-Analysis*, 43 (1962), pp. 306–10.

18 Ibid., pp. 306–10.

19 In the words of Cassirer: 'The reproducibility of the content is itself bound up with the production of a sign for it, and in producing this sign the consciousness operates freely and independently. The concept of "memory" thus takes on a richer and deeper meaning. In order to remember a content, consciousness must previously have possessed itself of that content in a way differing from mere sensation or perception. The mere repetition of the given at another time does not suffice; in this repetition a new kind of conception and formation must be

manifested. For every "reproduction" of a content embodies a new level of "reflection". By the mere fact that it no longer takes this content as something simply present, but confronts it in imagination as something past and yet not vanished, consciousness, by its changed *relations* to the content, gives both to itself and the content a changed ideal meaning. And this occurs more and more precisely and abundantly as the world of representations stemming from the "I" becomes differentiated. The "I" now exercises an original formative activity all the while developing a deeper understanding.' Cassirer, *The Philosophy of Symbolic Forms*, vol. 1: *Language*, p. 90.

20 D. W. Winnicott, *The Maturational Process and the Facilitating Environment: studies in the theory of emotional development* (London: Hogarth Press and the Institute of Psycho-Analysis, 1965), p. 145.

21 Salimbene de Adam of Parma (1221–88), 'Chronicon Parmense: Avvenimenti tra il 1167 e il 1287', reported in *La letteratura italiana: Storia e testi: Le origini*, ed. A. Viscardi, B. and T. Nardi, G. Vidossi and F. Arese (Milan and Naples: Riccardo Ricciardi Editore, 1946), p. 979.

Chapter 11   From Biological Life to Dialogic Relations

1 According to Gadamer all knowledge is clouded over by opaqueness and forgetfulness. 'Diotima knew this when she compared the knowing proper to humans with the life of a species that has its ongoing being only in the relentless process of the reproduction of its individual instances. Hermeneutics tries to establish this point inasmuch as it characterizes the context of tradition within which we exist as an ongoing reacquisition that proceeds into infinity. It endeavours to make its own just how every vital and productive conversation with someone else knows how to mediate the other's horizon with one's own.' H. G. Gadamer, *Reason in the Age of Science* (Cambridge, Mass.: MIT Press, 1979), p. 60.

2 E. Cassirer, *The Philosophy of Symbolic Forms*, vol. 1: *Language* (New Haven, Conn., and London: Yale University Press, 1953–5), ch. 5, 'Language and the expression of the forms of pure relation: the sphere of judgement and the concepts of relation', pp. 303–19.

3 D. W. Winnicott, *Playing and Reality* (New York: Basic Books, 1976), p. 65.

4 W. R. Bion, *Attention and Interpretation: a scientific approach to insight in psycho-analysis and groups* (London: Tavistock, 1970), p. 105.

5 D. W. Winnicott, *The Maturational Process and the Facilitating Environment: studies in the theory of emotional development* (London: Hogarth Press and the Institute of Psycho-Analysis, 1965), p. 57 (italics added).

6 Ibid, p. 57.

7 R. A. Spitz, 'The evolution of dialogue', in *Drives, Affects and Behavior*, vol. 2, ed. M. Schur (New York: International Universities Press, 1965), p. 177.

8 W. V. O. Quine, *Word and Object* (Cambridge, Mass.: MIT Press, 1981), Preface, p. ix (italics added).

9 T. E. Hill, *The Concept of Meaning* (London: Allen & Unwin; New York: Humanities Press, 1971), p. 27.

10 H. P. Grice, 'Utterer's meaning and intentions', *Philosophical Review*, 87 (1969), pp. 144–77.

11 Winnicott, *The Maturational Process and the Facilitating Environment*, p. 57.

12 In this connection, see G. Corradi Fiumara, *The Other Side of Language: a philosophy of listening* (London: Routledge, 1990), ch. 4, 'The power of discourse and the strength of listening', pp. 52–71.

13 Winnicott, *The Maturational Process and the Facilitating Environment*, pp. 57–8. In this connection Klein writes: 'We see that the child's earliest reality is wholly fantastic; he is surrounded with objects of anxiety, and in this respect ... things animate and inanimate are to begin with equivalent to one another.' M. Klein, *Contributions to Psycho-Analysis 1921–1945* (London: Hogarth Press and the Institute of Psycho-Analysis, 1973), p. 238.

14 W. R. Bion, 'A theory of thinking', *The International Journal of Psycho-Analysis*, 43 (1962), pp. 306–10.

15 M. S. Manfredi Turillazzi, 'Dalle interpretazioni mutative di Strachey alle interpretazioni delle relazioni tra gli oggetti interni', *Rivista di Psicoanalisi*, 1 (1974), pp. 127–43.

16 J. Strachey, 'The nature of the therapeutic action of psycho-analysis', *The International Journal of Psycho-Analysis*, 15 (1934), pp. 127–59.

17 Ibid., p. 132.

18 Ibid.

19 Ibid.

20 'It follows from this that the purely informative "dictionary" type of interpretation will be non-mutative, however useful it may be as a prelude to mutative interpretations.' Ibid., pp. 149–50.

21 Ibid., p. 150.

22 Manfredi Turillazzi, *Rivista di Psicoanalisi* (1974), p. 139 ff.

23 Strachey, *The International Journal of Psycho-Analysis* (1934), p. 154.

24 Ibid., p. 142.

25 Ibid., pp. 158–9.

Chapter 12   The Maturation of Knowledge

1 On this topic, see G. Corradi Fiumara, *The Other Side of Language: a philosophy of listening* (London: Routledge, 1990), section 1 'Maieutics: Socratic listening' in ch. 10, 'Midwifery and philosophy', pp. 143–68.

2   From notes of seminar discussions held in Rome from 1974 to 1984.

3   H. A. Rosenfeld, *Psychotic States: a psycho-analytical approach* (New York: International Universities Press, 1966), p. 178.

4   Ibid., p. 179.

5   J. Chevalier (ed.), *Dictionnaire des symboles* (Paris: Robert Laffont, 1969), p. 528.

6   J. Strachey, 'The nature of the therapeutic action of psycho-analysis', *The International Journal of Psycho-Analysis*, 15 (1934), pp. 127–59 (p. 129).

7   Ibid., p. 132.

8   H. A. Rosenfeld, 'L'accostamento clinico alla teoria psicoanalitica degli istinti di vita e di morte: una ricerca sugli aspetti aggressivi del narcisismo', *Rivista di Psicoanalisi*, 18 (1972), pp. 47–67 (p. 63).

9   The full remark is as follows: 'Where id was, there ego shall be. It is a work of culture – not unlike the draining of the Zuider Zee.' S. Freud, 'The dissection of the psychical personality', Lecture XXXI, *New Introductory Lectures on Psycho-Analysis* (1933 (1932)), *The Standard Edition of the Complete Psychological Works of Sigmund Freud* vol. 22 (London: Hogarth Press and the Institute of Psycho-Analysis, 1964), p. 80.

10 E. Cassirer, *The Philosophy of Symbolic Forms*, vol. 1: *Language* (New Haven, Conn., and London: Yale University Press, 1953–5), pp. 87–8.

Bibliography

Adler, G., *The Living Symbol: a case study in the process of individuation*, Toronto: McClelland, 1981.

Adler, J. E., 'Abstraction is uncooperative', *Journal for the Theory of Social Behaviour*, 14, 2, 1984, pp. 165–81.

Adorno, T. W., *The Jargon of Authenticity*, tr. K. Tarnowski and F. Will, London: Routledge & Kegan Paul, 1973.

Aenishanslin, M., *et al.*, *Systèmes symboliques, science et philosophie: Travaux du séminaire d'épistémologie comparative d'Aix-en-Provence*, ERA du CNRS 650, Paris: CNRS, 1978.

Anscombe, G. E. M., *From Parmenides to Wittgenstein: the collected philosophical papers of G. E. M. Anscombe*, Oxford: Basil Blackwell, 1981.

Anscombe, G. E. M., *Metaphysics and the Philosophy of Mind*, Oxford: Basil Blackwell, 1981.

Arendt, H., *The Life of the Mind*, New York: Harcourt, Brace, Jovanovich, 1978.

Aschen, S. T., *Symbols Around Us*, tr. R. Spink, New York and London: Van Nostrand Reinhold, 1978.

Atkin, S. 'Psychoanalytic considerations of language and thought', *Psychoanalytic Quarterly*, 38, 1969, pp. 171–80.

Austin, J. L., *Philosophical Papers*, Oxford: Clarendon Press, 1961.

Austin, J. L., *How to Do Things with Words*, William James Lectures delivered at Harvard University in 1955, ed. J. O. Urmson and Marina Sbisà, Oxford: Clarendon Press, 1975.

Barth, E. M., and Krabbe, E. C. W., *From Axiom to Dialogue: a philosophical study of logics and argumentation*, Berlin and New York: Walter de Gruyter, 1982.

Baudrillard, J., *L'Echange symbolique et la mort* (Italian trans. *Lo scambio simbolico e la morte*, Milan: Feltrinelli, 1979), Paris: Gallimard, 1976.

Benhabib, S., *Critique, Norm and Utopia: a study of the foundations of critical theory*, New York: Columbia University Press, 1986.

Berne, E., *Games People Play: the psychology of human relations*, Harmondsworth: Penguin, 1964.

Bion, W. R., *Transformations: change from learning to growth* (Italian trans. *Trasformazioni: Il passaggio dall'apprendimento alla crescita*, Rome: Armando, 1973), London: William Heinemann Medical Books, 1965.

Bion, W. R., *Attention and Interpretation: a scientific approach to insight in psycho-analysis and groups*, London: Tavistock, 1978.

Bion, W. R., 'A theory of thinking', *The International Journal of Psycho-Analysis*, 43, 1962, pp. 306–10.

Bjorklund, D. F., *Children's Thinking: developmental functions and individual differences*, Pacific Grove, Cal.: Brooks Cole, 1989.

Bregman, L., 'Death and its denial: definitions and perspectives from depth psychology and Christian thought', *Thought*, 61, 1986, pp. 150–61.

Bruner, J., Oliver, R. R., Greenfield, P. M., *et al.*, *Studies in Cognitive Growth*, New York: Wiley, 1966.

Bruner, J., *Actual Minds, Possible Worlds*, Cambridge, Mass., and London: Harvard University Press, 1986.

Bruner, J., 'The course of cognitive growth', *American Psychologist*, 19, 1964, pp. 1–15.

Bunge, M., 'The maturation of science', in J. Lakatos and A. Musgrave (eds), *Problems in the Philosophy of Science*, Amsterdam: North Holland, 1968.

Burke, K., *Language as Symbolic Action: essays on life, literature and method*, Berkeley and Los Angeles: University of California Press, 1968.

Butterworth, G. (ed.), *Infancy and Epistemology: an evaluation of Piaget's theory*, Brighton: Harvester Press, 1981.

Carey, S., *Conceptual Change in Childhood*, Cambridge, Mass.: MIT Press, 1985.

Carini, L. *The Theory of Symbolic Transformations: a humanistic scientific psychology*, Washington: University Press of America, 1983.

Carnap, R., *Philosophy and Logical Syntax*, London: Kegan Paul, Trench, Trubner & Co., 1935.

Cassirer, E., *The Philosophy of Symbolic Forms*, vol. 1: *Language*, tr. R. Manheim, Preface and Introduction by C. W. Hendel, New Haven and London: Yale University Press, 1953–5.

Cassirer, E., *The Philosophy of Symbolic Forms*, vol. 2: *Mythical Thought*, tr. Ralph Manheim, New Haven and London: Yale University Press, 1953–5.

Cassirer, E., *Symbol, Myth and Culture*, New Haven and London: Yale University Press, 1979.

Chase, S., *The Tyranny of Words*, New York: Harcourt Brace, 1938.

Chevalier, J. (ed.), *Dictionnaire des symboles*, Paris: Robert Laffont, 1969.

Chomsky, N., *Reflections on Language*, London: Fontana, 1976.

Chomsky, N., *Language and Responsibility: based on conversations with M. Ronat*, tr. J. Viertel, Hassocks: Harvester Press, 1979.

Chomsky, N., *Rules and Representations*, Oxford: Basil Blackwell, 1980.

Cohen, L. J., 'What sorts of machines can understand the symbols they use?', *Aristotelian Society: supplementary volume*, 60, 1986, pp. 81–96.

Cohn, N., *Europe's Inner Demons: an enquiry inspired by the great witch-hunt*, London: Chatto and Heinemann for Sussex University Press, 1975.

Cooper, D. E., *Metaphor*, Aristotelian Society series, vol. 5, Oxford: Basil Blackwell, 1986.

Corradi, G., *Philosophy and Coexistence*, Leyden: Sijthoff, 1966.

Corradi Fiumara, G., *The Other Side of Language: a philosophy of listening*, London: Routledge, 1990.

Corradi Fiumara, G., 'Filosofia del linguaggio e costruzione della realta', in P. Filiasi Carcano, *Introduzione alla lettura di 'Ricerche filosofiche' di Wittgenstein*, Rome: Bulzoni, 1976.

Corradi Fiumara, G., 'The symbolic function, transference and psychic reality', *The International Review of Psycho-Analysis*, 4, 1977, pp. 171–80.

Cowan, P. A., *Piaget, With Feeling: cognitive, social and emotional dimensions*, New York and London: Holt, Rinehart & Winston, 1978.

Coward, H. G., 'Symbolizing' (1), *Method. Sci.*, 16, 1983, pp. 17–41.

Danto, A., *Analytical Philosophy of Knowledge*, Cambridge and London: Cambridge University Press, 1968.

Davidson, D., *Inquiries into Truth and Interpretation*, Oxford: Clarendon Press, 1985.

Deri, S. K., *Symbolization and Creativity*, Madison, Conn.: International Universities Press, 1988.

De Sousa, R., *The Rationality of Emotions*, Cambridge, Mass.: MIT Press, 1987.

Dewey, J., *The Quest for Certainty: a study in the relation of thought and action*, New York: Minto, Balch, 1929.

Donaldson, M., and Wales, R., 'On the acquisition of some relational terms', in J. Hayer (ed.), *Cognition and the Development of Language*, New York: John Wiley, 1970.

Dummett, M., *Truth and Other Enigmas*, London: Duckworth, 1978.

Eaton, R. M., *Symbolism and Truth: an introduction to the theory of knowledge*, Dover: Dover Publications, 1964.

Eisenberg, N., *The Development of Prosocial Behaviour*, New York: Academic Press, 1982.

Ferenczi, S., *First Contributions to Psycho-Analysis*, tr. E. Jones, London: Hogarth Press and the Institute of Psycho-Analysis, 1952, 'The symbolic representation of the pleasure and reality principles in the Oedipus myth', pp. 253–4.

Filiasi Carcano, P., *Introduzione alla lettura del 'Tractatus' di Wittgenstein*, Rome: Editrice De Santis, 1966.

Filiasi Carcano, P., *Introduzione allo studio della filosofia linguistica: Guida alla lettura dei 'Principi della filosofia linguistica' di Waisman*, Rome: Bulzoni, 1972.

Filiasi Carcano, P., *Introduzione alla lettura di 'Ricerche filosofiche' di Wittgenstein*, Rome: Bulzoni, 1976.

Firth, R., *Symbols: Public and Private*, London: Allen & Unwin, 1973.

Fliess, R., *Symbol, Dream and Psychosis*, Psychoanalytic Series, vol. 3, New York: International Universities Press, 1973.

Fodor, J. A., *The Language of Thought*, New York: Crowell, 1975.

Fortesque, M., 'Why the "language of thought" is not a language: some inconsistencies of the computational analogy of thought', *J. Prag.*, 3, 1979, pp. 67–80.

Foulkes, D., 'Dreaming as language and cognition', *Scientia*, 113, 1978, pp. 481–99.

Freud, S., 'Instincts and their vicissitudes', *On the History of the Psycho-Analytic Movement: Papers on Metapsychology and Other Works* (1914–16), pp. 109–40, *The Standard Edition of the Complete Psychological Works of Sigmund Freud*, tr. under the general editorship of J. Strachey, in collaboration with A. Freud, assisted by A. Strachey and A. Tyson, vol. 14, London: Hogarth Press and the Institute of Psycho-Analysis, 1957.

Freud, S., 'Beyond the pleasure principle', *Beyond the Pleasure Principle, Group Psychology and Other Works* (1920), pp. 7–64, *Standard Edition*, vol. 17, London: Hogarth Press, 1955.

Freud, S., 'The loss of reality in neurosis and psychosis', and 'Negation', *The Ego and the Id and Other Works* (1923–5), *Standard Edition*, vol. 19, London: Hogarth Press, 1961.

Freud, S., 'Inhibitions, symptoms and anxiety', Addenda, 'Modifications of earlier views', C Repression and Defence, *An Autobiographical Study, Inhibitions, Symptoms and Anxiety, The Question of Lay Analysis and Other Works* (1926), *Standard Edition*, vol. 20, London: Hogarth Press, 1959.

Freud, S., 'The dissection of the psychical personality', *New Introductory Lectures on Psycho-Analysis*, Lecture XXXI (1933 (1932)), *Standard Edition*, vol. 22, London: Hogarth Press, 1964.

Freud, S., *Moses and Monotheism: three essays*, part II, section C, 'The advance in intellectuality' (1939), *Standard Edition*, vol. 23, London: Hogarth Press, 1964.

Gadamer, H. G., *Reason in the Age of Science*, tr. F. G. Lawrence, Cambridge, Mass.: MIT Press, 1979.

Gadamer, H. G., *Truth and Method*, tr. W. Glen-Doepel, J. Cumming and G. Barden, London: Sheed & Ward, 1979.

Ghosh, R. K., 'Artistic communication and symbol: some philosophical reflections', *British Journal of Aesthetics*, 27, 1987, pp. 319–25.

Gillet, G., 'Representation and cognitive science', *Inquiry*, 32, 1989, pp. 261–76.

Goodman, N., *Languages of Art: an approach to a theory of symbols*, Indianapolis and Cambridge: Hackett, 1976.

Goodman, N., *Ways of Worldmaking*, Hassocks, Sussex: Harvester Press, 1978; Indianapolis: Hackett, 1978.

Goodman, N., *Of Mind and Other Matters*, Cambridge, Mass.: Harvard University Press, 1984.

Grava, A., *A Structural Inquiry into the Symbolic Representation of Ideas*, The Hague and Paris: Mouton, 1969.

Green, A., *Il discorso vivente*, Rome: Astrolabio, 1974. *Le discours vivant*, Paris: Presses Universitaires de France, 1973.

Gregg, R. B., *Symbolic Inducement and Knowing: a study in the foundations of rhetoric*, Columbia: University of South Carolina Press, 1984.

Gregory, B., *Inventing Reality: physics as language*, New York: Wiley, 1988.

Grice, H. P., 'Meaning', *Philosophical Review*, 62, 1957, pp. 377–88.

Grice, H. P., 'Utterer, meaning and intentions', *Philosophical Review*, 87, 1969, pp. 144–77.

Haack, S., *Deviant Logic: some philosophical issues*, Cambridge: Cambridge University Press, 1974.

Habermas, J., *Knowledge and Human Interests*, tr. J. Shapiro, London: Heinemann Educational Books, 1978.

Habermas, J., *Communication and the Evolution of Society*, tr. T. McCarthy, Boston, Mass.: Beacon Press, 1979.

Habermas, J., *The Theory of Communicative Action*, vol. 1, Boston, Mass.: Beacon Press, 1984.

Hamburg, C. H., *Symbol and Reality: studies in the philosophy of Ernst Cassirer*, The Hague: Martinus Nijhoff, 1956.

Harris, R., *The Language Makers*, London: Duckworth, 1980.

Hayes, J. R. (ed.), *Cognition and the Development of Language*, New York: John Wiley, 1970.

Heidegger, M., *Being and Time*, tr. J. Macquarrie and E. Robinson, Oxford: Basil Blackwell, 1980.

Heim, M., *Electric Language: a philosophical study of word processing*, New Haven: Yale University Press, 1987.

Henle, P., *Language, Thought and Culture*, Ann Arbor: The University of Michigan Press, 1959.

Hill, T. E., *The Concept of Meaning*, London: Allen & Anwin; New York: Humanities Press, 1971.

Hillman, H., *Il suicidio e l'anima*, Rome: Astrolabio, 1972.

Hjemslev, L., *Prolegomena to a Theory of Language*, tr. F. J. Whitfield, Bloomington, Ind.: Indiana University Press, 1961.

Holt, R., and Peterfreund E., *Psychoanalysis and Contemporary Science: an annual of integrative and interdisciplinary studies*, New York: McMillan, 1972.

Jaspers, K., *Man in the Modern Age*, tr. E. and C. Paul, George Routledge & Sons, 1933.

Johnson, D. M., 'Forgetting dreams', *Philosophy*, 54, 1979, pp. 407–14.

Jovanovic, G., 'Symbolization and rationality', *Commun. Cog.*, 21, 1988, pp. 357–70.

Jung, C. G., *Symbols of Transformation*, in *The Collected Works of C. G. Jung*, tr. R. F. C. Hull, ed. Sir H. Read, M. Fordham and G. Adler, vol. 5, London: Routledge & Kegan Paul, 1956.

Jung, C. G., *The Structure and Dynamics of the Psyche*, in *The Collected Works of C. G. Jung*, tr. R. F. C. Hull, ed. Sir H. Read, M. Fordham and G. Adler, vol. 8, London: Routledge & Kegan Paul, 1960 ('The soul and death', 1934, pp. 404–15).

Jung, C. G., *Man and his Symbols*, London: Pan Books, 1978.

Kant, I., *Critique of Pure Reason*, tr. N. K. Smith, London: Macmillan, 1933.

Kegan, R., *The Evolving Self: problems and processes in human development*, Cambridge, Mass., and London: Harvard University Press, 1982.

Kenny, A., 'Wittgenstein on the nature of philosophy', in B. McGuinness (ed.), *Wittgenstein and his Times*, Oxford: Basil Blackwell, 1982, pp. 1–26.

Kierkegaard, S., *Fear and Trembling and the Sickness unto Death*, tr. W. Lowrie, Princeton, NJ: Princeton University Press, 1974.

Kierkegaard, S., *Sören Kierkegaard's Journals and Papers*, ed. and tr. H. V. Hong and E. H. Hong, Bloomington, Ind., and London: Indiana University Press, 1975.

Kierkegaard, S., *The Sickness unto Death: a Christian psychological exposition for upbuilding and awakening*, ed. and tr. H. V. Hong and E. H. Hong, Princeton, NJ: Princeton University Press, 1983.

Kittay, E. F., *Metaphor: its cognitive force and linguistic structure*, Oxford: Clarendon Press, 1987.

Klein, M., *Contributions to Psycho-Analysis 1921–1945*, London: Hogarth Press and the Institute of Psycho-Analysis, 1973.

Koffka, K., *Principles of Gestalt Psychology*, New York: Harcourt Brace, 1935.

Kubie, L. S., *Symbol and Neurosis*, Psychological Issues, Monograph 44, New York: International Universities Press, 1978.

Kuhn, T. S., *The Structure of Scientific Revolutions*, 2nd edn, Chicago and London: University of Chicago Press, 1970.

Kuhn, T. S., 'Second thoughts on paradigms', in F. Suppes (ed.), *The Structure of Scientific Theories*, Urbana, Ill.: University of Illinois Press, 1974.

Lakatos, I., and Musgrave, A. (eds), *Criticism and the Growth of Knowledge*, Cambridge: Cambridge University Press, 1970.

Langer, S., *Philosophy in a New Key: a study in the symbolism of reason, rite and art*, Cambridge, Mass., and London: Harvard University Press, 1979.

Leclaire, S., *Smascherare il reale: Saggio sull'oggetto in psicoanalisi*, Rome: Astrolabio, 1973.

Lee, D. S., 'The pragmatic origins of concepts and categories: Mead and Piaget', *Southern Journal of Philosophy*, 21, 1983, pp. 211–29.

Leibniz, G., *New Essays in the Human Understanding*, Cambridge University Press, 1981.

Leondar, B., 'Metaphor and infant cognition', *Poetics*, 4, 1975, pp. 273–87.

Le Pore, E. (ed.), *Truth and Interpretation: perspectives on the philosophy of Donald Davidson*, Oxford: Basil Blackwell, 1986.

Lugarini, L., *Esperienza e verità*, Urbino: Argalia, 1964.

Lugarini, L., 'Cassirer e il compito della fondazione delle scienze umane', *Il Pensiero*, 2, 1967, pp. 142–61.

McGuinness, B. (ed.), *Wittengenstein and his Times*, Oxford: Basil Blackwell, 1982.

McLuhan, M., and Fiore, Q., *The Medium is the Message*, New York: Bantam, 1967.

Manfredi Turillazzi, M., 'Dalle interpretazioni mutative di Strachey alle interpretazioni delle relazioni tra gli oggetti interni', *Rivista di Psicoanalisi*, 1, 1974, pp. 127–43.

Markey, J. F., *The Symbolic Process and its Integration in Children: a study in social psychology*, Chicago and London: University of Chicago Press, 1978.

Martinelli Tomellini, P., 'Precedenti psicologici della formazione del pensiero razionale', in P. Filiasi Carcano (ed.), *Analisi metafilosofica e storia della filosofia*, Rome: Bulzoni, 1974.

Masterman, M., 'The nature of a paradigm', in I. Lakatos and A. Musgrave (eds), *Criticism and the Growth of Knowledge*, Proceedings of the International Colloquium in the Philosophy of Science, vol. 4 (London, 1965), Cambridge: Cambridge University Press, 1970, pp. 59–89.

Matte Blanco, I., *The Unconscious as Infinite Sets: an essay in bi-logic*, London: Duckworth, 1975.

Menendez Urena, E., 'Psicoanalisis y lenguage en Alfred Lorenzer', *Pensamiento*, 30, 1974, pp. 437–51.

Milner, M., 'Aspects of symbolism in comprehension of the not-self', *International Journal of Psycho-Analysis*, 33, 1952, pp. 181–95.

Milner, M., 'The role of illusion in symbol formation', in M. Klein, P. Heimann and R. E. Money-Kyrle (eds), *New Directions in Psycho-Analysis: the significance of infant conflict in the pattern of adult behaviour*, London: Tavistock, 1955.

Money-Kyrle, R. E., *Man's Picture of the World: a psycho-analytic study*, London: Duckworth, 1961.

Morris, C., *Foundations of the Theory of Signs*, Foundations of the Unity of Science: Toward an International Encyclopedia of Unified Sciences, vol. 1, Chicago: University of Chicago Press, 1938.

Murawski, R., 'The development of symbolism in logic', *Proceedings of the Aristotelian Society*, 89, 1988–9, pp. 65–78.

Murray, E. L., *Imaginative Thinking and Human Existence*, Pittsburg: Duquesne University Press, 1986.

Nagel, E., and Newman, F. R., *La prova di Gödel*, Turin: Bosinghieri, 1961.

Nietzsche, F., 'The genealogy of morals', *The Birth of Tragedy and The Genealogy of Morals*, Garden City, NY: Doubleday Anchor Books, 1956.

Nietzsche, F., 'On truth and lies in the nonmoral sense', *Philosophy and Truth: selection from Nietzsche's notebooks of the early 1870s*, tr. and ed. D. Breazeale, Atlantic Hyland, NJ: Humanities Press, 1979, pp. 79–97.

Neumann, E., *The Child: structure and dynamics of the nascent personality*, New York: Harper & Row, 1976.

Ong, N., *La presenza della parola*, Bologna: Il Mulino, 1970.

Peill, E. Y., *Invention and Discovery of Reality: the acquisition and conservation of amount*, New York: John Wiley, 1975.

Pepper, S., *World Hypotheses*, Berkeley, Cal.: University of California Press, 1961.

Piaget, J., *The Origin of Intelligence in the Child*, tr. M. Cook, Routledge & Kegan Paul, 1953.

Piaget, J., *Science and Education and the Psychology of the Child*, tr. D. Coltman, Harmondsworth: Penguin, 1977.

Piaget, J., *et al.*, *Epistemology and Psychology of Functions*, with the collaboration of C. Fot, tr. F. X. Castillanos and V. D. Anderson, Dordrecht: D. Reidel, 1977.

Piattelli Palmarini, M. (ed.), *Language and Learning: the debate between Jean Piaget and Noam Chomsky*, London: Routledge & Kegan Paul, 1960.

Pikas, A., *Abstraction and Concept Formation*, Copenhagen: Munksgaard, 1965.

Plato, *Symposium*, ed. K. Dover, Cambridge: Cambridge University Press, 1986.

Popper, K., *Objective Knowledge: an evolutionary approach*, rev. edn, Oxford: Clarendon Press, 1979.

Putnam, H., *Mind, Language and Reality: philosophical papers*, Cambridge University Press, 1975.

Quine, W. V. O., *Ontological Relativity and Other Essays*, New York: Columbia University Press, 1969.

Quine, W. V. O., *Word and Object*, Cambridge, Mass.: MIT Press, 1981.

Rapaport, D. (ed.), *Organization and Pathology of Thought*, New York: Columbia University Press, 1951.

Ricœur, P., *Finitude et culpabilité: La symbolique du mal*, Paris: Aubier Editions Montaigne, 1960.

Ricœur, P., *Freud and Philosophy: an essay on interpretation*, tr. D. Savage, New Haven, Conn.: Yale University Press, 1972.

Ricœur, P., *The Conflict of Interpretations: essays in hermeneutics*, ed. D. Ihde, Evanston, Ill.: Northwestern University Press, 1989.

Rifflet-Lemaire, A., *Introduzione a Jacques Lacan*, Rome: Astrolabio, 1972.

Rorty, R., *Philosophy and the Mirror of Nature*, Oxford: Basil Blackwell, 1980.

Rosch, E. H., 'Principles of categorization', in E. H. Rosch and B. B. Lloyd (eds), *Cognition and Categorization*, Hillsdale, NY: Erlbaum, 1978.

Rosenfeld, H. A., *Psychotic States: a psycho-analytical approach*, New York: International Universities Press, 1966.

Rossi-Landi, F., *Il linguaggio come lavoro e come mercato*, Milan: Bompiani, 1968.

Royce, J. R., 'The implications of Langer's philosophy of mind for a science of psychology', *J. Mind Behav.*, 4, 1983, pp. 491–506.

Russell, J., *The Acquisition of Knowledge*, London: Macmillan, 1978.

Ryle, G., *Dilemmas: the Tarner Lectures 1953*, Cambridge: Cambridge University Press, 1966.

Salimbene de Adam of Parma, 'Chronicon Parmense: Avvenimenti, tra il 1167 e il 1287', in Viscardi, A., *et al.* (eds), *La letteratura italiana: Storia e testi: Le origini*, Milan and Naples: Ricciardi Editore, 1946.

Schilpp, P. A. (ed.), *The Philosophy of G. E. Moore*, The Library of Living Philosophers, vol. 4, La Salle, Ill.: Northwestern University and Southern Illinois University, 1968.

Schmidt, D. D., *Hellenistic Greek Grammar and Noam Chomsky: nominalizing transformations*, Chico, Cal.: Scholars Press for the Society of Biblical Literature, 1981.

Schrag, C., *Communicative Praxis and the Space of Subjectivity*, Bloonington, Ind.: Indiana University Press, 1986.

Schur, M (ed.), *Drives, Affects and Behavior*, vol. 2, New York: International Universities Press, 1965.

Scott, C. E., 'The pathology of the father's rule: Lacan and the symbolic order', *Thought*, 61, 1986, pp. 118–30.

Searle, J. R., *Speech Acts*, London: Cambridge University Press, 1969.

Segal, H., 'Notes on symbol formation', *The International Journal of Psycho-Analysis*, 37, 1957, pp. 391–7.

Sperber, D., *Rethinking Symbolism*, tr. A. R. Morton, Cambridge: Cambridge University Press, 1975.

Spitz, R. A., *No and Yes: on the genesis of human communication*, New York: International Universities Press, 1957.

Spitz, R. A., 'The evolution of dialogue', in M. Schur (ed.), *Drives, Affects and Behavior*, vol. 2, New York: International Universities Press, 1965.

Stern, N. D., *The Interpersonal World of the Infant*, New York: Basic Books, 1985.

Strachey, J., 'The nature of the therapeutic action of psycho-analysis', *The International Journal of Psycho-Analysis*, 15, 1934, pp. 127–59.

Suber, P., 'What is software?', *Journal of Speculative Philosophy*, 2, 1988, pp. 89–119.

Taylor, J. R., *Linguistic Categorization: prototypes in linguistic theory*, Oxford: Clarendon Press, 1989.

Thass-Thienemann, T., *The Interpretation of Language*, vol. 1: *Understanding the Symbolic Meaning of Language*, New York: Jason Aronson, 1973.

Vernant, J. P., *Myth and Thought among the Greeks*, London: Routledge & Kegan Paul, 1983.

Walkup, J., 'When a psychoanalyst makes sense, what does he make it out of?', *J. Brit. Soc. Phenomenal*, 15, 1984, pp. 180–96.

Weihr, C. F., 'Knowing and symbolic functioning', *New Scholas.*, 62, 1988, pp. 412–37.

Weimer, W. B., and Palermo, D. S. (eds), *Cognition and the Symbolic Process*, Hillsdale: Lawrence, 1974.

Whitehead, A. N., *Science in the Modern World*, New York: Macmillan, 1924.

Whorf, B. L., *Language, Thought and Reality: selected writings of Benjamin Lee Whorf*, ed. J. B. Carroll, Cambridge, Mass.: MIT Press, 1973.

Wilden, A., *System and Structure: essays in communication and exchange*, London: Tavistock, 1980.

Winnicott, D. W., *The Maturational Process and the Facilitating Environment: studies in the theory of emotional development*, London: Hogarth Press and the Institute of Psycho-Analysis, 1965.

Winnicott, D. W., *Between Reality and Phantasy: transitional objects and phenomena*, ed. S. A. Grolnick and L. Boskin in collaboration with W. Muensterberger, New York: Aronson, 1974.

Winnicott, D. W., *Playing and Reality*, New York: Basic Books, 1976.

Winnicott, D. W., *The Spontaneous Gesture: selected letters of D. W. Winnicott*, ed. F. R. Rodman, Cambridge, Mass.: Harvard University Press, 1987.

Wisdom, J., *Philosophy and Psychoanalysis*, Oxford: Basil Blackwell, 1953.

Wittgenstein, L., *Tractatus Logico-Philosophicus*, tr. D. F. Pears and B. F. McGuinness, London: Routledge & Kegan Paul; New York: The Humanities Press, 1961.

Wittgenstein, L., *On Certainty*, tr. D. Paul and G. E. M. Anscombe, ed. G. E. M. Anscombe and G. H. von Wright, Oxford: Basil Blackwell, 1979.

Wittgenstein, L., *Culture and Value*, tr. P. Winch, ed. G. H. von Wright in collaboration with H. Nyman, Oxford: Basil Blackwell, 1980.

Wittgenstein, L., *Remarks on the Philosophy of Psychology*, vol. 1, tr. G. E. M. Anscombe, ed. G. E. M. Anscombe and G. H. von Wright, Oxford: Basil Blackwell, 1980.

Wittgenstein, L., *Philosophical Investigations*, tr. G. E. M. Anscombe, Oxford: Basil Blackwell, 1988.

Woodger, G. H., *Biology and Language: an introduction to the methodology of the biological sciences including medicine*, Cambridge: Cambridge University Press, 1952.

Wright, G. H. von, 'The Wittgenstein papers', *Philosophical Review*, 79, 1969, pp. 483–503.

Wurmser, L., 'Is psychoanalysis a separate field of symbolic forms?', *Human Soc.*, 4, 1981, pp. 263–94.

Index

230 *Index*